MW00586376

'It's more than just a long motorcycle trip; as well as battling with endless bad roads and, often worse, endless bad bureaucracy, Heather is also fighting a killer disease. That in the end she overcomes them all—roads, bureaucrats and the killer disease— feels like a miracle in all sorts of ways. She also proves, again and again, that the old line about the 'kindness of strangers' really does hold true, particularly when the road you're on is a rough one and what you really need is a little love and compassion.'

–Tony Wheeler, author, travel writer
and co-founder of Lonely Planet

'Heather Ellis weaves a raw and thrilling adventure tale that is exciting, inspiring, and refreshingly honest in its telling.'
–Lois Pryce, author of motorcycle adventure travel books

'The road may be silken but it's far from smooth. Heather Ellis delivers a devastating punch and that's even before the going gets tough. If you want a taste of life on the road, though nowhere, this is as good as it gets.'
–Ted Simon, author of *Jupiter's Travels*

'This is so much more than a riveting travel story. Throughout her journey Heather Ellis struggles with the knowledge that she will inevitably confront her demise and death. As a fellow traveller, I was engrossed in her poignant descriptions of the people and the challenges she encountered along her journey. As a person living with HIV, I related to the author's self-stigma and fear of HIV disclosure, as well as her determination to keep going, just because. But you need not be a traveller or a person living with HIV to relish this read. The ending is astounding, inspiring and a testament to human spirit.'

–Susan Paxton, PhD, author of *Lifting the Burden of Secrecy -
Positive Speakers' Guide*

'Heather travels on her motorbike with vision hope and resilience under a cloud of uncertainty about her own health and wellbeing. Turning the pages I loved travelling with her.
A woman of courage and perseverance even in times of despair. Heather is a true warrior woman and a total inspiration to others, especially women to not give up when faced with adversity.'

–Bev Greet OAM, co-founder of Positive Women VIC

'Heather Ellis opens your eyes to the life of the long distance overlander; the uncertainties, the unique solutions, the moments of awe, and the times of pure joy. She does so in such a way that will have you there with her, with all your senses alive. Without a hint of overkill she weaves in historical fact and describes the landscapes so well that the combination had me wanting to climb on my bike and head out. I think that most readers are going to want to read this book at least twice. Once so they can see what happens next; it's a real page turner. And the second time so they can revel in all the details. Heather Ellis tugs at your heartstrings, opens your mind, and thoroughly entertains. What a journey!'

–Sam Manicom, author of motorcycle adventure travel books

TIMELESS on the SILK ROAD

AN ODYSSEY FROM LONDON TO HANOI

Heather Ellis

PUBLISHING

Published by Phonte Publishing
PO Box 567
Healesville Vic 3777
Australia
enquiries@phontepublishing.com
www.phontepublishing.com

National Library of Australia Cataloguing-in-Publication entry:
Ellis, Heather, 1964–author.
Timeless On The Silk Road: an odyssey from London to Hanoi / Heather Ellis
9780648496908 (paperback)
9780648496915 (ebook)
Ellis, Heather–Travel–Europe–Central Asia–China. Motorcycle touring–Europe–
Central Asia–China. Central Asia–Silk Road–Description and travel. Central Asia–
Silk Road–Social life, history and customs.

 A catalogue record for this
book is available from the
National Library of Australia

Cover design by Peter Long
Cover photograph (Kalyan minaret, Bukhara, Uzbekistan) by Heather Ellis
Text design and typesetting by Libby Austen
Map by Mapping Specialists Ltd.

For
all whom 1996 was too late

A year after I was diagnosed with HIV in September 1995, my travels along the Silk Road from London to Hanoi was to be my last adventure: my one last search for meaning. No real preparation went into this journey. There was no detailed study of maps; research into what equipment might be needed; hotspots of political unrest to avoid; and what vaccinations and visas were required. I threw caution to the wind, packed my motorcycle and rode east and then south. I rode across half our planet.

The story of that year-long journey came from my diary, my memories, my interpretation of those events, and from researched facts. To preserve anonymity, I have changed the names and identifying details of some of the people in this book. Other names used, I recalled from memory as I didn't always record these details in my diary. I apologise for any inaccuracies. Other people named in this book have kindly given me permission to use their name and include their photo. Thank you.

—Heather Ellis, 2019
www.heather-ellis.com

BY THE SAME AUTHOR
Ubuntu: One Woman's Motorcycle Odyssey Across Africa

HEATHER ELLIS has worked as a radiation safety technician, a motorcycle courier in London, a journalist for News Ltd and in international community development. She was diagnosed with HIV in London in 1995, and after her motorcycle ride across Europe and Asia, nearly died from AIDS in Australia in 1997. Heather is an advocate for the empowerment of women living with HIV, particularly through ending stigma. She is also a motivational speaker. Heather lives with her three children in Victoria, Australia where she is writing her next book, a novel. And she still rides motorcycles.

Photo by Lawrence Pinder

The trouble is, you think you have time.
Buddha's Little Instruction Book compiled by Jack Kornfield

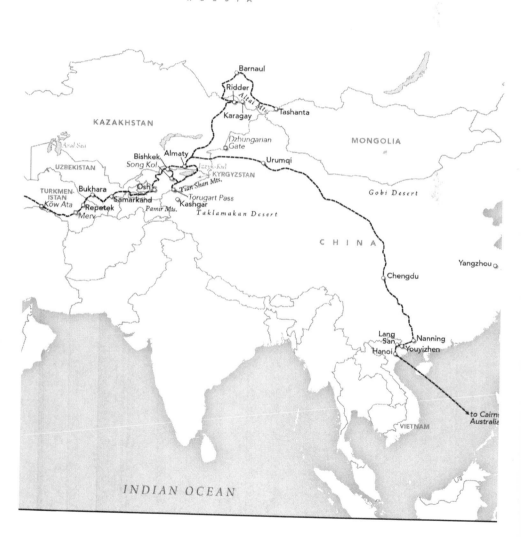

Contents

Part 4 CHINA TO AUSTRALIA

Part 1

LONDON TO GREECE

1

A ROOM OF MY OWN

London

I sat alone in the upstairs room of a ground-floor council flat off Old Street in the heart of London's East End. All day, I'd scrubbed and disinfected the room. Cleaned and wiped all traces of the two dogs who'd occasionally failed to hang on for 'walkies'. The room had been theirs before I moved in. I'd rented the unfurnished digs with its smelly floral carpet for £50 a week from a skeletal old lady who lived mostly in her lounge room downstairs, now with her dogs, watching television and smoking cigarettes. Outside, locked to a steel post in the stairwell, was my motorcycle, a Yamaha TT600. This toughest of off-road motorcycles was once favoured by desert racers when it dominated the Paris Dakar in the 1980s.

My TT600 had given its all on our ride from south to north Africa, a journey of fifteen months that started in April 1993 and had recently ended. I say, 'our ride' because, after months on the road together, this motorcycle had become my companion, my loyal friend. It was simply referred to as the TT. But it was much more than steel and plastic; nuts and bolts and had developed its own aura of indestructibility that could not be snuffed out, even when its engine failed as I rode along the Nouadhibou docks, in Mauritania, to the cargo ship that carried us away from Africa to Europe. That was two months ago. It was September 1994, and the TT was rebuilt—reborn and ready for our next adventure.

It was Sunday night and with a bottle of shiraz, and a plate of cheese and crusty bread, I sat on my makeshift bed: my camping mattress and sleeping bag, which still held the scent of Africa, of dirt and wood smoke. I leaned against the wall, satisfied I could comfortably call the room home.

I was thirty years old. My shoulder-length light brown hair was still tinged with streaks of blond. My skin was still bronzed from an everlasting African sun. My body still lean and strong from riding a motorcycle, which weighed upwards of 200 kilograms, through mud, sand, pot-holed and corrugated roads. The plan was to rent the room during the coming winter. I would work as a motorcycle courier then ride home to Australia next spring through Russia, Central Asia, China, and South East Asia. I'd be riding along the world's oldest trade route: The Silk Road, which meanders as a network of roads for more than 4000 kilometres over mountains and across deserts until it forks into China and India. These ancient trade routes were never just one road and collectively, provided several options for merchants, migrants, armies, refugees, artisans and pilgrims to travel from east to west or west to east. People travelled this way as far back as 200BC, the golden age of ancient Greece, exchanging skills, ideas and goods—mostly silk—but also spices, tea, gold and jade.

Admittedly, the plan for this next journey was still quite vague. It was still so far away. Next spring? 'Maybe, I don't know'. This had become my catchphrase in Africa. When asked by the locals where I planned to go next or where I'd sleep that night or if I'd take this road or that, this was often my response. It was because I'd learned to move with the ebb and flow of life. Things had always worked out for me, and I reasoned this next journey would be no different.

The ride home along the Silk Road was merely something that would happen at some point in the future. What occupied my thoughts more was my very next journey: working as a motorcycle courier. Before Africa, I'd toyed with ideas of what I'd do when I reached Europe, how I'd top up my travelling funds, and how I'd keep us, the TT and me, together.

I wanted London to be a continuation of our journey, not an interlude where my motorcycle collected dust if I got a job in a pub or an office or something else that would keep us apart. Before my odyssey across Africa, I found out about couriering when I worked as a radiation safety technician at the Ranger uranium mine in Australia's Northern Territory. An English guy working as a haul truck driver told me I should give motorcycle couriering a try. 'You'll make a shit load of money,' he'd said.

I hoped he was right. My bank balance sat at A$8000, but a month ago I'd been A$500 away from being broke. I was eternally grateful to Mobil for paying the equivalent of A$3000, the cost of repairs to the TT. Without their support, garnered by the Letter of Introduction from the Australian arm of this multi-billion dollar oil giant before the ride through Africa, I'd still be stuck on the docks in Antwerp with a broken and busted motorcycle. My refund of A$7500, the deposit I'd paid for a Carnet de Passage, had improved my financial situation overnight. A Carnet de Passage is the customs document to import and export a vehicle through countries without paying duty. In future years, rather than paying such a hefty deposit, overland travellers can easily buy carnet insurance for a few hundred dollars. My deposit was returned when I sent the paperwork to the Royal Australian Automobile Club of Western Australia, the holding authority for my carnet. Fortunately, a Carnet de Passage was not required by those countries I'd be crossing on the ride home.

My funds of A$8000 would be more than enough to get me back to Australia, but I had no idea how long I'd be on the road. It could be one, two or more years. I would travel until my journey took another path. The money earned from motorcycle couriering would help with unplanned expenses and unexpected emergencies. Besides, the idea of taking my riding skill to the next level excited me. After all, I was a motorcyclist.

I was under no delusion though about the dangers of motorcycle couriering. I'd be riding up to ten hours a day dicing through traffic as I made pick-ups and deliveries. I'd also been warned often enough by the British motorcycle travellers I met in Africa. 'You'll get yourself fucking killed,' they'd say when I excitedly, and somewhat naively, told them of my plans. But despite these risks, couriering would be as much a part of my motorcycle journey as Africa had been and as the Silk Road soon would be.

2

THE ROAD WARRIOR

London

I woke early and left the room with its lingering smell of dog-poo to wait outside a motorcycle accessories shop on Old Street. I'd ridden past it the previous afternoon when I went to check out the room, which I found through an advert in the *Evening Standard*. Before the next stage of my journey could begin, right here in London, I needed to ditch my travel-worn ripped and faded jeans and my grease-stained Burberry trench for the armour of a motorcycle courier. The trench coat was all I could find in a market in Kinshasa when my motorcycle jacket had been stolen.

When the sales assistant unlocked the door, I told him I would be working as a courier and needed some gear. He glanced over at the TT parked on the pavement.

'Who the fuck are you? Mad Max's fucking sister?' he said in a thick Cockney accent. 'Bloody crazy Aussies,' he added with a mix of jovial good humour and respect when I told him my story. As he led me to the off-road section, I learnt he too had done his time as a despatch rider back in the 1980s; the heady economic boom days of big money before email and PDFs.

Looking at my well-worn lace-up work boots, he asked: 'You'll need motocross boots. What size are you?'

'Five,' I said, and he pulled a box from the shelf and unpacked a pair of black Sidi boots with a price tag of £180. They felt stiff on my feet, but my ankles and calves were encased in a protective shell that could quite comfortably slide down the tarmac or bounce off car fenders. I also needed new gloves to replace the pair worn through to the palms. Next was a motorcycle jacket and leather pants, then wet weathers for the rain. My helmet, although well-worn from my travels, would have to do.

'You'll need a jacket with lots of pockets,' he said, and led me to the racks at the back of the store. 'There's nothing better than Belstaff. Just layer up in the winter. Get yourself some decent thermals and a polar fleece. That'll keep you warm enough.'

It was late September, and already winter was closing in. Soon I'd be riding in freezing temperatures.

I'd walked into that shop as a vagrant. I looked at home with the homeless. But when I walked out, I was a road warrior ready for battle. I was ready to take on London and its traffic, and so was the TT with its *Mad Max* persona. But inside, I was raw nerves and fear. After a short ride along Old Street, I pulled up outside a motorcycle courier office at the end of a cobblestone lane. I'd called the manager earlier in response to an ad for motorcycle couriers that appeared in the same *Evening Standard* as the room. As I walked into the drab office, a tired man, podgy and with thinning hair, looked up from a desk stacked with paperwork.

'I'm here for the courier job,' I announced with false confidence.

'Ever used one of these?' he said and handed me a two-way radio. I nodded. The radio felt familiar, and I was taken back to my days when I worked at the uranium mine fringing Kakadu National Park. It seemed a lifetime ago and I suddenly felt a longing for its hidden gorges where I'd swim naked in rock pools and bask in the sun like a lizard.

'So you've just ridden through Africa. You got more fucking guts than most. This will be a piece of piss for you. Ride down the road a bit. We'll radio you with a job,' he said and returned to his stack of papers.

'Is that it?' I asked in disbelief. There were no questions about my experience. No forms to complete.

He threw a crumpled piece of paper into a bin. 'You get paid cash on Friday.'

I picked up the radio, slung it across my shoulder and turned to leave.

'Look,' he said. I stopped and turned. 'If you survive the first three weeks, you'll be okay.'

I knew that survive didn't mean just staying with the job. And if I didn't survive, it would be no concern of his. As I walked back to the TT, I hoped the forces that protected and guided me in Africa were still with me now. I hoped events would continue to unfold effortlessly in my favour as they always had.

I rode into the flow of traffic, which was orderly, as the British sense of queuing also applied to driving. After a few blocks, I stopped and the radio operator barked an address. I quickly pulled out the *A to Z London* street directory from the Gearsack and looked it up. This was the 1990s, before the widespread use of GPS. My heart sank. The job was an office block near the Tower Bridge. It was in London's financial centre, the oldest part of the city. An area of narrow lanes, one-way streets and modern office towers. I found the street, but to reach it would be like navigating a maze.

'Excuse me,' I called through my helmet to a man in a dark-grey suit carrying a briefcase. I'd pulled up beside him at the fringe of the old city. He looked to be some kind of financial professional, and I assumed he would know this maze of office buildings that rose up from the cobblestones of old London. As I neared, he quickened his pace. I jumped the TT over the gutter and onto the pavement and stopped beside him. My mark was not going to escape so easily.

'Excuse me,' I called again. The man stared at me stunned, but when he saw I was a woman, his look turned to relief. I showed him the address, and he gave out the directions.

'Go right, then left, then through the arch. It's the building on the right,' he said and hurried off into the stream of pedestrians shuffling along the pavement like an army of ants dutifully serving their purpose.

I would never have found the address without his help. A few minutes later I arrived at my destination, picked up the package and radioed in. The office gave me another job and asked what took me so long. This next job was easy. Ride down past the Tower of London, past Trafalgar Square and cut up into Soho, an area of narrow one-way streets in an ordered grid. After I'd picked up and delivered the second package, I radioed in and was told to wait.

It was a bright autumn day, and I stood in the sunshine with a coffee. A Honda CB500 painted in matt black pulled up. The rider spoke a few quick words into the two-way slung across his shoulder and glanced at me as he bounded up the steps of the offices where I'd just delivered my package. A moment later, he bounded out and stood beside me.

'Haven't seen a TT600 over here. I see you're well travelled,' the rider said and leaned close to look at the world map traced into the TT's side-cover. He had thick curly black hair, and his accent was unmistakably Australian. Dressed in black leather both he and his motorcycle looked to have slid down the tarmac more than a few times.

'Hi, I'm Chris. I'm from Sydney,' he said and told me he'd been working as a motorcycle courier for about three years. He did the winters in London when there was money to be made, and then the winters in Sydney when much of London's business world took summer holidays. I told him my story and how it was my first day with a courier company near Old Street.

'Naw. You don't wanna work for them. You'll get nothing but short jobs. You'll earn nothing. Come work for Wings. There are heaps of Aussies and Kiwis. We'll look after ya,' he said.

'Okay,' I replied feeling as though we were of the same tribe and I would soon be amongst my own kind.

'We're all at the King George IV on Portugal Street every Friday. Come along,' he said, and his radio crackled with another job. 'Got to go. See you Friday. Give Wings a call,' and handed me their business card.

I got back to the old lady's flat around 7.00 p.m. exhausted from nearly nine hours of constant riding. As I sat with a bottle of shiraz, and fish and greasy chips, I knew the short jobs around the old city would kill the TT. It was air-cooled, and the long stints of idling in traffic would soon fry the newly rebuilt engine.

'Yes. Chris told us about you. Come on in. We don't see many girls couriering. But all you Aussies are mad,' said the male voice on the phone the following morning. It was 8.00 a.m. and after I'd called Wings, I headed over to the courier office near Old Street and told the manager I'd found another job. He looked disappointed. He then added up my one day of couriering, £67.50, and paid me in cash.

'Good luck,' he said, and I was gone.

'Here's your radio. You're six four,' said the man in the control room at Wings Couriers when I was given my first job an hour later. Sixty-four, it was my lucky number. I was born in 1964, and I saw it as an omen.

After just two days, I knew the TT and I were made for couriering. Riding through my fair share of Africa's cities, I knew all about traffic and how to get through it unscathed. And by the end of the first week, the streets and the districts of London no longer confused me. I was learning the shortcuts. Learning those areas where I needed to be even more vigilant—districts where there were no road rules. One moment, I was riding through Kensington and British orderliness and good manners. The next through Wembley, home to a thriving Indian community. I'd enter the chaos of downtown Delhi with beeping horns and market stalls filled with the aroma of spices. Then I was in Brixton and back in the chaos of Nairobi where I dodged drivers or filtered past African men driving their fancy BMW convertibles. Their big thick gold chains glinting in the afternoon sun as doof-doof music bleared from an enormous stereo.

London slowly started to make sense. Sometimes, I delivered packages to recording studios. Once it was English rock band Blur and lead vocalist Damon Albarn stopped and asked me about my day. I nervously mumbled something incomprehensible, and he replied, 'Take care out there, okay'.

From my first week with Wings, I earned £300, which was half what the other couriers earned as they whizzed passed in a blur of black. They were the untouchables. They ruled London's roads. But my skills improved quickly, and a few weeks later, I too was earning on average £600 a week. Each day was a full tank of fuel and I often covered over 500 kilometres as the TT and I became one with the traffic.

With my growing skill as a motorcycle courier, I earned my stripes as a road warrior and like the rest of the black-leather-clad couriers, I too owned London. We thrived on adrenaline. Our senses were finely tuned, and we could identify hazards long before a driver disobeyed the road rules. I rode as if invisible. I assumed nothing. This was the hazard perception of the motorcycle courier. As I weaved through the traffic, my perception, calculation and aversion to not crash, worked in perfect harmony. It was an awareness that was addictive, a high better than any drug.

After a week in the flea-infested room with its stained floral carpet and odour of dog-poo, I moved to a share house in Perivale, near Wembley. It was a semi-detached double-storey place filled with Aussies and Kiwis working in London. The girls were all nurses and the blokes had jobs in construction. I'd answered an ad in the *Evening Standard* for a room for £50 per week.

'It's too expensive for one person. We'd prefer a couple,' I was told when questioned over my ability to pay, so I paid two weeks in advance. But for my indulgence, I had the biggest and warmest room in the house. It was upstairs, and the hot water system was housed in a cupboard next to my bed. It would prove its worth as winter closed in, and I could put my feet into warm socks and boots in the morning. Wings paid in cash too. I had no bank account, but there was no point because £600 did not last long in London. After stashing £100 a week, often less, under the carpet in my room, my savings for the ride home, there was not much left after paying rent, food, drinks, petrol, and going out on weekends. I was often close to broke by payday.

The Perivale house was always busy. There was always a mountain of coffee cups in the sink, and the lounge was perpetually filled with the friends of my Aussie and Kiwi housemates and their oversized backpacks as they dossed for a night or two or three. One Friday night I sat in the lounge with a tin of Guinness. As one of only five rent payers, space was immediately vacated for me on the saggy brown couch. The landlord's son, Ahmed, a Pakistani boy aged about fifteen, who lived with his family next door, sat beside me dishing out the weekend's drugs to my fellow tenants and their travelling friends. He eagerly answered my questions about the effect of each drug— and which was the best high.

'Cocaine is the best. It is the drug of choice for those who can afford it,' he said, pleased I showed respect for his extensive knowledge of recreational drugs. 'Cocaine makes you feel invincible. You're full of energy. Like you can take on the world, and nothing can stop you.'

'That's how I feel all the time. Sounds like motorcycle couriering,' I said.

'Ecstasy is the poor man's drug. What people take who can't afford cocaine,' he said, summarising the advantages and disadvantages of each drug stashed inside his daypack. 'But ecstasy is cool. It just makes you want to love. You'll enjoy the music too. Heroin. That's a shit drug. Just makes you want to lie around like a zombie. Someone could come up and stick a gun at your head, and you wouldn't give a fuck. Crystal meth is the devil's poison. Fucks people up real quick. Makes you turn into a real angry fucker. Speed, now the nurses love speed.' He winked at the four girls fidgeting nervously on the couch opposite as they watched TV. They ignored him, they'd already scored. 'Keeps 'em awake on night shift,' he whispered. 'LSD will open your mind. Are you ready to see the other side?' Ahmed asked raising a thick black eyebrow, a mischievous glint in his dark eyes as he held up a strip of paper with a row of little dark green dots.

'Yes,' I said eagerly.

3

DOWN THE RABBIT HOLE

London

It wasn't the first time I'd dropped acid. I'd done it before, years ago, when I was twenty and working at the uranium mine in Northern Australia. Back then it was all about the visuals. At night, the lights of the processing plant had an iridescence encased in a green and purple otherworldly halo. But there was nothing about seeing the other side back then. Or even a hint of the kaleidoscope of brilliant flashes of light and colour I'd seen when I had a vision in Mauritania—if that's what it was—while staying at a village on the edge of the Sahara.

This time I was with Andy, another Wings courier I'd met earlier. It was Friday evening, and we'd met at the King George IV on Portugal Street. I'd been couriering for three weeks and was out of the danger zone. I'd survived. We had all survived yet another day, another week and we celebrated with a few beers and games of pool. Andy asked me if I wanted to drop acid at a party with Chris and some of the other couriers who lived in a squat, a deserted old house, on the outskirts of London. It was an acid party, and we'd go places, Andy assured me with a smile that revealed an inner knowing. In the space of a few hours, my life had begun an unstoppable spiral into the nether world.

Andy was from New Zealand with Maori heritage and had the stance of a man who carried the genes of tribal royalty. Even before I met him, I'd felt drawn to him as if he'd sent out a spark of energy that had barbed my heart and all he had to do was reel me in. I first heard about him when I started with Wings: 'Did ya hear? Andy made 850 quid this week,' someone would say in awe. Over the past few weeks, I'd also caught brief glimpses of him. 'Who's that?' I asked the other couriers when I saw this knight in black leather bound up the stairs to the office building where we were parked in Soho. He was tall with broad shoulders and looked as though he could effortlessly carry chain mail. He gave us a brief look and nod before disappearing into the traffic. 'That's Andy. The fucker can ride,' someone had said.

I'd been playing pool when I first met Andy. Chris introduced us.

'Here's that Aussie chick who's fucking crazier than you,' he said, shoving a pool cue in my hand. 'Your shot.'

'So you rode through Africa. I'd love to hear about it,' crooned the demi-god gazing down at me with smokey-grey eyes that glinted with a mix of mischief and promise. I looked up and for a brief moment had the vision of a small furry creature mesmerised by an enormous cobra before it strikes its fatal bite. I was utterly lost; completely infatuated. I felt myself falling down into a deep dark hole with no return. My gut feeling was to run.

'Sure,' I said and reached for my half-empty pint. 'What ya drinking?' he asked. 'Lager,' I said. Escape was futile.

From our very first night together Andy appointed himself my protector, my Roman centurion. 'Ready to go down the rabbit hole?' Andy asked later when we arrived at the squat. I nodded and pulled out my contribution I'd bought from Ahmed earlier.

'Put that away. You've got no idea about quality. That could be hard shit and really blow your mind. Now, this is the fucking best,' he said, and placed a small piece of white paper with a dark dot in the palm of my hand. I popped it into my mouth.

'Just let it dissolve on your tongue,' he said with a hug, his strong arms wrapped tightly around me.

Shortly after, my world morphed into a kind of brilliant fluidity. Colours and people blended together to form one huge melting-pot of atoms held together by an energy that ebbed and flowed around the room. About a dozen people lounged on couches talking intensely with each other. For a moment it all made sense, life, the universe and everything—but then it was gone.

'It's like you can almost grasp it and then nothing,' Andy said as though he was with me, in my mind, as we hurtled together through space and time.

We woke mid-afternoon, a tangle of bodies amongst the couches. Later, a group of us rode back to London, meeting up again at midnight at Slimelight, a Goth night spot in a centuries-old bluestone warehouse behind the Angel Station in Islington. I followed Andy down the narrow cobblestone lane and we parked our motorcycles next to the other couriers from the squat party. The bouncers, two burly guys in black leather jackets, waved us through ahead of the twenty or so other patrons dressed in biker fetish gear queuing in the cold and rain. I felt like I was part of some special elite group; as though we were the real deal and dicing with death somehow made us superior.

Once inside, Andy handed me a small white pill. 'Ever taken ecstasy?' he asked, a smile spreading across his broad face.

'No,' I said holding the pill between my fingers.

'You're in for some fun,' he said. 'The first time on ecstasy is unbelievable. Take half now and the other half in about an hour.'

When the ecstasy hit my brain, my body moved involuntarily to the deafening beat of the music that reverberated off the dark stone walls. An all-consuming sense of love gripped me, and I smiled uncontrollably.

'Pretty good, huh,' Andy said leaning close.

Slimelight was on three levels connected by a maze of staircases. In the chill-out area upstairs on comfy old couches, I sat close to Andy squeezing his hand, entwining my arm in his, pressing my leg against his as I transferred my love into every cell of his powerful body—feelings made a thousand times more intense with the ecstasy. As I sat with him, I was mesmerised by the images of capitalism projected onto one of the stone walls. Just like the LSD, the ecstasy also stimulated my brain sparking synapses that had lain dormant all my life. To my drugged mind, the images were a moment of revelation. As designed to do, each image portrayed a system of consumerist control. But they also backed up what I felt intuitively after Africa, when I arrived back in the developed world.

'I see it now,' I said to Andy, leaning even closer, pressing my leg even tighter and holding his hand with even more intensity. It was now so obvious after being away from western society for so long. Before, I'd been oblivious. But in Africa, where I was embraced by its people who have nothing in material wealth, but everything in family and tribe, I was shown a different order. The African people had shown me human kindness, a meal because I looked hungry and a place to sleep because I looked tired. I was often told 'You are on a journey, we help you.'

'People here just want more—more money, more gadgets, more clothes, more cars, more everything. They are slaves. They will never escape, and then they will die,' Andy said, and he put a strong arm around me. I snuggled into his chest. I felt safe and protected, like I had arrived home. Like we had spent thousands of years searching for each other, and after many adventures and even greater hardships, we had found each other.

'No one needs to live this way when freedom to follow their dreams is within their reach,' I said as the slides revealed another reality.

Andy took a deep drag on a joint and blew the smoke toward the ceiling to mix with the cloud floating above us in a grey haze in the dimly lit room. 'Work is a state of mind. A job can be their passion. It's up to them to make it happen,' he added.

The slides also portrayed an economic order that fuelled the pillage of the earth's resources and polluted it with reckless abandon. It was a system that was unsustainable, and as I watched, I could see it clearly now—the slow death of our beautiful blue planet that shone like a lone jewel in the blackness of space.

'What's the answer?' I asked looking up at Andy with wanton adoration as though he alone could save us all.

'We're all fucked. The end is inevitable so make the most of it,' he replied and then kissed me deeply on the mouth, and I melted into him.

Without Andy, I would never have had the courage to venture into this underworld of drug-fuelled parties at London squats and derelict farmhouses. This was when we had our downtime and partied till dawn most Saturday nights during that winter. My attraction to Andy was pure: my whole body was perpetually on fire in his presence. He would only have to touch me, and I would be swollen and moist with receptivity. But my sexual intensity was never reciprocated. I always had a condom at the ready, but there was never a need for it. At first, I thought it was me even though we always talked so comfortably about a myriad of things, or he'd listen for hours to my stories about Africa. For him though, this wasn't that kind of friendship. We'd drop acid and exclaim we understood what it all meant, then our realisation would be gone as suddenly as it appeared. On ecstasy, our embrace held the infinite power of soul mates. Then, as suddenly as the universe had bought him to me, it took him away. As winter ended, so did our time together.

'I've met another girl,' he casually announced in Soho one crisp spring morning where we were parked up with a half-dozen other couriers. 'She's from New Zealand. She's the one. I'm sorry,' he said as the tears welled in my eyes and I stood looking up at him like an abandoned puppy cast aside, unwanted and unloved. 'You'll be alright,' he continued.

'But I love you,' I stammered as the weight of his rejection began to crush me as though the entire planet was collapsing in on me.

'I know,' he said as his radio crackled and the operator barked an address. 'Got to go.'

And then he was gone, leaving me quivering and sobbing uncontrollably on the street. I turned and walked over to the TT hoping the other couriers hadn't noticed. I placed my hands on the petrol tank, seeking comfort from my loyal friend and protector that had never once deserted me.

I cried myself to sleep that night and the one after that, and still, it went on. I had never experienced a broken heart, and the pain was a dull relentless ache, as real as an open wound that felt like it would never heal. But as spring turned to summer, my sadness turned to acceptance and thoughts of my ride home. With Andy, while down the rabbit hole, nothing else mattered. I'd gone down deeper all the time seeking the source of the secret energy shown to me in that vision in Africa, but instead, I'd lost all sense of my search, and of reality. My plans for the ride home along the Silk Road were forgotten, even abandoned.

Summer brought new friends. I moved onto a 64-foot narrowboat called *Hedgehog* on London's canals. The deal was to pay half its rental of a hundred quid a week with another Australian, Steve. He was a lanky, dark-haired, good-natured guy, a friend of one of the backpackers living at the Perivale house. He managed a second-hand motorcycle shop and was hardly ever on the narrowboat as he spent most evenings with his girlfriend in her warm and cosy flat a few blocks up the road. It was a fortuitous turn of events, and when my motorcycle ground to a halt as I crossed London Bridge while couriering, Steve came to my rescue with a trailer. Through a combination of drugs and heartbreak, I had ignored the TT. It had never abandoned me, but I'd abandoned it. I couldn't remember the last time I changed or even checked its oil. I had ridden it into the ground and killed it. The TT would need another rebuild and with it went half my savings. I needed to keep working, and that required another motorcycle.

Steve sold me a somewhat rusted 1984 Moto Guzzi V50 MK III for £400. It was red once; it was instant love. The V50 was perfect for filtering through London's gridlock traffic: a quick, nimble beast of a thing. Buying that old V50, which proved to be as reliable and faithful as the TT, was another turning point that opened up the world of Guzzistis—those unusual folk who ride Moto Guzzi motorcycles. They come from all walks of life, and the Mole Valley Guzzi Club had an odd assortment of members including lawyers, business managers, labourers and office workers. But they all shared a unifying passion for Moto Guzzi: the Italian motorcycle with grunt and soul. Notably, they worshipped the early models like my V50, which were lovingly crafted by hand at a factory in Mandelo, Northern Italy.

I soon became a regular at the club's weekly social sips at a pub in Surry. Club stalwarts Serena Powis and Paul Harris would invite all and sundry, about a dozen of us, back to their house for red wine, gorgonzola, and floor space to spread a sleeping bag. It was at one of these social sips I met Don. Another fortuitous meeting, as he was of all things, a motorcycle mechanic. He was also gorgeous, with that perfectly smooth honey-coloured English skin, sandy blond hair and green eyes that glinted with a devilish sense of fun and sexiness. When our eyes first connected, his gaze made me feel a little uncomfortable, as though I was standing in the pub naked. He smiled at me, knowing exactly what he would soon do to me. I smiled back. We were destined to meet, not only to rebuild the TT's burnt out engine, but also to rebuild me.

4

DIAGNOSIS

London

I knew something was wrong the moment I walked into the medical clinic in Uxbridge, in outer suburban London. It was a short ride from where I lived on *Hedgehog*, which was now moored at Cowley Lock. There was a sadness in the room that hung like a dense fog and I gasped for breath. Other little things also gave it away. I noticed the downcast eyes of the receptionist when I gave my name.

'Go in. The doctor is waiting,' she said, unable to meet my questioning gaze.

I looked up at the clock behind her. It was 2.30 p.m. I was on time, but it felt strange; I did not have to take a seat and wait my turn. Surely the others, an old man, a woman nursing a baby, a middle-aged woman who looked at me with a scowl, were before me. Doctors' appointments always ran behind schedule. Why had I been given preferential treatment?

This follow-up appointment was scheduled after I had an HIV test two weeks earlier. I had not been anxious for those two weeks as I believed I had nothing to fear. My one unguarded moment of unprotected sex in Africa was long forgotten. The test was just a bureaucratic requirement to get a three-month Russian visa. It was 14 September 1995, and in two months I would be riding to Moscow to spend the winter at Moscow University studying Russian in preparation for the ride home along the Silk Road. For a young Australian girl who grew up in the 'bush', partly in the dry heat of the outback, but mostly in tropical northern Australia, I had a romanticised view of Moscow in the winter. Of ice crunching under my boots as I walked past the Kremlin with its imposing colourful domes dusted with snow.

The door was slightly ajar. I pushed it open.

'Take a seat,' said the doctor. He was in his sixties, I guessed, with thinning silver hair and white, almost translucent skin. I sat down. He turned, and his look of regret, of sadness, told me everything.

'You have HIV,' he said and placed a box of tissues on the desk beside me.

The first sob racked my body like a fierce gust of wind striking from nowhere. Like the rain of a violent storm, then came the tears and mucus. I dropped a sodden tissue on the desk and pulled another from the box. With a ballpoint, he flicked it into the bin at his feet. My life was over. I would never have all the things I'd expected were my right—things that would be mine, one day, in the distant future. I would never be a wife, a mother. I would never have children. Another violent sob wracked my body. Another wave of tears and mucus flowed uncontrollably. I'd never given much thought to children. It was just something I fully expected would happen eventually, but now it would never happen, not ever. I suddenly realised procreation was the meaning of life, but I would soon be dead.

The doctor was speaking, but his words were garbled as though I was listening from under water. I only heard him say, 'you've got five years'. It repeated over and over in my head: five years, five years, five years. This was not meant to happen. Until now, everything had continued to work out for me. Since arriving in London, that guiding protective force I'd felt in Africa was still with me. I'd just been through a glorious English summer, and its warm glow lingered as a permanent smile and a sparkle of anticipation in my bright blue eyes. A stranger would be mistaken for thinking I was madly in love or I'd been bestowed with good fortune. They would be right, but my good fortune was not money, and I was not in love.

Lately, I smiled as though I'd been let in on a special secret. It came from a sense of expectation that life would always be one grand adventure where things would effortlessly unfold in my favour. I was at one of those exceedingly happy moments in my life, and I saw no reason for this to change now, not ever. But it had. And that thing— the universal energy that had ebbed and flowed to my thoughts just as I wished it too—that thing I'd come to believe in so completely, had suddenly deserted me.

I looked down at my hands resting on the black leather of my motorcycle pants. London soot was embedded under my fingernails, and grime stained my skin. It was the sort of dirtiness that comes from riding ten hours a day, five days a week in city traffic. Against the doctor's pale skin and white-collared-shirt, my hands—all of me—was noticeably unclean. The doctor kept talking about some couple with HIV. When they were diagnosed, they decided to go travelling to spend all their money before they died, but they came back to nothing, and they were still alive. It was the only glimmer of hope he could give when there was none. In 1995, there were no effective drugs to control HIV and stop the virus destroying the immune system and progressing to AIDS and certain death.

'They're finding new treatments all the time,' the doctor said as though reading my thoughts. 'But you're better off going back to Australia for care. You Aussies have a lot more money to spend on health than we do here in Britain. Go home to your family,' he added and handed me several brochures. It was all he could offer. 'Get in touch with these support groups. You'll need to talk to someone.'

I noticed that the first was a support group for HIV positive women. I pulled another tissue from the box and stood to leave.

'You'll need to tell your sexual partners,' he said and turned back to his notes. There was nothing more he could do.

With heavy legs, and head downturned to hide my tears, my shame, I walked out of the clinic and into a world that no longer held that special glow. I walked into a world as dull as the row upon row of semi-detached speckled grey houses shrouded in drizzle on that cold autumn day in suburban London. It was a world, I felt that now shunned me. It was as though I was a different species: as though I was no longer part of the human race and I shared nothing in common with the people who walked past me.

As I pulled on my gloves, I thought of how and where I'd been infected. In my denial it would never happen to me, I'd purposefully forgotten my one night of unprotected sex in Africa. It was with

Muhammad, a man I'd met briefly in Mali in May 1994, sixteen months ago. I thought of how I'd said no. I thought of my naivety that I did not carry condoms because I wasn't going there. Sex was too dangerous in Africa. It was the epicentre of HIV. I knew this, but it was a fact that made no difference after I'd smoked the joint that was passed around and drank a few too many of the beers offered—a deadly combination. I thought of how I'd let my guard down and let his hands caress me later that night when he crooned, 'Relax, and I will bring you pleasure'. How I'd moved away from him in the room we shared. How he'd followed me and reached out to me, his touch burning my skin as his hand moved under my shirt. How I'd gone too long without sex: more than a year. And how my body had failed me and how ultimately, I had failed myself.

That unguarded moment happened when I found myself at a house in suburban Bamako in Mali. I felt safe. It was Sunday afternoon. I was with people I knew—friends almost—although I'd only met the tenants of the house, an American girl and her Malian boyfriend, that afternoon. I'd first met Muhammad two weeks before in another part of the country when we shared a lunch of goat meat stew. I met him again by chance, earlier on that Sunday.

Riding back to *Hedgehog*, I remembered that Muhammad was not the only man with whom I had intimate relations. HIV may have travelled through another, a German man I'd met in Hamlin while my motorcycle was being repaired. He'd also travelled by motorcycle across Africa. Maybe he had an unguarded moment too?

While my letter sent to Muhammad went unanswered, the German assured me all was okay when I phoned him after my diagnosis. I briefly thought of the gorgeous Indian man with shoulder-length glossy black hair and ink-black eyes who melted all my defences. I was a lost cause and was about to fall, without resistance, into his strong arms when I realised where I was; Africa, a continent gripped by an epidemic of HIV and AIDS.

But I could go back even further—even before Africa to Australia. To Jabiru, where I lived as I worked at the nearby uranium mine. We were a town of mostly twenty-something singles in our hormonal prime. This was my home for nine years with a break of two years when I was just nineteen and went backpacking to Europe. During those intensely sexual years of our youth, we were linked by an intricate web of liaisons until the Grim Reaper campaign was launched on our television screens in 1987 alerting Australians of the danger of HIV. Secure in my negative test result, I vowed never to have unprotected sex again, a vow that was soon forgotten. But it hardly matters how I caught the virus. The end result was the same.

5

HOPE

London

Don's hand was warm, large and soft as it held mine. His skin seemed too smooth for a motorcycle mechanic. Together, over autumn, we'd spent two months rebuilding my motorcycle in the garage of his parents' house where he lived in Ilford. It was all in preparation for my trip to Moscow and then the ride home through Central Asia. It was odd that even though we'd become so close, so compatible, so inseparable in every way, he would not be joining me. Our conversations were relaxed, comfortable: a sharing of thoughts, hopes and dreams. Our intimacy was always a fusion of our souls that left us both quivering, our naked bodies entwined in the afterglow.

When we first met, I'd told Don about my plans to spend the winter in Moscow to study Russian. As we grew closer, I'd asked if he wanted to travel with me back to Australia. I'd suggested he could meet me in Greece in spring and then we'd ride along the Silk Road together. But he showed none of my passion for motorcycle adventure travel, so we left it out of our conversations—my departure from his life. There was no question of me staying, in my mind or his. It was just accepted our liaison would end and then I would be gone. I don't know why I thought this way, or why Don didn't try to talk me out of my travel plans. It was as though we both knew the next leg of my motorcycle journey was something I had to do. But all these plans had vanished into the ether of my despair on the day of my diagnosis.

It was three weeks after my diagnosis delivered at the Uxbridge clinic, and Don and I were sitting in a small private waiting room at the HIV clinic on an upper level of the Chelsea Westminster Hospital. We'd been ushered in there by a nurse, a pleasant young woman who oozed understanding, having consoled so many after a doctor delivered news of death. We were there to receive the results from my second HIV test. Just a precaution, we'd told the doctor when asked if we had any concerns when we had the test a few days after my first diagnosis.

'We always used condoms,' I said relieved that we always had. I'd insisted as I didn't want to go on the pill and Don didn't object. Using condoms made no difference to him he'd said when I told him what a rare beast he was: that most men preferred sex without one.

I squeezed his hand, and his smile gave me no doubt what we'd do later when we got back to Ilford and he closed his bedroom door. I smiled back, but the light that had been there for so many months was now gone. In its place was sadness for all the happiness that would no longer be mine.

'We'll beat this,' Don whispered, and I looked into his eyes framed with thick black lashes. His eyes showed love and hope when there should have been fear and rejection. He'd said the same words when I told him, the day after I was first diagnosed.

From the Uxbridge medical clinic on that day, I'd radioed Ricochet Couriers, telling them I didn't feel well and needed a few days off. I'd moved to Ricochet after I understandably got the sack from Wings after an expensive designer handbag needed for a magazine photo shoot was stolen from the Gearsack strapped to the TT. I'd parked directly outside the large window of an office to deliver another package, but when I came back, it was gone. Ricochet worked out well. They were based alongside the canal just up the road from *Hedgehog*, and most of my jobs were collecting movie film rolls from Pinewood Studios with delivery to various post-production studios in the city.

From the medical clinic, I'd ridden back to *Hedgehog* and sobbed and sobbed until there were no more tears. I woke Friday morning in a daze and sat on the futon, which doubled as the lounge and my bed, and stared at the wood paneling lining the inside of the narrowboat. The words 'five years' rolled over and over in my head. I sat all day alone, sometimes sleeping, sometimes making tea and Vegemite on toast (comfort food on that cold grey day). I did not want to see anyone, even Don. He would be expecting me at Ilford later that

Friday night. But I could not move, not even to walk the hundred or so metres to The Shovel, to the pub's pay phone to call him at work, a Moto Guzzi spares shop in London's south-east. The day had turned to night, and instead, I sat in the dark, eyes still wet with tears. The hours passed. I dozed.

'Heather, are you there?' a voice had called. It was Don. 'What's up? I was worried when you didn't show,' he'd said and lit the gas lamp before sitting on the futon beside me.

I buried my head in my hands and sobbed. 'I'm HIV positive.'

He'd hugged me, and another wave of tears wracked my body.

'They might have got the result wrong. We'll do another test,' he'd said and hugged me even tighter. I'd nodded, but I knew the result would be the same.

On the day I received the results of that second test, the nurse ushered us into a small room, where the doctor, a young dark-haired man who appeared not long out of med school, looked directly at me, his eyes filled with regret. I returned his gaze and sensed his intake of breath before he delivered the inevitable bad news.

'Heather, your result came back positive. You've got HIV,' he said. 'Don, yours was negative.'

'What a relief,' I said as I squeezed Don's hand.

'Are you okay?' the doctor asked looking directly at me and placed a box of tissues beside me, but there were no more tears. 'You're taking this well,' he said.

Calm and tearless was not the usual reaction when one is told their life is finished, that there is no hope. We hadn't told the doctor that I'd already had a test and knew the result.

'What can we do?' Don asked as if there was a magic cure for HIV and I would be fixed, rebuilt as easily as he'd rebuilt the TT.

'There's nothing we can do,' he replied looking at me. 'You're still healthy. There's no point taking any of the treatments until you start getting sick.' By treatments he meant, AZT, ddI, 3TC and d4T. I'd read about these drugs in a brochure given to me by the elderly doctor in Uxbridge. All these medications, the pamphlet warned, came with side effects: severe headaches, nausea, nerve damage, muscle wasting and anaemia. None of these drugs stopped HIV destroying the immune system and the body developing AIDS. They might delay death by a year or two. There was no hope of long-term survival.

'How long do we have?' Don asked, and I squeezed his hand again thinking how lucky I was to have his support. He saw this as 'our' fight, and not just mine. He had no intention of deserting me.

'You're still well, and we don't recommend starting treatments early,' he said repeating his advice. 'The best you can do is stay healthy.' He handed me a bundle of brochures offering support for people with HIV. The same brochures given to me previously. 'Go see a support group,' he said. 'And you'll need to tell any other sexual partners.'

One of the brochures was for an HIV women's support group in East London. After I assured Don I was okay, he returned to work, and I rode over to an old three-storey brick building wedged between high-rise offices. Inside, I was greeted by a young woman with a mass of tiny blond ringlets framing an angelic face.

'Hi. I'm Maggie. Welcome. Come upstairs,' she said. Her smile seemed to light up the darkened foyer and I followed her up a narrow staircase and past hallways leading to a maze of rooms.

'I've just found out,' I blurted when we reached a room on the top floor. A golden-green light streamed through a large stained-glass window that towered behind an oversized antique wooden desk. A tall, slender woman with auburn hair, tied in a thick plat that rested on her shoulder, stood beside it.

'Hi. I'm Liz,' she said and walked towards me. It felt like I was part of a secret sisterhood fighting for survival: a minority within a minority. A sisterhood that would always be there for each other. Liz gave me a hug and Maggie squeezed my motorcycle-jacket-clad shoulder.

'I've been positive for five years,' Maggie said as if she knew this would give me the hope I craved. She looked fantastic: beautiful and full of exuberance for life and her future. Not a woman who had lived up her decreed time and would soon die.

'Wow,' I replied.

'Wow,' she said nodding and her ringlets bounced as if dancing in celebration.

'The doctor gave me five years before I'll develop AIDS,' I said.

'Don't listen to them. They know nothing about this virus. No one knows how long any of us have got.' With her hand on my elbow, she led me to the couch as though I was one of the shell-shocked come in from the battlefront. She sat beside me.

'Are you on medications?' I asked.

'No way. Stay away from those drugs. They'll make you sicker than the HIV.'

'I'm travelling by motorcycle. I rode through Africa. I got it...' She nodded. There was no need to explain how I was infected or expectation to do so. 'I'd planned to ride home to Australia through Russia and Central Asia, but I don't know what to do now,' I said the words tumbling over themselves with the relief of speaking to someone who understood. Someone with HIV. Someone who gave me hope.

'Not everyone gets sick,' she said. And with those four words, everything became clear.

I rode back to Uxbridge, to *Hedgehog*, my head spinning with renewed enthusiasm. After speaking with Maggie and Liz, I felt hope where before there'd only been despondence. Maybe I too would not get sick. Maybe Don was right, and we would beat this insidious thing that was amassing its forces to wage war inside me. He would be here soon, and we would celebrate my good news with a pint or two of Guinness at The Shovel.

Inside the narrowboat, I filled the pot-belly stove with coal and as I waited for the first flicker of heat to warm my chilled bones, a plan slowly began to form. I would write my story. I would write a book. I saw it as an evolutionary call to action to do my bit to help make the world a better place. I could not let all that had been revealed in Africa die with me. All those experiences, I believed, happened for a reason. It was all evidence that humanity had the power to tap into an energy that could help us achieve our dreams, our goals and turn our ideas into reality. Although, as I devised this plan, I failed to make the connection that this very energy had recently deserted me.

My motives to write my memoir were not entirely altruistic. I wanted to leave my legacy: something to show that I had existed on this earth.

With my grand plan taking shape, I turned to the practicalities. I'd need to retrieve the £500 deposit I'd paid for the Russian language course. The balance of £2000 was due next week. Without a three-month visa, winter in Moscow was out of the question. Motorcycle couriering no longer seemed like the exciting adrenaline-fuelled adventure it had been over the past year. But if I was not working, I could no longer live in London. To write my book, I would have to go home to my parents' banana farm in Queensland. Tropical far northern Australia seemed a far more attractive option than another winter in London.

I was still well. My parents would never need to know about the HIV. I wanted things to stay the same as long as possible. I wanted my parents to love me as they always had: to be proud of me. Not admonish me for my stupidity, confront me with the shame I'd brought on our family. I knew they would still care for me even as I lay dying, but at what cost? Don was working part-time. He'd never travelled overseas. He'd jump at the chance to come with me. I'd pay. Don had rebuilt the TT, and the flight was my way of saying thank you for his labour and expertise, and all his support. He had made me feel normal, wanted, and more importantly, loved, at a time when I only saw myself as diseased: as death.

After the parts to rebuild the TT and buying the Moto Guzzi V50, I'd saved nearly £2000 from couriering. It was enough to pay for the flights, plus I hadn't touched the A$8000 in my bank account back home. It'd take me six months to write my book, and we'd be back in April, just in time for summer. I'd still be well: I'd still have four and a half years, or even longer. Maybe the elderly doctor in Uxbridge was right and new treatments, even a cure, would be discovered by then.

For the first time in weeks, I had something to look forward to. We'd leave in November. We'd escape the biting cold and grey drizzle of London for sun-drenched tropical far north Queensland.

6

POINTING THE BONE

Cairns to London

It was mid-November 1995 when Don and I took a flight from London to Cairns in northern Australia. My mother was there to collect us for the hour-drive to their banana farm. My parents were happy to have me home, but they weren't entirely sure of Don or his motives.

'I wouldn't trust him,' my mother said quietly as we washed up after dinner a week later. 'He'll spend all your money and then leave you.'

I assured her she was wrong and explained why I had paid for the flights.

'He's lazy,' my father said as I worked beside him in the packing shed.

'He's not used to banana work or the heat,' I replied in Don's defence.

The deal was that we'd stay with my parents until April. I would write my book; they'd even bought me a computer and printer. To pay our way, we'd work on the farm three days a week.

But the heat and unrelenting humidity of a tropical summer was too much for an English boy with delicate skin and a constitution for a more civilised, cooler climate. Don lasted several weeks then returned to London and his family in time for Christmas. His first ever overseas trip amounted to nothing more than day after day of sweaty back-breaking work where he was covered in banana sap, bitten by insects and his only reward was the occasional trip to a nearby beach where the rainforest meets the sand. We had no money for sightseeing, and having seen it all before, I had no interest in it anyway. It had been an unfair arrangement filled with mismanaged expectations.

At the Cairns airport, we hugged and kissed and said how much we'd miss each other, but secretly, I was relieved he was going, and I expected he felt the same. I'd have no more distractions. I had discovered writing and was possessed by a frenzied drive to recount all that had happened in Africa. Through writing, I had also found my catharsis. Writing helped me forget the truth. Writing carried me back to Africa, to that happy time when my world held so much hope and promise—before HIV. The writing stopped the torment, and on those four days when I was not working with my parents, I wrote feverishly from sun up to sundown.

Outwardly, I looked no different. I looked healthy and still saw no reason to tell my parents. But when I was not writing, when I worked in the banana paddocks, and the packing shed, the real truth filled my every thought. I was caught in a perpetual loop: 'I'm going to die. I'm going to die'. It was like a 'pointing' had been called against me. When I was a child living in outback Australia where my parents were mining opal, my father had often recounted stories about Aboriginal culture. I'd listened wide-eyed when he told me about the kurdaitcha man, the tribe's spiritual leader who administers the execution ritual: pointing the bone. It is carried out against those who commit a serious crime and the victim of a 'pointing' soon loses the will to live. They are told they will die. They believe this and eventually, they succumb.

In April 1996, after six months with my parents, my manuscript was finished. I copied it on several disks, just in case one failed, and also printed it to lug the weighty tome back to London.

There was no one to meet me at the airport. Don was working. I caught the tube to the city and then another to Ilford where I sat down to a cup of tea and slice of chocolate cake with his parents. They were kindly, gentle retirees who'd first welcomed me into their home soon after Don and I met nearly a year earlier.

Don returned late afternoon, and for those first few weeks, everything was beautiful again. I prepared my submission to publishers and even gained the interest of the UK office of Little Brown, but a meeting with editorial staff in their boardroom did not extend to an offer. The rejection was even more devastating as I'd stepped inside the hallowed halls of an international publishing house and felt like I was just inches away from signing a contract. The meeting had held so much promise, but neither I, nor my manuscript, were ready. It was very much an unpolished first draft, and I showed no commitment to write a second book.

The reignited spark between Don and me was never quite the same, and as it faded, I moved back to the *Hedgehog*. Steve had returned to Melbourne, and the new tenant was Tim, one of the guys from the Moto Guzzi Club. Ignorant that I carried the scythe of death, he welcomed me on board for both someone with whom to chat and to share the rent.

Tim was a jolly red-haired Londoner in his mid-thirties who worked as a welder building the Heathrow Airport extension, so I saw little of him. I went back to couriering with Ricochet, but the thrill of dicing with death was gone. London's traffic felt as though it had become even more chaotic with even more double-decker red buses belching black smoke, and I no longer had the nerve for it. In my new-found vulnerability, I no longer felt invincible, an untouchable, a road warrior. Instead, I saw motorcycle couriering for what it was: a dangerous occupation where my body of flesh and bone was no match for large hard objects hurtling toward me at speed.

I continued submitting my manuscript to publishers in the hope my evolutionary duty would be done, and I would not be forgotten. But I received only rejection slips. As winter closed in, I sank deeper into my dark world. I closed myself off from friends and spent all my spare time in the alternative therapy section of self-help bookshops where I searched the healing arts of the ancients hoping to find a miraculous cure. I then turned back to the only thing I had left—the ride home along the Silk Road. I turned back to the road because it was on the road in Africa that I had stumbled across something that was profoundly important. Travelling alone, I had no one to fill my head with doubts, and in this void, I turned to my own gut feeling. I learnt to trust my intuition, and in this trust, I felt an all-consuming sense of knowing that there was some greater meaning to our existence. I felt all those chance encounters and coincidences that came my way, often to save me in the nick of time, were more than just good luck. Maybe, just maybe, I would be saved again.

First, I'd ride through Europe and take a brief hiatus to work in a ski resort in the Alps; anywhere but another winter in London. And then along the Silk Road through Central Asia and down through China to South East Asia. There was no real planning, no poring over maps, no researching road conditions or what visas I'd need. No purchase of travel insurance. What was the point with my days numbered? I had no plan of how long this journey would take or even if I would make it, because none of this really mattered.

Two weeks before leaving London, I booked an appointment at the specialist HIV clinic at the Chelsea Westminster Hospital. I was still healthy, but in the months to follow I wanted to know what to expect. I wanted to know my enemy.

'Jane Smith,' the nurse called. 'Jane Smith,' she repeated as I sat reading the *Evening Standard*. 'Are you Jane?' the nurse asked tapping me on the shoulder. 'Ah, yes,' I replied, looking around the room and realising I was the only woman among a room full of emaciated young men, all hope gone from their slumped bony shoulders. I'd given a false name even though there was no one here who knew me or who even cared.

The doctor was a young man with a chiselled jaw and a stock of perfectly groomed brown hair. I told him of my plan to ride my motorcycle back to Australia via Central Asia and China. I would leave in a fortnight. I told him if I had less than four years of my five years left, I wanted to do this; I wanted to have one last adventure.

He did not try to discourage me. How I lived my last years was of no interest to him.

'Before you go, we need to see what the HIV is doing. How active it is. There's a new test to find out how much virus is in your blood. It's a viral load test. It's not funded by the NHS yet. It'll cost you £80,' he said. I nodded. 'We'll do a CD4 count as well.'

The results would be available in a week. The CD4 count showed the strength of my immune system or how much of it the HIV had destroyed. A healthy person's CD4 count sits typically between 800 to 1500.

My CD4 or T-cell count was 450 and my viral load was 1300. My coiffured doctor assured me this was of no real concern because my viral load was considered low.

'You're still healthy. There's no sign of illness. It might be years before you get sick,' he said. 'But I'd like you to take Bactrim with you just in case. It's an antibiotic. The HIV might get aggressive, and then you'll be susceptible to PCP.' And he went on to tell me that PCP stood for pneumocystis pneumonia, and that it would rapidly smoother my lungs and kill me if my immune system became too weak to fight the infection. Those with a healthy immunity are not susceptible to PCP.

'You'll know when you've got it. You'll feel like you're suffocating,' he said and with a manicured hand, wrote out a prescription. 'Here's my phone number. If you run out, call me. I'll send more.'

Despite his good intentions with the Bactrim, he made no mention of the hope that had emerged on the horizon a year earlier. No mention of the new generation of HIV medications, protease inhibitors, that had been discovered by Dr David Ho and his team of researchers in the US.

This discovery, heralded by some back then as the first step in a potential cure, was presented at the International AIDS Conference in Vancouver in July 1996. This conference would become a landmark moment in the history of HIV/AIDS. Saquinavir, the first protease inhibitor was rushed through US Food and Drug Approval on 6 December 1995 after scientists found, when combined with existing HIV medications, it had the 'Lazarus Effect' on AIDS patients close to death. Already, more than six million people had died globally from AIDS. Saquinavir, and a number of other protease inhibitors that soon followed, were to save millions of people. These new drugs effectively controlled HIV to undetectable levels and stopped it from destroying the immune system and killing its host from a cohort of illnesses collectively known as AIDS.

But I knew nothing of these medicines at the time, and presumably neither did those young men in that waiting room, young men whose lives held so much promise. How many died needlessly? The doctor likely was as ignorant of the potential of these discoveries as his ill-fated patients. The discovery had not long been out of the test tube, and there was nervousness around side-effects and when to treat patients. Some also thought it was just another medicine that would buy a bit more time.

I was still healthy and could stay that way for five or more years. If I showed no sign of illness, it was understandable to err on the side of caution. So with several packets of Bactrim and reassurance that the virus was presently in a state of suspended animation, I packed my motorcycle for my one last adventure—my one last search for meaning.

7

SNOW SEASON

London to St Johann

'Ya can crack a smile can't ya!' the photographer for *Motor Cycle News*, one of the UK's leading motorcycle magazines, yelled above the din of traffic that honked, tooted and belched black smoke as it circled London's Trafalgar Square. I forced a smile, but I winced with worry and a little pain. A few minutes before, I'd burnt my hand on the muffler when I'd tightened the straps securing a bag to my motorcycle like one would secure a bag on their horse. With the TT packed for the long journey ahead, I felt reassured that my trusty steed would do its best for me on this our last crusade.

It was 4 November 1996, as bleak a day as London can throw up as it heads into winter. But there was no sense of excitement for this second journey: no expectation of the grand adventure that had revealed so much in Africa.

'Ya a bit fucking overloaded aren't ya?' the stony-faced photographer yelled as he snapped off a few more photos. In the Gearsack bag that sat on the seat behind me was a printed copy of my manuscript, *Ubuntu: One Woman's Motorcycle Odyssey Across Africa*. The manuscript tracked a journey on which the African people, through their kindness, showed me the way of *ubuntu*, a Bantu word, which means the universal bond that connects us all as one.

I carried the manuscript as I'd received a letter from Gustav Lübbe Verlag, a German publisher, asking to see more. I'd lodged my submission after meeting one of their staff at the Frankfurt Book Fair in October. My trip to the world's largest literary marketplace of publishers and agents brokering book deals was my last-ditch attempt to gain attention, anyone's attention. I must have looked a sad cause lugging my manuscript from stall to stall in the cavernous halls housing publishers from around the world. It was just fortunate that Anna, whom I'd met in Mauritania, North Africa, and her partner Bernd, lived in Frankfurt and offered me a bed in their apartment near the city centre.

The photographer was done and packed his camera and tripod into a small rucksack. I was anything but excited about the media coverage. I'd only contacted the magazine out of a sense of duty to Mobil UK who'd kindly given me a Letter of Introduction. It replaced the one provided by Mobil Australia I used in Africa. When I'd presented it at Mobil depots, I'd been furnished with quite a few litres of oil and petrol.

'Good luck to ya. You'll fucking need it,' he said and strode past me toward the underground and into the throng of people that was the constant busyness of London.

I'd grown to love London. Even own it. I knew my way around this city of seven million people as I diced with death as a motorcycle courier. But now I hated it. I hated its greyness, drizzle and damp. I hated its bone-chilling cold that was steadily closing in. I wanted to escape this bleakness that had descended to permeate my every thought since that day I was diagnosed. At first, I'd gone through denial. Then hope as I searched for a cure in alternative therapies. When I'd returned to London from my parents' banana farm, I'd tried it all. Crystal therapy, spiritually charged water therapy, a multitude of vitamins and minerals and even ozone therapy, where a middle-aged tight-lipped Indian woman charged me a small fortune to aerate a litre of my blood and feed it back into my veins. I had been the modern-day snake-oil salesman's best customer. But in the nick of time, before I'd spent all my savings, I'd accepted none would be found.

I wasn't really sure what stage of mental anguish I had reached as I sat on my motorcycle posing for magazine photos with Nelson on his column towering above me, gazing southwards toward Dover where I would catch the ferry to France later that day. I was somewhere, I felt, between being the victim of a 'pointing' and a faint glimmer of hope.

To avoid the very real possibility of a rear-end collision from cars travelling at well over 200 km/hr, I kept off Germany's autobahns for this was a country with no speed limits on its freeways. When there was no alternative on my map, I rode in the slow lane, wedged between trucks hauling all manner of goods bumper to bumper between its utopian cities to fuel a nation that knew no bounds to its prosperity. Any overtaking maneuvers had to be made with deft precision as the speck in my mirror one moment was a Mercedes, BMW or Audi hurtling past me the next.

After leaving London, I reached Frankfurt in two days. It was a cold ride through an unrelenting drizzle, and I rumbled into Frankfurt mid-afternoon to Anna and Bernd's apartment. I'd phoned Anna from London, and she was overjoyed when I asked if I could visit. I was welcomed with open arms, and they insisted I stay a week as they'd planned a string of outings to show off their beloved hometown. While it was a vibrant modern metropolis with flashy skyscrapers that stretched into a cloudless azure sky, Frankfurt was also a city steeped in culture and history with grandeur churches, museums and art galleries where I viewed the works of Botticelli and Rembrandt. We strolled through the Palmengarten, a sprawling botanical garden spread over twenty-two hectares and later drank *apfelwein* at a rustic tavern. We browsed markets in medieval Römerberg and attended the opera of *Don Giovanni*, where I soared to the heights of emotion as the voices of the sopranos reverberated into the very depths of my soul.

On my first day in Frankfurt, I'd posted my manuscript to Gustav Lübbe Verlag and eagerly awaited a reply, but a week later my excitement turned to crushing disappointment when the rejection letter arrived. Bernd and Anna consoled me with a delicious meal of slow-cooked beef and a bottle of red, advising I should finish my travels first and try again when I returned to Australia.

When I first arrived in Frankfurt, I'd told them of my plan to work in a ski resort, and they'd kindly offered to store my motorcycle in the basement of their apartment. I'd skied the Alps while on a backpacking trip in the 1980s and then again more recently with motorcycle couriering friends before my diagnosis.

'Leave your *moto* here. Best you catch the train,' Bernd said. And as a keen skier himself, suggested I try St Johann near Kitzbühel. 'It is a beautiful village. The skiing is excellent.'

After an overnight train from Frankfurt, I arrived in Kitzbühel and moved into a dorm room at an ageing three-storey alpine hotel near the station. It housed an assortment of backpackers all in search of a job for the upcoming ski season, which started in early December, two weeks away. The snow had not yet arrived, but I was told the best jobs went quick, so everyone arrived in the mountains early. The most coveted positions were in the upmarket hotels and nightclubs where staff made just as much in tips as they did in wages.

But of course, it all depended on whether you could speak German and had a passport from a country in the European Union, which enabled the holder to work without a permit. While I couldn't speak German, I did have a British passport. My choice was for something a little more genteel than Kitzbühel, and I followed Bernd's suggestion. Besides, St Johann was my layover, somewhere bright and fresh to sit out the winter rather than gloomy London.

I was offered a job from the first advert I phoned. 'You have British passport?' the lady asked when I told her I was Australian. 'Very good. Australians very good workers.' She gave me the address, and an hour later, after I'd trudged halfway up a mountain, the Kitzbüheler Horn, I arrived at Gasthof Hirschberg, a quaint guesthouse overlooking St Johann. I was employed as a waitress and chambermaid. I'd start in two weeks, and while the job paid the equivalent of about US$200 per week, it included all meals, skis and ski pass, and a room, which I'd share with another Australian girl whom the owner had already employed. 'We have Australian boy too,' she told me.

Winter came early to the Alps, and by the end of the two weeks, the valley and mountains were blanketed in snow. From my first day, the slopes were busy with skiers, and I quickly fell into a pleasant routine of serving lunch, cleaning rooms and skiing most afternoons with Penny, the Australian girl with whom I shared a room.

But despite living in a winter wonderland where the skiing was perfect and the days were filled with sun and blue skies, I could not shake the depression that perpetually lingered in me. Penny, and Jeff, the other young Australian who worked in the kitchen were always bursting with energy, and at the end of our shift, at around 10.00 p.m. would walk down the mountain to St Johann's bars. I'd always find an excuse to stay behind. By the end of the night, I was exhausted and would crave sleep in the warmth of my bed.

As the weeks rolled into months, I was consumed by a sadness that hung like a dark cloud above me. My health slowly deteriorated and with this deterioration came the realisation that I may not be spared. With bumper snow falls, the slopes got busier, and despite the fatigue penetrating into the very depths of my being, I worked just as hard. I put on a 'happy face' to serve the house guests their meals, clean their rooms and serve hot chocolate and chips to hordes of hungry skiers. To avoid suspicion as to why I wasn't enjoying the snow, most afternoons I'd catch a few runs before the lifts closed.

In early January my body could take it no more, and during the early hours while Penny slept soundly in her bed a few feet away, I suffered an attack of PCP, an ordinarily innocuous strain of pneumonia that is fatal to those with weakened immunity such as myself. Just as the HIV doctor in London had advised, I felt I was suffocating.

I popped two Bactrim, the antibiotic he'd given me, and propped myself up on pillows to drain the fluid from the top half of my lungs. I wheezed through the night, too afraid to go to sleep in case I should end up horizontal and unable to breathe.

I'd caught the PCP in the nick of time. From fear of my dark secret being revealed, I struggled through my shift, every step leaving me breathless. Late that afternoon, I tobogganed down the mountain to the post office in St Johann and phoned the doctor in London. He asked nothing about my symptoms and instructed I take two pills three times a day for a week and then, as a prophylactic, one every three days. There was no insistence I go immediately to a hospital where I would undoubtedly have been told about the new generation of HIV medications that would save me. As promised, he would post a four-month supply of Bactrim to the St Johann post office.

With my head held low in front of the beautiful people in their fur-trimmed ski jackets, I walked through the village, all festive with snow-covered roofs and multi-coloured lights hanging from the eaves. In near-darkness, I trudged back up the mountain on the toboggan track, my boots crunching on the snow as I dragged the toboggan behind me. Every step was an insurmountable effect. I struggled to breathe and rested often. The conifers tall, their branches laden with snow, stood silent and foreboding around me.

In the weeks that followed, the Bactrim cleared my lungs of all infection, and I was able to breathe to full capacity. With lungs filled with pure mountain air, I regained my energy, but my face was flushed bright red as though I'd reclined on a deck chair all day at a mountain-top bar where the air is thin and the sun burns with its full intensity. The HIV doctor had asked nothing of my allergies, and as Bactrim is a sulphur-based medication, it left me looking permanently sunburnt. I read this in the medication notes, but hypersensitive skin, which I covered with foundation, was irrelevant compared to the alternative. Years later, I also found out that Bactrim caused pronounced facial redness in HIV patients with high viral load, but the doctor would likely not have known this either.

I'd also discovered pumpkin seed oil, much to the dislike of Gasthof Hirshberg's chef. And I can't say I blame him. Cold pressed by a local farmer, it was the key ingredient in the house speciality: *spaetzle*, an Austrian pasta dish. *Kürbiskeröl* is very expensive, he told me every time I poured lashings of it on just about everything I ate, such was my body's craving for this dark green oil packed full of nutrients.

In early March, the ski season ended. With what I'd saved from my wages, the equivalent in Austrian shillings to just over US$1500, I returned to Frankfurt, spending a few days with Anna and Bernd before packing the TT for the ride along the Silk Road.

From Frankfurt, I rode south to Italy over the Alps on the Brenner Pass, riding through snow and sleet that blew across the high mountain peaks. Numb with cold, every part of me wanted to give up. 'Turn back,' my mind screamed. Ride to the Munich airport, dump the TT, and with my American Express card, buy a ticket on the next flight to Australia. It would be so easy. I could give up, go home and die. The thought tantalised me with each bone-chilling second of that ride, and in my need to survive, I'd been so ready to cast aside my beloved motorcycle. But I pushed on as if the TT had taken control: as if it understood I'd reached rock bottom.

As I rode down the lower slopes of the northern Italian Alps and into the warm sunshine, I peeled off most of the clothing under my jacket. The road wound down into a valley and through quaint villages until it leveled and I rode across flat grazing land. As I would not reach Ancona, the Italian port where I'd catch the ferry to Greece, before nightfall, I searched for a place to stay. Just as the sun sank below the grassy plains, I found the Hotel Maria, a two-storey, dark wood structure that sat alone on a crossroads. It had a shed to safely store my motorcycle, a room with a hot shower for US$25 and served a generous portion of spaghetti Neapolitan with a complimentary jug of red wine. While it was beyond my budget, it was my reward, and that night I fell asleep feeling warm, intoxicated and grateful for what had been provided when everything had seemed so bleak only a few hours before.

8

APOLLO RISING

Greece

On the side of a rocky hill in Greece, surrounded by the ruins of the Temple of Apollo at Delphi, I stood in a small cellar-like room: the *adyton*. Outside, scattered and in disarray, were broken pillars and slabs of grey stone that once formed Apollo's imposing temple.

It was late afternoon, and the hordes of tourists had left on their convoy of buses. In the semi-darkness of the *adyton*, a restricted area, once the exclusive domain of the religious elite, I was alone. Mike, the tall, bearded Greek-German man I'd met last night on the ferry from Italy, was outside smoking a cigarette. He'd had enough of wandering the ruins. Mike was aged about forty, I guessed, and was also travelling by motorcycle, riding his Harley Davidson through the Middle East to the Sinai and Egypt. He was on his way to visit Greek friends near Delphi, and suggested, as we were going in the same direction, we ride together.

I sat down. The slab of rock felt cold in this darkened place sheltered from the sun that cast long shadows outside. I closed my eyes, and in the silence, imagined what it was like back then, when no important decision was made without consultation with the oracle.

In London, after my diagnosis when I spent hours trawling through the alternative therapy sections of bookshops, I stumbled across a book about the oracles of Delphi. In an instant, I was captivated and read everything I could about these women, the high priestesses, appointed to speak the words of Apollo, the ancient Greek god of the sun, music, prophecy—and healing. But also, if he was angered, disease and plague. I was drawn to the oracles' secret sisterhood because I felt we shared a common thread: a sense of knowing an energy permeates all creation.

Like thousands of others from all over the ancient Greek world, as far as Persia (what is Iran and parts of Central Asia today), I too was a pilgrim. While my journey had just begun, for those pilgrims who'd travelled the Silk Roads of antiquity, Delphi was the end of a very long journey.

In ancient times, Delphi was considered the centre of the world. For a thousand years or more, from about 600BC to 600AD, many a priestess in a trance-like state had spoken Apollo's words of wisdom from this sacred place. It is believed these women, who were often middle-aged, were recruited from their villages and townships for their reputation as wise women. Historians have found evidence that cannabis was widely smoked in Ancient Greece, and the perceived wisdoms they uttered may have been particularly prolific when high; when they issued forth a stream of consciousness. For this reason, they may have been chosen to speak the words of Apollo. Their audience came from all levels of society. Generals, politicians, merchants, farmers, and anyone seeking prophecy on life's important decisions and concerns: predictions for crop yields, marriage, children, career, investment. And as Apollo was the god of healing, the sick too, in their search for a cure, came to Delphi.

In the *adyton*, the oracle inhaled clouds of smoke. Some historians proclaim these vapours came from a fissure in the rocks deep under its floor. Others say it was cannabis, picked and dried to the prime of its stickiness to smoulder under a throne-like lattice chair made of hardened smoke-blackened timbers.

While the oracles had long been engulfed by the mists of time, I called them forth from the dimension of the dead, hoping they would hear me and I would be bestowed with Apollo's healing powers. But maybe the oracles had gotten bored with the petty wants and concerns of tourists and moved on? Were they, instead, moving through a timeless dimension along with all the other souls who were no longer part of the living? Earlier, Mike and I, in our heavy motorcycle boots, had trudged uphill through the ruins to reach the games arena. Breathless, we'd sat on the smooth stones where I had a sudden moment of revelation.

'I know what it's like when we die,' I blurted. 'Death releases us from time. It is when we are dead that we can, on a whim, at any moment, be witness to the past, the present, and maybe the future too. We could come back here and watch the games,' I prattled and held my arms wide to embrace it all. 'We could walk amongst these people.'

Everything at Delphi had existed for no other purpose than to meet the needs of hundreds, if not thousands, who waited their turn for an audience with an oracle. The games arena where athletes competed for glory and gold. The amphitheatre where Greek tragedies were performed. The rooms where men and women took bodily pleasures. The courtyards where they indulged in wine and food. The pools where they bathed. And the stalls where merchants sold their wares from far distant lands carried over the mountains and deserts along the network of Silk Roads.

I felt all of this, and my skin had tingled with the undeniable feeling of knowing. For a moment, my depression had lifted and was replaced with great joy: an expectation of what was to come rather than fear and regret. In a brief moment of illumination, I no longer feared death. Instead, I knew that when my life ended, I would not be snuffed out by blackness, by nothingness. I would enter a new world, a new dimension, a new beginning.

'There'll probably be nothing left in the future,' Mike had said raising a bushy black eyebrow. His dark brown, almost black, eyes held the squint of a playful smile. 'But I could handle hanging with the Greeks.'

'It was just a thought,' I replied to quickly quell any suspicions I was a little bit crazy.

'Well, sounds like being dead might not be so bad,' he said with a gentle pat on my shoulder to reassure me it was perfectly reasonable to have such ideas and to share them.

In the semi-darkness of the *adyton*, as I sat on that cold slab of rock, I hoped Mike was right. I hoped I was right. Or had my mind been trying to make good a bad situation? Was it trying to counteract the onslaught of negative thoughts I'd bombarded it with for the past year and a half when death, in all its guises, had been in my every thought?

In the stillness of the *adyton*, I asked for reassurance; a sign that everything would be okay. But there was nothing, only silence. There was no signal, no voice from above to guide me.

From Delphi, I rode with Mike to Larissa, a three-hour ride, where we stayed for two days with his friends Poppi and Sam. And then for another two days with more friends, George and Lisa, who ran a small hotel in Stomio, a fishing village on a beach of golden sand lapped by clear blue water. We dined on large plates of pan-fried calamari served with Greek salad and cold beer followed by shots of ouzo.

I could not bring myself to tell Mike and his friends I had HIV. I'd internalised the stigma, and my fear of rejection stopped me. Despite my permanently flushed face, and my generally sad demeanour, they showed no sign of knowing that there was something wrong with me. Instead, they treated me with a warmth and generosity of spirit that was the Greek way of doing things. It was as if they wanted to do all they could to help this fearless young Australian girl ride her motorcycle alone all the way to Australia. Their kindness helped me forget what awaited me, and my time in Stomio was relaxed and carefree. It was here that my thirty-third birthday also passed. I kept it to myself as I didn't want Mike and his friends to make a fuss; they'd already showered me with so much hospitality. It didn't matter anyway, because every day was a celebration in Stomio as we dined on delicious Greek food, beers and ouzo. Between these celebrations, I'd swim in the ocean, the gentle waves washing over my body, which absorbed the immune-boosting minerals while my lungs breathed in the ionised sea air.

I felt no sexual desire towards Mike. We were just two like-minded souls whose paths had crossed to share some thought-provoking conversations. In fact, after breaking up with Don, I no longer felt any desire for sex at all—even with myself. The loss of sexual desire wasn't a conscious decision. It wasn't like I thought about it and wanted it, but couldn't have it, because I carried the kiss of death. It was merely that I, both physically and emotionally, had no desire for it. Understandable, with the voice of doom my constant companion. My brief reprieve from its vile chatter would come flooding back the moment I moved on from Greece.

Before leaving Stomio, I offered to pay Mike for my room and all the delicious Greek food and drinks, which I knew he'd paid for.

'You've got a long journey. You'll need all your money,' Mike told me. So many times, I'd been told this on my travels, and I hoped, one day I would be in a position to bestow the same generosity on others who passed through my life. Then I realised, I may not have a life for others to pass through. But like a person shipwrecked—adrift at sea, alone, drowning in a deep, dark ocean—I reached for a lone piece of flotsam. It was faith, and I grabbed hold of it and held it, my grip tight and firm.

Part 2

TURKEY TO AZERBAIJAN

9

COURAGE

Turkey

Chilled-to-the bone, I crossed into Turkey at Ipsala in the late afternoon. Soon after leaving Stomio that morning, I'd ridden into a cold front that had suddenly descended from the north, the last of the Russian winter. It would soon be dark, and I had to endure the cold for another hour before reaching Gallipoli. Clothing-wise, I was unprepared.

'Much cold. You have warm clothings?' the kindly border guard asked and hugged his arms, feigning a shiver.

I nodded, but my warm 'clothings' included my entire wardrobe. Under my jeans, I wore leggings. Over my socks, I wore Gore-Tex booties. And under my Belstaff jacket, two T-shirts, a long-sleeved shirt, and a polar fleece.

With my passport stamped, I walked back to the TT, the effort leaving me struggling to breathe. For the past three days, I'd been blessed with the warmth of a Greek sun, but with this late season cold, the tightness in my chest—all the signs of PCP—had returned. I popped two Bactrim just in case.

The sky ahead was filled with clouds, dark and heavy with snow. To cut down wind chill, I pulled on my rainproof pants and jacket over the top of my 'wardrobe' and morphed into Michelin man.

As I refuelled, I'd hoped to buy something hot to eat, but the petrol station kiosk only sold soft drink. My destination was Gallipoli, where I planned to free camp hidden amongst bushes or a gully. It was an hour's ride and I would arrive as day turned to night. The tourists would be gone. I would be alone, and I would also save money. I carried about US$2500 as a combination of travellers cheques and cash, but was unsure if this would be enough as I had no idea how much I'd spend on the ride through Central Asia, China and South East Asia. But if money got low, I could always withdraw more from my bank account via American Express, although I doubted I'd find an office until I reached Hanoi or even Bangkok.

My journey on the Silk Road, like thousands before me, was merely the quickest overland route to reach the east, then turn south for Asia. Delphi and Gallipoli were rare exceptions. At Delphi, I had hoped to connect with the spiritual forces that may still linger there. Gallipoli was to pay homage to the Anzacs of World War I: to honour the needless death of so many Australian and New Zealand soldiers. I wanted to lay down on the ground where they were shot and where they died, where their blood had soaked into the soil. I wanted to pay my respects and honour their sacrifice.

Every mile of that ride along the peninsula to Gallipoli, a desolate, windswept landscape, was agony and I whooped with joy as I passed a sign that advised it was just ten more kilometres. My only knowledge of Gallipoli was what I'd learnt at school. As a child, I'd attended ANZAC Day parades and listened with awe to the speeches recounting acts of bravery in the face of certain death that made the world take notice of Australia as a nation. The soldiers' courage, strength and mateship left a legacy that formed our identity. Their sacrifice shaped the Australian culture that has endured today, and will endure long into the future.

My only map was of Europe, and while it included Turkey, it lacked detail. I'd picked it up at a service station before boarding the ferry for France. Instead of the Gallipoli I had envisioned, I arrived at a fishing village also known as Gelibolu. I rode past bland cement block houses that overlooked the Dardanelles. It was nothing like the images of trenches I'd seen in books at school and on television back home during ANZAC Day commemorations. Gallipoli was the entire peninsula and the title of the World War I campaign, not the actual location of the battlefield, which was near Anzac Cove. It was nearly dark and there was no chance of free camping in a gully at the battlefront, which was another fifty kilometres along the peninsula,

I'd realised when I checked my map more closely. I continued on until the road ended at a pizza restaurant next to a small harbour filled with fishing boats. I stumbled inside, shivering uncontrollably from the cold that had penetrated deep into my bones. Finding a hotel would have to wait; first I needed to eat. My last meal was breakfast in Stomio: spinach pie and strong sweet black coffee.

'Table for one?' the young waiter asked as he flipped a mop of black wavy hair from his eyes, then glanced through the window at my motorcycle illuminated by a single light bulb. 'You ride the big *moto*. Where you from?'

'Australia,' I nodded to confirm the big moto was mine and lowered my head a little to hide my red face.

'Welcome. Please come. Sit.' In the poor light, he didn't seem to notice, so I looked up and smiled.

He smiled back. 'Long journey.'

'Yes,' I said and followed him to a table by the window, and as I sat down, he placed a menu in front of me. 'I am looking for a hotel,' I said.

'No hotel, but you can stay there,' and pointed to a row of flat-roofed cement-block units overlooking the harbour on the low hill opposite. There were no lights and nothing to indicate accommodation was available.

He read my questioning look. 'Yes, you can stay. The caretakers work as cleaners, but they will return soon. After you finish your meal.'

I ordered a pizza, the house special, and while it was cooking, I asked for bread and salad. It arrived in minutes, and I polished it off along with the small bowl of olive oil. The pizza came soon after. It was huge, enough to feed four, and I regretted gorging on the bread and oil, but still I ate every last piece. I called the waiter and asked for the bill.

'No, no. It is all for you. Australians are good. You are welcome,' he said and waved his hands in front of himself to refuse the payment I offered.

'Thank you,' I said, humbled by the generosity. It was strange, this camaraderie when we were enemies and so many died on both sides. But while that World War I battle was steeped in the blood of both nations, it was also steeped in their bravery.

As I prepared to climb on the TT and ride it back up the hill, I looked up at the row of units abandoned and run-down. Previously, in darkness, a light glowed outside the first unit, the one closest to the road.

After I'd parked, I knocked on the door and was greeted by an old man in a baggy faded tracksuit. He was shorter than me with a paunch and thinning grey hair. He stared bewildered chewing a mouthful of food. After swallowing, he bellowed a few words in Turkish and a portly woman with wiry black hair, flecked with grey, appeared beside him.

'What you want?' she asked almost in a low growl. She looked tired, as though her whole life had been one long struggle devoid of even a brief moment of happiness.

'Do you have a room?' I asked and looked purposefully along the line of about ten units.

'Hotel closed. We are caretakers,' she replied. I stared back, momentarily at a loss. It started to rain.

'I can camp. I have a tent,' I said and pointed to a small patch of grass in front of the third unit down from theirs.

'Come in. Sit down. I find key. You sleep in room,' she replied, and I sat on a single bed, on a lumpy mattress that doubled as both bed and couch, grateful for her change of heart. A Turkish soapie blared on the television, and their half-eaten meal was on a coffee table. Against the opposite wall was another single bed and a bench used to prepare food. The woman removed the two plates, and I felt guilty I'd disturbed their dinner. A small dog and three cats stared at me.

'We eat later,' she said as if reading my mind. 'Come, I show you room.'

She waddled along the veranda, and I followed. Inside was a single wrought-iron wire bed without linen. The mattress was stained and lumpy.

'You have bedding?' she asked.

'Yes, I have a sleeping bag.'

I thanked her and then retrieved the TT parked on the edge of the road, pushing it along the veranda to my room where it would be undercover. The drizzle had turned to soaking rain, and I said a prayer of thanks for the meal that filled my belly; for somewhere dry to sleep; for the kindness of Mike and his friends in Greece; and so many others who had offered their help and hospitality if I went back even further since leaving London.

I began my pilgrimage to the battlefield and Anzac Cove early, well before the hordes of tourists ferried by bus from Istanbul arrived. Alone, I stood on a wind-swept hill dotted with spindly bushes that struggled to survive in the barren soil that was once soaked with the blood of Australian and New Zealander troops, British and French, and even more Turkish soldiers. It was a senseless loss of so many, mostly young, lives.

The Allied forces landed on the beach at Anzac Cove on the 25 April 1915, and the first 2000 men never made it more than a few steps towards the ridge where the Turks fired down on them. In that split-second, what did they think—if they had time to think at all.

Later, in the museum, I read each letter with a growing sense of sadness, but also a deep respect for their bravery. I stared at the photos where the hardship of battle was etched eternally on the soldiers' faces. Outside, a cold drizzle fell, and mist blanketed the gullies. It was a miserable cold place, and before leaving, I wandered along one of the gullies and sat down sheltering from the biting wind. I hugged my knees and closed my eyes to think of the men who died there—11,488 Australian and New Zealander soldiers who joined the 44,150 Allied troops killed. But it was nearly double for the Turks who lost more than 86,692 fathers, husbands, brothers and sons before the Allies retreated eight months later. In the face of certain death, neither side gave up. I took strength from their bravery as though they sat beside me, encouraging me to also be brave when there are no safe places.

As another cold front moved across the peninsula, I returned to my room at the block of units. It rained heavily that night and the old couple, Hussain and Fatima, insisted I stay another day. It was so cold, even colder than when I crossed the Alps, and I was convinced I'd never feel the warmth of the sun again. All day, wearing most of my clothes, I lay huddled in my sleeping bag. There was a leak and rainwater had seeped across the bare cement floor.

There was no running water in any of the units except in Hussain and Fatima's, but they had kindly allowed me to use their shower and toilet. I felt like a stray, just like their brown short-haired terrier cross and the cats that called their unit home.

After my shower that second night, Fatima invited me to sit with them in their room warmed by a small electric heater. I looked at the cats, who like myself, had come in from the cold. They stared back from under the bed opposite, out of reach of Hussain who constantly tried to kick them. Together we watched television. A voluptuous woman was singing cabaret and the audience danced and gyrated to the beat of the Turkish music. Fatima had prepared a meal and plates of feta cheese and spinach pastries, mutton stew, rice, salad, olives and bread were placed on the coffee table in front of the single bed where Hussain and I sat.

'You eat,' she said waving a chubby arm over the feast.

'*Teşekkür ederim*,' I said, faltering over the Turkish words for thank you.

'You are welcome,' she said handing me a plate and then one to Hussain.

The food was delicious, the mutton stew hearty and warming. When the meal was over, I offered to help Fatima clean up, but she insisted I stay seated. Hussain then stood beside Fatima, as she spooned leftovers into plastic containers, which she stacked into a small fridge. They started to argue and Hussain looked over at me and I heard him say *para*, the Turkish word for money. Despite putting no effort into learning Turkish, after two days I had picked up the basics by merely being there. But words were superfluous in this situation. The tone of their voices and sideways glances told me enough that the argument was about me, and about how much I would be asked to pay. So far, there had been no talk of money.

'Yes, I will pay,' I offered.

They stopped mid-sentence. A desperate meow from outside broke the tense moment and when Hussain opened the door, a wet, bedraggled tabby rushed in.

He picked it up and sat beside me towelling it dry. 'Three years we have this cat,' he said as he fed the purring tabby a piece of meat from the small plate Fatima had placed on the table at his request. 'The dog and all the cats come to us. We welcome them,' he said as if to explain why they had so many pets.

'I will leave tomorrow,' I announced, realising I had overstayed my welcome. The rain continued to fall as a constant patter on the tin roof.

'Snow tomorrow,' Hussain replied and Fatima nodded in vigorous agreement. 'No problem. You stay,' he added as if reading my thoughts.

Please let it be fine tomorrow, I prayed. But regardless of whether my prayer was answered, I would leave. Earlier, they had asked probing questions about how I could afford to travel.

'It is very expensive. Hotel, food, petrol,' Hussain had said.

'I have a tent. I camp. I do not eat in restaurants. Petrol is cheap, and my *motosiklet* can go far on just a little,' I'd explained hoping this was enough to end the conversation.

'Maybe you can help us. We can live in Australia?' Hussain had asked, and Fatima spoke a few quick words to reprimand him for his rudeness.

'I have no money. No job. No home in Australia. I must have these things to sponsor you. I am sorry,' I'd said.

'Turkey is our home. This is where we belong,' Fatima added and looked toward the harbour beyond the window of their tiny unit. While it was a cramped derelict motel unit, it was a home nonetheless, and they'd opened it to a mongrel dog, four stray cats, and me.

I woke early to pack the TT and say goodbye to Fatima and

Hussain, before they left for work.

'*Snee,*' Fatima said, when I knocked and she'd opened their door, and pointed to the distant clouds that were dark and heavy. I shivered.

'Tea?' Fatima asked.

'For you,' I said handing Fatima one million lira (about US$8), as I sipped on the sweet black tea and nibbled a sweet dry biscuit. 'For my stay,' I said pushing the money closer to her when she recoiled.

'No, for *benzin*. For food. It is far to Australia,' Fatima replied, raising her hands in front of her. I did not insist further, because I needed every dollar I had. I'd done next to no research for this ride home. I had no idea of costs and therefore no idea how much money I'd need. One part of me saw no reason to care about such things as I may not even make it that far, but the other, more practical side, had to plan: had to ensure my money would last.

Earlier I'd pushed the bike down the veranda and parked it on the driveway. I was ready to leave. Hussain and Fatima, along with the dog and the four cats, were lined up to bid me farewell.

'No, problem. You stay,' Fatima said and looked again toward the dark grey clouds that seemed to have edged closer and grown bigger and heavier with the threat of snow.

'*Teşekkür ederim*. But it is time to go. I will ride to Istanbul. It is not far,' I said and climbed onto the TT. Packed, it looked a cumbersome thing, and I was always surprised how I actually managed to ride it with such ease. The engine fired first kick as it usually always did. The cats scattered and the dog barked. I was as familiar with this motorcycle and all its idiosyncrasies as one is with an old friend, a husband or a wife, of many years.

As the engine warmed, Fatima and Hussain gave me a hug filled with their blessing for my journey.

'*Teşekkür ederim*,' I said again grateful they'd taken me in when I'd first knocked on their door on that cold rainy night. As I waved goodbye, I realised other than a few days of riding in the rain and biting cold, no catastrophe had befallen me. So far, I'd been showered with hospitality and kindness and each day everything worked out. So what was the point of worry?

10

ANZAC DAY

Istanbul

I rode away from Gallipoli towards a range of low hills blanketed with snow and clouds, dark and heavy. After just a few kilometres my toes and fingers were numb.

An hour later, I passed through a small township, where I refuelled and tried to warm my chilled-to-the-bone body with the glass of steaming sweet black tea offered by the young Turk operating the petrol station. Memories of chilblains from motorcycle couriering during a London winter came flooding back. I then braved the next range of snow-covered hills, not stopping until I reached the next township, a short but freezing thirty-minute ride. I did not need fuel, but stopped at a Mobil petrol station, taking refuge with the staff in their cramped booth.

As I warmed myself on the gas fire, two middle-aged men and a teenager stared at me perplexed. I still carried my letter of introduction from Mobil and unfolded the copy I carried in a jacket pocket hoping it would explain my sudden appearance—and desperation. One of them poured sweet black tea, and I swallowed three warming cups in quick succession, declining the fourth.

'You like some food?' one of them asked.

'No,' I replied not wanting to abuse their hospitality further even though hunger gnawed at the emptiness in my stomach, which rumbled in protest. 'I am going to Istanbul. Thank you.'

Once outside, I quickly scoffed a bread roll I'd stashed in my Gearsack, left over from lunch I'd bought at a bakery the day before. As I ate, one of the petrol attendants, the teenage boy, approached with a hot dog steaming and covered in tomato sauce and mayonnaise.

'Please, for you,' he said, and as I thanked him, I looked over to the booth and waved to the men inside. They waved back.

As I neared Istanbul, I left the snow behind, and the sun finally broke through the clouds. Mid-afternoon, I rode through the city centre and towards the dome of the Sultan Ahmed Mosque, commonly known as the Blue Mosque, which pulled me in like a shining beacon of light. I'd already decided, I could not travel through Turkey, and over the mountains to Georgia, for at least another month. I would not survive the biting cold that had seeped into my bones and left my toes and fingers numb. Spring was late this year. I needed to find somewhere I could bide my time for a few weeks. A hostel offering a job, with bed and meals, was the obvious choice. With ANZAC Day commemorations only ten days away, Istanbul would be filling with Australians and New Zealanders, including hundreds of backpackers who'd worked the winter in London or in Europe's ski resorts. Cashed up, they'd pay homage to the Anzacs and then the summer travelling season would begin.

I rode slowly through the old city's narrow streets, the TT bouncing gently over the cobblestones until I came across the Orient Hostel. I had no map, no guide book for Turkey, and no recommendations of where to stay. But still, it was no surprise, when by chance, I pulled up outside what appeared to be one of Istanbul's larger backpacker hostels, a four-storey rooming house, a stone's throw from the majestic Blue Mosque.

A sign on the Orient's heavy timber door announced: We celebrate ANZAC Day. Welcome. I pushed it open. Inside, the foyer was strewn with the backpacks of those waiting to check in. Most of the young people who loitered nearby, it seemed, had just arrived on buses or flights from London. A bed in an eight-bed dorm including continental breakfast was 600,000 lira a night, about US$5.

'I'll take the job,' I said pointing to the sign on the counter: Staff wanted for roof-top café.

'You speak to manager,' said the young Turk and raised a chiseled chin toward the office behind me. The door was closed.

'You come back later,' he grunted after I'd knocked and there was no answer.

'I have a motorcycle. Is there a garage, a storeroom?' I asked.

He sighed. 'At back of hostel.'

After I rode the bike down a narrow side street, he appeared, standing at the back door to a room packed with boxes and assorted junk.

'I'm sorry. I don't want to be any trouble, but my motorcycle is very important.'

'Bike stay here. You not come go. Only when you leave,' he said running a hand over his black hair oiled to sleek perfection.

'Yes, yes. Thank you so much,' I said and began moving the boxes to make space for the TT.

'It is no problem. I am Ali,' he said, the annoyance in his voice replaced with the first signs of understanding. 'You ask for me if you need visit your bike for any belongings, but better you take now.' And then he was gone up a low flight of stairs partially hidden behind all the junk. After stacking the boxes and making space for the TT, I pushed it inside where it would be safe.

Later, I spoke with Tanner, the manager, about the job and asked what I would be paid: 'We see how it goes,' he'd said. I was, however, grateful for the opportunity to save money and not pay for a bed and food.

During my first week at the Orient, with time on my hands, I fell into a deeper state of misery. The dull ache of uncertainty pushed me further into despair.

Every afternoon, when I finished my shift at the roof-top café, I'd walk down to the seafront and sit on the foreshore bannisters. With my legs dangling over the edge, I would watch the ships arrive and depart from Istanbul. The same sense of longing to leave I'd lived with all winter in Austria, when I'd watched the vapour trails above St Johann, washed over me. Every part of me wished to be embraced by those who loved me: by my family. I longed to be held and told all would be well and there was nothing to worry about. But there was no one to embrace me—no one to reassure me. I could not go home. I could not face rejection and shame.

Instead, I breathed in deeply the salt air blown on a cool breeze across the Bosporus, my body hungry for any life-giving elements it could find. Increasingly, I felt as though my body had become a separate entity to my mind, which cowered in a corner wallowing in sadness and regret for my life lost. My body and its trillions of cells, on the other hand, was on its own mission—that of survival. It was a mission based on a pure and determined instinct, which had evolved over millions of years to reach this point in humanity's collective journey.

As I gazed over the Bosporus, I thought: what choice did I have but to continue my journey? I knew nothing of the recent discovery of effective treatments that were saving thousands from dying from AIDS, giving them back their health and their life. I still lived in a world with no hope other than what I might find on the road.

'If you are real, then save me!' I shouted into the wind to that greater force that I'd thanked just a few days ago in that moment of positive reflection.

The day after I'd arrived at the Orient, I lodged my application for a Russian visa. I was told to come back in a week, but it could take longer. It all depends on Moscow, the buxom middle-aged Russian woman told me. It also depended on the validity of my letter of invitation, which was from Lena. Surprisingly, it was accepted.

I'd met Lena in London at the introduction evening for the Russian language course I'd attended just before my diagnosis. Lena had given me her phone number, saying if I needed any help, to call her. So just before leaving London, I did, and without hesitation, she gave me the highly prized letter. Without it, I would not have been issued with a one-month Russian visa, which unlike a three-month visa, did not need an HIV test. My one-month visa would allow me to travel along the Silk Roads through the former Soviet countries of Central Asia, which had not yet cut immigration ties with the motherland.

After a week, my Russian visa, valid from 15 May 1997, was issued free of charge. I told Tanner I'd leave on 7 May, which would give me a week to reach Azerbaijan, the first of the Central Asian countries where I'd use the visa.

The hostel soon filled to capacity with backpackers, so much so that with all bunk beds taken, people slept on the floor in the rooms. There were beds for one hundred, but guests numbered nearly double that. Most were Australians and New Zealanders there to pay homage to the Anzacs on 25 April.

But despite so many of my own countrymen and women at the hostel, I was unbearably lonely. I was shunned, to be avoided it seemed. Did they innately know I was diseased, I asked myself? Even though I hid my facial redness with a layer of foundation, it still showed through. There was also the question I'd often been asked: 'How can you work for the Turks?' But what ultimately nailed it, was my own aura of depression. The negativity radiating from me must have been stifling for the full-of-life adventure-loving backpackers with whom I was in daily contact as I served them in the Orient's roof-top café.

I worked either in the café or in the hostel's basement bar, which at midnight morphed into a nightclub until 3.00 a.m. It was a long day working from 8.00 a.m. to 5.00 p.m. or 8.00 p.m. to 3.00 a.m. with no breaks other than snacking on free food during the serving lulls. Breakfast was busy then we'd have a few stragglers come up for lunch, but it'd be hectic again from 4.00 p.m. for afternoon snacks and beers. Most of the time, I sat around either reading or chatting to the Turkish staff. After the breakfast rush, each hour dragged on and Joseph, who managed the café, was dictatorial and enjoyed ordering me to polish cutlery, fold napkins and clean table legs. I preferred the basement bar where I worked mostly with Ebor, a stocky young Turk with a gentleness that was refreshing after Joseph's imperiousness upstairs. I helped cook hamburgers and chips and served beers. Ebor treated me as a colleague and tried his best to cheer me up, insisting I needed to brighten my wardrobe.

'You must wear white shirt,' he said.

'Is there a market that sells second-hand clothes?'

'In Turkey, the people only wear new clothes,' he said, indignant I would consider such a thing. 'It is important to look good, to wear good jeans and good shirt. And shoes. Your shoes are not good,' he said flaring his nostrils at my scuffed and faded black canvas runners.

'I am travelling on a motorcycle. There is no room for going-out clothes.'

'When you not ride the bike, you can look good. It is important to how you feel,' he said, and I thought of the tour guides, the young men, I'd met in West Africa. I'd asked them why they did not save their money when they'd been paid by a tourist for their guiding services. Instead, they spent it all on fake designer sneakers, jeans and T-shirts. They'd replied: 'The "look" is everything.'

Ebor looked me up and down. 'Tomorrow, we go. You buy some nice clothes. Then you look good.'

I'd been in no mood to buy clothes, but Ebor, after some serious convincing from me that I was happy with second-hand clothes from a market, chose a nearly new pair of black Levis for less than US$1 in lira. Eventually I relented and bought a new white collared shirt and a white T-shirt for just a few dollars each.

'See, now you look good,' he'd said when I turned up for my shift at 5.00 p.m.

After my dark grey T-shirt and faded black jeans, which were both as dull as my sense of wellbeing, the change in my attitude from this minor wardrobe revamp was miraculous. For the first time in weeks, I felt good.

Ebor and I became firm friends. He was Muslim and we discussed all manner of spirituality. I often questioned him about the meaning behind the time-honoured hospitality of the Muslim people shown to me in North Africa, which I'd also experienced in Turkey. There was a newfound sense of happiness—a spring to my step—and I smiled often. It was the old me, the me before diagnosis. While the voice of doom was not entirely silenced, it was temporarily quietened. It no longer consumed my every waking and dreaming moment, and this realisation came to me one day with a jolt. I was telling Ebor a funny story from my travels when I suddenly stopped mid-sentence.

'Is problem?' he asked.

'No,' I smiled. 'Everything is good.'

The day before ANZAC Day, buses transported most of the backpackers from the Orient to Eceabat, near Anzac Cove. I was given a free ticket, and after the bus off-loaded us at RSL house, with a beer in hand, I wandered amongst the backpackers searching for someone to talk to, someone like me who was also alone. Many of the backpackers had no time for strangers as they knew each other, either from Australia and New Zealand or had worked together and lived in share houses in London.

'Heather,' I heard my name called. It was Justin, a ginger-haired Australian in his twenties, who I'd worked with in the basement bar at the Orient. He invited me to join his group of friends, all in their mid-twenties. We talked about our travel plans, and then they moved away to talk to others. As I stood alone, I saw Kalm, one of the motorcycle couriers from Wings in London. 'Small world,' I thought smiling. We embraced then caught up on the gossip from London and what we'd done over the winter.

More than 8000 attended the ANZAC Day services. It was a cold, windy day with the buses ferrying us from RSL House to Anzac Cove at 3.00 a.m. in time for the dawn service. Late afternoon, the buses transported us back to Istanbul and the party that had lasted over the past two weeks ended.

*****

Twelve days later, spring finally arrived. It was time to leave the Orient and ride over the mountains to the Black Sea, and into Georgia.

'You Australians are good workers,' Tanner said when I collected my wages. Happy with my work ethic, he paid me US$20 a day in lira, about US$400. Most went to pay for a new set of Metzeler tyres. Then, with Ebor's help, we pushed my motorcycle out of the storeroom, and once I'd packed my bags, said goodbye.

'You will be a rich businessman one day,' I said. Ebor and his friend had set up a shuttle bus service to the airport. They also planned to open an internet café opposite the Orient, tapping into this new online world, which I knew nothing about. But Ebor spoke with excitement about the opportunities the internet would bring: how it would connect the world as one. I never considered, for a moment, that it would link me to a global network of support for people living with HIV, and to news of the protease inhibitors discovered by Dr David Ho. But I knew none of this. Instead, I lived in a world were death from AIDS was still inevitable.

'Thank you. I have been blessed to meet you. You helped me feel good about myself. I felt so bad, so low,' I said to Ebor, blurting out my true feelings.

'I know,' he replied and patted my shoulder. 'You must smile, even if it is artificial. Even when you don't feel like smiling. Then you will feel happy. Even when you are not. I feel you carry a big problem, and it weighs heavy on you, but I know you are strong. Allah is with you.'

I managed a faint thankyou as I held back the tears that brimmed in my eyes.

After nearly a month in the storeroom, it took just a few kicks, and the TT fired into life once again. I quickly put on my helmet, pulled on my gloves, and with the engine warm, climbed on and then I was gone.

With new tyres fitted, I rode through Istanbul's chaotic traffic and then its sprawling suburbs, which soon gave way to undulating hills. It felt good to be back on the road, and that familiar sense of expectation for the unknown washed over me.

11

THE WILL OF ALLAH

Turkey

After leaving Istanbul, I headed toward the arid region of Cappadocia and its 'fairy chimneys', cone-shaped rock formations that pepper a massive area across central Turkey. There is just as much to see underground as there is above ground, I was told by the backpackers at the Orient. It was a two-day detour from my planned route to ride over the mountains towards Georgia, the gateway to Central Asia.

On my first night, by chance, I found myself at a health spa and thermal springs after I passed the turn-off late afternoon. I'd been riding through an arid valley, the sun highlighting the bare rock in hues of pink and orange, when I rounded a sweeping bend and saw a sign, a piece of whitewashed tin attached to a rusted pole: Ayos Icmeleri 3kms, it read. 'Ah, a village,' I thought and turned off the tarmac to follow a narrow dirt road that disappeared behind a low rocky hill dotted with clumps of spindly bushes. I envisioned this small village where free camping looked a likely possibility.

As I'd often done in Africa, I'd ask permission to camp and once granted by the chief or headman, I would have their protection. Ebor told me it was the same in Turkey. 'The village people will welcome you too. All you must do is ask,' he said when I told him how the African people had welcomed me into their homes. And just as Ebor said they would, I was welcomed at Ayos Icmeleri too.

The health spa, a collection of cement block buildings painted in pastels of pink, blue and green, was closed for renovations. However, the caretaker and his wife gave me dinner and breakfast and allowed me to pitch my tent on the lawn of their bungalow at the entrance to the spa complex. When I arrived, I asked how much lira for camping, fully assuming that such a thing was possible. The response was 'No money', and I was given a spa brochure in English.

'I speak little English,' she said as she handed it to me, knowing the brochure would answer all my questions.

The mineral waters of the hot springs cure many health ailments, it read and I later inched my way into a pool where the water was a scorching 50°C. While I slowly boiled for the recommended ten minutes, my body absorbed a plethora of immune-boosting minerals including sulphur, boron, magnesium, potassium, sodium, silica, selenium and lithium, which the brochure said treats depression. The hot springs were just what I needed for both my body and my mind.

Before descending into the valleys of honeycombed hills and lunarscape of Cappadocia, I parked the TT to take photos. Below lay a mesmerising panorama bathed in hues of dusky oranges, soft pinks and creams.

Kaymakli is the largest of over 200 underground cities where Christians hid from persecution for hundreds of years beginning in 200AD; first, it was the Romans and later the Muslims. The area was one of Turkey's most popular tourist destinations, and several buses lined the narrow road.

For a while, I tagged along with an English-speaking tour group as their guide brought to life the history of this subterranean Christian refuge. But I soon wandered off along a dimly lit passage to explore the underground labyrinth of rooms carved out of the soft rock. The rabbit warren of rooms was once home to over 3000 Christians hiding for days, weeks and sometimes months at a time from those who sought to annihilate them. When these persecutors had lost interest and moved on, the Christians returned to the surface, to their villages and farmlands, or what was left after being ransacked. I had the advantage of electric light and signage arrows to find my way, but the Christians endured air thick with dust, light from a hemp oil torch and the rancid stench of shit. Clay pots were used as toilets.

Late afternoon, I moved on, stopping at a vantage point above the village of Goreme to admire the stunning scene spread across the valley of 'fairy chimneys', tall, conical stone pillars, the last of the sun highlighting the soft cream and pinkish ochres. A campsite

'Panoramic Camping' was opposite, and after taking photos, I pushed the TT across the road.

Later, I ate dinner of salad drenched in olive oil, which I mopped up with bread, but wished it was steak, medium rare, the size of a dinner plate. All day I'd been craving such a meal, but the campsite, which undoubtedly had one of the best views of Cappadocia, was a bare patch of dirt with a few picnic tables, and one shower and toilet. Tomatoes, cucumber, red onion, olive oil, cheese and bread had become the mainstay of my diet.

Leaving Cappadocia early the next morning, I rode all day on smooth black tarmac that wound through endless fields of spring grass shimmering in the gentle breeze, a distant towering mountain range an ever-present backdrop. I'll be riding over those mountains tomorrow, I thought and opened the throttle.

Just before sunset, I approached a small lake, still and calm, its mirrored surface reflecting the hills that fringed its opposite shore. A small building sat perched on the lake's edge. I turned off the main road where a rusty sign read: Tödürge Gölü with the symbols of a crossed knife and fork. Ah, a restaurant! And likely place to camp. I followed a two-wheeled track, and as I rode through the opened gate, two large cream-coloured dogs barked their welcome. I was in the Sivas region, the home of the Kangal sheepdog, the national dog of Turkey. With their thick creamy coat, black nose and ears, these magnificent gentle giants stood at nearly a metre. At first, I was filled with fear of these enormous guardians, but with their curled tails wagging, I could see they merely wanted to say hello. They trotted after me. The restaurant was a cement block building with a wide timber veranda on its three sides, giving diners a perfect setting to enjoy a fish meal.

'I am Feridun. Welcome to my restaurant,' a stocky middle-aged dark-haired man called as he approached where I'd parked. I introduced myself.

'How much to camp?' I asked.

'Camping, yes. No money,' he replied beaming a broad smile and pointing to a nearby patch of thick green grass under the shade of a leafy tree, its trunk thick and gnarled.

'It is very beautiful here. Can I swim?' I asked. It had been a warm day, and the cool waters of the lake beckoned.

'Yes, no problem,' he said then turned on his heel to disappear inside the restaurant.

As I set up my tent, a moment later he returned with a can of beer in one hand and a bottle of Fanta in the other.

I reached for the beer. 'Thank you.'

'You will have fish? Yes. Come to restaurant at 8.00 p.m.'

'*Teşekkür ederim,*' I said to show my gratitude. As I had no watch, I estimated the time to be around 6.00 p.m. Sunset was at 8.00 p.m.

As I slipped into the lake, the water slightly alkaline, I felt the fatigue drain away. My body tingled in the coolness, and I floated, frolicked and dived luxuriating, in this moment of perfection—this timeless moment when nothing else mattered.

I'd been in Turkey just over a month and had fallen under its spell. But in this Muslim country where women were mostly hidden, I had only met Fatima and the women at the hot springs. Even though most of my contact with the Turkish people had been with men, all had treated me with respect, as an honoured guest as is the Muslim way. But I had also been charmed by a different Turkey? A hidden Turkey only accessible off-the-beaten track, away from the tourist trail? I questioned too, if my sudden arrival on people's doorsteps did not elicit a certain amount of pity—that innately human trait to help another in need. Was this kindness of strangers shown to me because I, and my motorcycle, looked a little worse for wear?

'Come. Sit,' Feridun ushered when I'd walked into the restaurant, and I was directed to a table on the veranda set for one. He then produced a whole fried fish, salad and bread. I ate it all, savouring every mouthful of its succulent freshness. When I'd finished, I carried my plates to the kitchen where Feridun and two other men were finishing the last of the cleaning after a busy day.

'I want to pay,' I said, and held out a handful of lira.

'No pay. You have long travel. Please,' he said shaking his head.

'Please, you sleep inside. Come.' I followed him to a back room of the restaurant. 'We go soon, and no one is here at night. You bring your *motosiklet* inside. You sleep here. It is safe for you.'

'I will be okay in my tent. The dogs will protect me,' I said and went 'woof woof.' The room was hot and stuffy. I would be much cooler and more comfortable outside, and safe, with the dogs standing guard. He laughed and nodded to acknowledge that yes, the dogs would protect me.

In the last rays of soft light, I walked back to my tent. The two dogs immediately rose from where they'd been lying near the entrance and followed as if instinctively knowing I was their charge; the lone sheep that needed protecting from the wolves. The dogs lay outside my tent, each like a sphinx—my sentinels. I gave each a pat on their large soft, creamy heads and crawled inside to fall into a relaxed and contented sleep.

I woke as the first rays of sun glistened off the mist rising from the lake, the dogs were waiting. 'Come,' I called, and they bounded ahead as I strode in my bathers, a towel thrown over my shoulder. After a swim, I stood on the shore to soak in the warmth of the sun, the dogs sitting one either side of me. Feridun said he'd return to the restaurant at mid-day, but I'd told him I needed to leave early to make it over the mountains for the six-hour ride to Trabzon where I'd get my transit visa for Georgia.

After leaving the peaceful shores of the lake and giving each of the Kangal dogs a good pat and cuddle, I rode over the high mountain passes still covered in patches of snow. Rather than follow the main road, I opted for the longer route over the Olukbel Baglari mountains, a decision that was to stretch a day's ride to Trabzon into three, but I had no regrets. It would become one of the most memorable roads of all my travels, and while mostly all on dirt, it meandered through conifer forest, fields of spring flowers and snow-capped mountain passes. I stopped to rest and drink sweet black tea at each small village, the inhabitants staring at me befuddled as they rarely saw tourists, especially a single woman on a motorcycle.

'Tea,' said a well-dressed man aged about fifty, offering a glass of it after I'd stopped to check my map in one such mountain village, Siran.

'*Teşekkür ederim,*' I replied and sipped on the sweet, warm tea as a small crowd of onlookers, again all boys and young men, gathered around me.

'Sit,' he said, producing a flimsy wooden chair. 'I am a teacher,' he said. 'Of English.'

I told of my travels, and he translated to the crowd, who hung off his every word and now numbered about twenty.

'You do this all alone?' he asked.

'Mostly,' I replied, and the crowd let out a unified sigh of wonder at such a feat.

'Where you go now?'

'I take this small road to Torul,' I replied, and pointed to the squiggly line on my map. I preferred this scenic route to the shorter route on the main tarmac road to Trabzon, which would easily get me there late in the afternoon. The squiggly line followed a high ridge climbing 2000 metres. It would be a slow two-hour ride of eighty kilometres and still another eighty to Trabzon, which I would ride tomorrow. 'Is it okay. Is the snow gone?' I asked.

'Is good. No problem on the *motosiklet,*' he replied, and I thought of all the times I'd heard this and ended up on something that was an enduro rider's dream, but my worst nightmare.

'Is good,' he repeated, sensing my hesitation and pouring me a second glass of tea. 'There is no signpost for this road. Turn left at the mosque. Then he asked, 'But where you sleep tonight?' He translated the question for the crowd who waited expectantly for what I'd do alone, deep in the mountains amongst the wolves.

'I would like to camp at a farm. Is it okay to do this?' I asked.

'No problem. The mountain people will welcome you,' he said, and the crowd nodded in agreement. I turned, and with a smile, cast my gratitude to all who had gathered.

Camping at a mountain farm was my back-up plan if I found the going too difficult. If I was caught out and could not reach Torul before nightfall.

'You must visit Sümela Monastery. It is near Torul at Zigana. It is built on the side of a cliff. It is very old. You must see this,' he said.

The road, while narrow at first, was well-graded dirt, but it soon deteriorated into pot-holes, and tight hairpin turns as it climbed through a thick conifer forest. Late afternoon, after eighty kilometres or so, I arrived in Torul and asked a local man directions for Zigana. But after five kilometres, exhausted, I stopped at a small roadside cafè. A freshly killed goat hung from a beam near a barbeque, a pile of firewood stacked against it. My stomach rumbled, and I parked on a grassy rise beside the cafè that overlooked an apple orchid, the trees covered in tiny pink blossoms. Down a steep bank, a mountain stream flowed from the distant snow-capped mountains. A man, aged about sixty, approached.

'Come, sit,' he said and pointed to the table and chairs near the barbeque. As I sat down, he offered a glass of yoghurt milk. 'For you. Drink.'

'I am heading to Zigana, to the campsite,' I said sneaking a glance at the nearby goat carcass.

'You stay here. You camp here. We cook meat.'

'Okay,' I said. I guessed by the angle of the sun that it was about 6.00 p.m. I could not have wished for a better place. All was provided, including the red meat I'd been salivating over for the past two days.

As the man lit the fire, I set up my tent then headed down a narrow, overgrown path to the fast-running stream to wash away the day's dust in the icy water.

When I returned, I was greeted by the smell of grilling meat and my mouth watered in anticipation. A young man, his dark hair cropped short and neat, sat at the table chatting to the older man who grilled strips of meat on hot coals.

'Hello. I am Mohammad,' he said as I sat down. 'This *motosiklet* is very big for you.'

'Yes,' I agreed then told him my story, and he told me his. Mohammad was a tax inspector from Trabzon and was in the mountains visiting his parents, who lived a short distance down the road growing apples and grazing their small herd of cattle. A plate of grilled meat, a salad and bread were placed on the table while we spoke.

'Eat,' he said. You will be safe here. Hussain is the caretaker, but he speaks only a little English. I see you are on a long journey. This is very good. Is it not difficult for a woman on her own? How do you find Turkey?'

'I am overwhelmed by the generous hospitality. Every night I find somewhere to camp, and the people are very kind. They give me food and don't take any money when I offer to pay. These people are poor. Why do they do this?' I asked puzzled.

'This is the Muslim way. This is what we do. It is our culture. You give us honour to travel through our country. You go alone. This shows you do not fear us. You trust us. You respect us.'

'Thank you,' I replied, but I hardly heard his words as with a belly full of meat, I was fighting sleep.

I slept through the trucks roaring past and even the violent shaking of my tent thinking it was a bad dream, but realising when I emerged soon after daylight, that Hussain had tried to get my attention. The reason was all too obvious as I packed my tent and found a congealed blob of cum sticking to one of the panels. As I turned to vent my disgust, Hussain, who was watering the plants fringing the café's veranda, waved with a grin, fully aware of what I had just discovered. It made me realise just how naive and trusting I'd been. While all the men I'd met so far in Turkey had treated me with respect, they were still men, and I was surrounded by unreleased testosterone that threatened to erupt at any moment. Could I have fended off his groping hands? Would he have stopped when I screamed out, 'I've got HIV'? The letters were universally understood in every language, and in that brief moment it would have been my only protection, but then my secret would have been revealed. Would I then suffer the full wrath of his anger while he saw me as the aggressor and he the victim?

As I came out of the bathroom, he was waiting, a glass of tea held in an outstretched hand. With the other, he pointed to a table laden with a feast of olives, boiled eggs, bread and salad. Was this his apology? I ate quickly and accepted the leftovers he insisted I take for the day's ride.

The Sümela Monastery defies all rules of physics as it sits seemingly glued to a towering cliff-face. Built by Greek Orthodox monks, it is dedicated to the Virgin Mary and is one of the world's oldest Christian churches. Construction began in 386AD as a refuge from the barbarians, the marauding tribes (Huns and others), who came as an unstoppable force from the Russian steppe into Central Asia and across western Europe. In later years, funds from a string of local rulers and other benefactors, as well as donations from pilgrims, flowed to the monastery. And Sümela, over several hundred years, became a feat of architectural wonder.

I'd climbed the narrow path to the monastery early, before the tour groups had arrived, and the church was eerily quiet. Morning sun filtered through the high square windows, highlighting the vibrancy of the multi-coloured frescos. I stood before Jesus, or what remained of him. His head was woefully pitted, and very little was left of the intricate multi-coloured fresco depicting his last hours nailed to the cross. I wondered who was responsible for this vandalism. Perhaps the damage was from stones thrown by devout Christians who follow an overly literal interpretation of the Ten Commandments, which forbids the worship of graven images or likenesses.

Or it may have been angry teenage Muslim boys, who'd grown up with the religious story of Ishmael and his banishment by his father, Abraham. Some believe this casting out of Ishmael, the first-born son, to be the root cause of humanity's calamitous division along religious lines.

Or was the stone throwing simply the result of senseless vandalism from tourists in times past?

As I stood gazing at the pitted head of Jesus, I voiced the words, 'Thank you', as if this would make my gratitude all the more meaningful—for the hospitality bestowed upon me, and for the fortuitous outcome of my travels so far. My peaceful solitude soon ended as a group of schoolgirls arrived, their giggles growing ever louder as they neared the church. I moved on, riding down the mountain and along the Black Sea coast to Trabzon.

'You travel alone on *motosiklet*?' a man asked as he sat down beside me raising a hand to the waiter. I sat outside a hotel drinking a beer as I watched the late afternoon promenade. I'd treated myself to a room and the TT was yet to be wheeled inside to spend the night parked securely in the foyer.

'Yes,' I replied welcoming the man's company as I hoped he'd know the situation in Georgia and the other former Soviet countries of Central Asia. 'I'm going to Georgia and then through the Stans,' I said. Stans was the term used by the Turks for Central Asia. 'I have a Russian visa. Hopefully, it is all I need.'

'You get a visa for Georgia no problem. Russia visa for Stans no problem, but who knows. No one knows what is going on over there,' he said, tilting his head towards the east and offering me a cigarette. It was the first I'd had since leaving the Orient Hostel where both the Turks and the backpackers smoked non-stop. Cigarettes throughout my travels were an ice-breaker, a shared moment of camaraderie with a stranger.

'They are Russian Natashas,' he said flicking his lighter as two women, proactively dressed in mini-skirts, tight tops and high heels, sauntered past. They cast me a quick glance with eyes rimmed in black, their lips painted red, their faces framed with bleached blond hair, the dark roots an inch grown. 'Many come here from across the Black Sea. They make much money in Trabzon. It is famous for Natashas.'

'I've been warned Georgia is dangerous. Do you know about this?' I asked, and he called to a man selling velvet-covered couches across the narrow street.

'He travels to Baku to do business,' he said as the man approached. They exchanged greetings, and after a few words in Turkish, the man returned to his store.

'He says you go through Nachicevan and Igdir on the Erevan

road. This is the long way, but is the safe way. You must not travel at night. You must not go over the mountains. May Allah be with you,' he said and then strode off down the narrow street.

This long way would be through Armenia and would completely avoid Georgia.

Ordinarily, I'd sleep soundly in the softness of a 'real' bed after sleeping in my tent for a few days, but I tossed and turned with worry about Georgia. So many of the Turks had told me I would almost certainly be robbed. It was understandable as nearly a quarter of Georgia's five million people lived in poverty. Another niggling issue was my chest. Since the previous day, it was increasingly feeling tight, the beginning of another attack of pneumonia. I decided to pop two Bactrim and deal with my red face tomorrow.

'What you doin' here, girl?' the man's voice asked. It sounded Cockney, from East London, but I later learnt he was from Southern Wales. I turned and was welcomed by a short, wiry man, a covering of grey stubble on his thin face. A few unmissable tufts of grey hair protruded defiantly from his nose. I was standing in the queue of about ten people at the Georgian consulate to lodge my application for a transit visa.

'Hi, I'm Alan Kendall,' he said, offering a calloused hand. As we inched forward, he told me he was a truck driver heading to Baku in Azerbaijan with a freezer full of food for the oil companies drilling the Caspian. I looked at him with interest.

'All the big oil companies are there. The Caspian is full of oil,' he said, sensing my inquisitiveness and nodding when I asked if Mobil was one of them.

Alan had been on the road a week, loading out of Holland, and now looked every bit the scruffy truck driver in his dirty jeans and once-white T-shirt.

'Is it true what I've heard about Georgia? The crime? The mafia?' I asked.

'Just keep rolling. You don't want to stop anywhere. Don't give them a chance to get at you. Stick with me, I'll see you right.'

The Georgian transit visa was US$13 and issued within ten minutes. It was nearly 2.00 p.m. and Alan invited me for afternoon tea at a layby on the outskirts of Trabzon.

'I'll brew a pot of English tea. You must be getting sick of this shit the Turks drink.' But, in fact, I'd gotten used to it and looked forward to a glass or two wherever I stopped.

'I'll look out for you!' I shouted up to him as he climbed into his enormous red and silver rig parked up the road from the consulate.

Before leaving Trabzon for the Georgia border, I bought two large packs of effervescent Vitamin C tablets. I'd never bothered with vitamin and mineral supplements before, even on my travels through Africa, when I probably should have after getting scurvy in Mauritania, the result of weeks without fresh fruit and vegetables. Despite a diet that included tomatoes for breakfast, lunch and dinner, I craved vitamins. An hour later, I rode along sweeping bends on smooth black tarmac skirting the Black Sea. In the distance, the sun glinted off the polished chrome of Alan's truck.

'Come on girl, kettle's on,' he called as I parked beside where he'd set up two camp chairs and a table.

'I've boiled you a couple of eggs too. Help yourself to cheese. It's cambozola,' he offered, and I smeared the creamy blue-vein cheese on a thick slice of English bread I'd plucked from a Sainsbury's packet. It was a little stale and flavourless compared to the freshly baked Turkish bread I'd been eating for over a month. Alan passed me a mug of strong English tea with milk, and in the warm afternoon sun, we leaned back in the chairs overlooking the mirror calmness of the sea and in unison, let out a contented sigh.

'This is absolutely perfect,' I said and smiled at how good life felt at that very moment: how good and how very simple. 'What more could you want.'

'You got that right, girl,' he replied. 'I'll be driving over the mountains in Georgia, stopping about halfway. It's shorter than going all the way around. You'll be safe with me.' Alan was still adamant I travel with him as he'd suggested at the consulate earlier.

'The TT only has a six-volt light. It's no better than a torch. I won't travel at night. I'll camp at a roadside café near the border and cross early tomorrow, reaching Tbilisi before dark. I'm sure I'll pass you on the mountain. I'll look forward to another cuppa,' I said, my voice gentle to reassure him. 'You said I was street smart, so don't worry—I'll be okay.'

'Well, don't stop anywhere or the *mafiosos* will get you. Just don't stop, okay,' he repeated, his tone ending in seriousness.

While I sounded confident, street smart as he called me, inside I was nervous. Alan had done the trip through Georgia eight times and had good reason to be concerned.

'Make sure you fuel up at the border, so you don't have to stop anywhere until you reach Tbilisi,' he added.

But fuel in Turkey was expensive. In Georgia, it was half the price and higher octane at 95, but I kept these thoughts to myself to save Alan the torment of worry.

With the sun sinking over the mountains behind us, I helped Alan pack away the chairs, table, camp stove and food. He then gave me a fatherly pat on the back before leaving.

'See you on the mountain,' I called through my helmet and then I was gone and riding off toward the border where I'd find a roadside café to camp before crossing into Georgia early tomorrow.

A roadside café soon appeared. It was perched on a low grassy hill next to a small mosque where a stream babbled over rocks into the glistening mirror-like waters of the Black Sea. I parked the bike and climbed the few steps to where several men sat at a picnic table under a large leafy tree.

'Welcome. Come sit,' one of them called, and an old man appeared with a bottle of Coke and a huge cheese sandwich—a half-loaf cut down the middle. Despite a belly full of cambozola, boiled eggs and bread, I accepted it, not wanting to offend the man's hospitality.

'I'm travelling through Georgia to Baku and then across the Caspian. Is it okay to camp here?' I asked the old man, who I assumed was the owner.

'No problem. You are welcome.'

After setting up my tent and changing into my bathers and sarong, towel tossed over my shoulder, I headed down a narrow rocky path to a beach of black and grey speckled stones. After the heat of the day, the water was cool, almost fresh: more like a lake than a sea. I floated on my back and looked up at snow-capped mountains and the dark green of the hills that ended at the beach. After washing in the icy water of a stream flowing into the sea, I returned to my tent. Later, as the sun sank behind the hills, I found a quiet spot to write under the leafy tree, its thick branches now adorned with several kerosene lamps.

'Please, join me,' a voice beckoned, startling me from that deep place I'd found. I looked up. The voice belonged to a handsome, well-dressed young man.

'I am Mustafa,' he said and I introduced myself. 'I invite you to dinner. I see you are a writer. I too am a writer,' he said flicking back a thick strand of black hair to reveal dark eyes that glinted with a sense of expectation for life and all its promise.

I followed him to a table laid with plates of sliced tomatoes, cucumber, olives, a soft white cheese and bread.

'You ride the *motosiklet*?' He glanced over at the TT parked next to my tent. I nodded. 'I see your map.' He spoke of the map on the side cover. 'You travel very far. From Australia... and through Africa. Unbelievable.'

I smiled and sat down. He poured a glass of Fanta.

'What do you write of your travels?'

'All that I've seen, and the people I've met, in Turkey. I've been here over a month.'

'And what of the Turkish people? What do you write about them?'

'Everyone, or should I say, the men, because I've rarely met any women, have treated me with kindness. They have been most generous, just like you,' I said, spreading my arms over the food laid out between us.

'This is Islam,' he replied.

95

'But what of the women. Where are they?' I asked.

'This too is Islam as written in the Quran. In the cities, it is changing, but in the villages, it is still the way. It is like your Bible,' he said, having made the assumption I was Christian. 'Some people follow the words. Others interpret their own meaning for our world today. The Quran was written for a different time when it was dangerous for women to be away from home. In Turkey, some people still live in these old times. Tell me, how was it in Africa? I read Africa is very dangerous?' He lent closer, fully expecting me to confirm his preconceived fears of the dark continent.

'In Africa, a woman told me, the African people would help me. That this is *ubuntu*. And she was right. And it has been the same in Turkey.'

'This is also the way of Islam. We see you alone on a long journey, and we want to help you. We give you food because everyone needs to eat.' And we both broke into an easy laugh over the truth of it.

A torrent of words then fell out of me: 'You think I am a Christian and yes I am, but I find it difficult to believe in a God, as written in the Bible, where we are told to ask forgiveness for our sins, even when we've done nothing wrong. God is universal, an energy surrounding us all. An energy like a guiding hand that connects to us through our intuition, our gut feelings, and through all those coincidences and chance encounters that come our way. There is meaning in these things,' I said in response to his puzzled look. 'But mostly we ignore all this, because we are so consumed by our worries and fears. I too was like this, but in Africa, and here in Turkey, nothing bad happened to me, so I do not expect it too. This way of thinking became a habit,' I explained. Then added: 'In the Bible, there is a saying, "Thou shalt decree a thing, and it shall be established unto thee". So many times this has happened for me. I believed I would be saved, but...' I stammered, suddenly ending my rhapsody.

'Saved?' he asked, confused. 'Saved from what?'

'Like you said, it is very dangerous to travel alone. Tell me, is there such a verse in the Quran?' I asked, my question a well-aimed distraction from his enquiring mind and from my own vulnerability.

'Yes.' His eyes narrowed as though sensing a whiff of deceit. 'But our reward does not come from just asking. The Quran writes that the reward comes to those who work.' His tone now changed to defiance and he crossed his arms as if to show we were two opposing forces in that age-old debate. 'This is the will of Allah.'

'Yes, of course, we must take the first steps to make our dreams come true no matter what faith we follow,' I said, to defuse the subtle air of conflict that had suddenly drifted between us.

I looked directly into his dark eyes: 'There is also another meaning to *ubuntu*, a deeper meaning. It means we are all the same. We are all connected. If you are hurting, then I am hurting.'

'Yes,' he said, his tone now calm, non-judgemental. 'The Quran says people of different faiths need not argue about their beliefs when they follow the one God. The Prophet Muhammad writes, they must never be divided.'

12

IN MAFIOSO TERRITORY

Georgia

I crossed the border at Sarpi into Georgia about 9.00 a.m. a little later than I'd planned. But I estimated I still had plenty of time to complete the six-hour ride to Tbilisi, the capital, before dark. I changed money, US$10, just enough to get me there.

I'd decided to take the main highway rather than the shorter route over the mountains, as Alan had suggested. At a police check-point just after the border, the two officials, more in awe than objectionable, flicked through my passport and studied the map on the TT's side cover both repeating '*dzalian kargi*', which I later found out meant, 'very good'. I asked them about the mountain road, pointing to it on my road map, saying, 'I go to Tbilisi. Is this road okay?'

'*T'ovli, t'ovli*,' they repeated, and I looked confused until one said 'snow' and crossed his arms, which I interpreted as 'road closed'. It would be a disaster to go this way and end up stuck at night on a mountain road in the middle of *mafioso* territory. I would take the long way round to Tbilisi. Near the turn-off to the mountains, I rechecked my decision when I stopped for fuel at a surprisingly modern Shell service station in Batumi, where petrol was less than half the price of Turkey's. A small crowd gathered, all stared dumb-founded when I pulled off my helmet and realised I was a woman... and I was alone. The petrol attendant, a boy aged about fifteen, spoke a little English, and told me, 'much snow'. My only option was the main road skirting the Black Sea until it turned east.

As I left Batumi, the highway to Tbilisi, a two-lane road, deteriorated to broken tarmac and pot-holes. Later, I took a minor road thinking it would cut 100 kilometres from my route, but instead it slowed my ride to a crawl. For several hours, I negotiated crater-like pot-holes as the road wound through thickly wooded forests and over rolling green hills. Finally, it opened to an expanse of lush pasture, thick and green with spring rains. I passed several hamlets of old timber cabins, the villagers staring at me from where they tilled their fields. It was untouched by the modern world, as though I'd fallen through a time warp to the 1800s. My arms ached to steer the TT, and it was a welcome relief when I reached the intersection to the main road, but it was littered with pot-holes too. I had it pretty much to myself passing the occasional truck and car, mostly small Russian-made sedans.

I'd underestimated just how long it would take to reach Tbilisi and only stopped briefly at a roadside shack for lunch of flatbread and a bottle of naturally sparkling Georgian mineral water, the list of minerals on its label mind-boggling. I guzzled it down.

By late afternoon, the road gradually improved. The pot-holes were soon replaced by smooth black tarmac that wound through a valley of steep hills fringing the fast flowing Dzirule River. As I rode towards a bank of heavy black clouds, I tried to push away the first twinges of panic: it would soon be dark; I was in the heart of *mafioso* territory; I would soon be drenched. Then I would also be cold. The Turks and Alan had explicitly told me not to stop in Georgia. And definitely do not stop anywhere near Kutaisi. 'Very bad men there,' I was told by one man at the border that morning. Kutaisi, I later read, was the home of the Kutaisi Clan, one of the biggest, most ruthless and powerful crime gangs in the world. Its networks stretch right across Europe and into Russia.

The first raindrops hit me. Lightly at first, then forcefully, turning to marble-sized hail. I rode on, hoping it would pass, but the hail fell harder, pummeling my arms and shoulders. I'd never ridden in hail, and the pain was intense. I searched for shelter and as I rounded a bend, up ahead was a roadside shack with a timber lean-to. I parked under it to the surprise of a gangly youth, all arms and legs on the cusp of growing into a man. His eyes bulged in disbelief when I pulled off my helmet and beamed a smile.

'Couldn't have taken that for much longer,' I said, and he relaxed, smiling back. The hail turned to a steady downpour.

'Where am I?' I asked pointing to my map. He shook his head, having no idea what I was talking about. The rain eased a little, but torrents still ran down the sides of the road.

'Toilet?' I asked hoping he'd understand. The word was pretty much universal in most languages… and I was busting for a pee. He nodded and pointed to a narrow track framed by an arch of thick dark green vines. '*Restorani.*'

'Restaurant?'

'*Diakh restorani,*' he said, pointing down the narrow two-wheeled track.

'Here. A restaurant. Wow. Unbelievable,' I said, and prayed it would be the same as those I'd come across in Turkey. There would surely be a place to camp. It may even have rooms, a cabin by the river perhaps. On this day, more than any other, I needed things to work out.

I rode slowly down the narrow track. The rain was still a steady drizzle. The track ended after about a hundred metres to reveal a grand old mansion. A disused water fountain, overgrown with vines, stood like a majestic icon of a bygone era of prosperity. Thick timber railings ran around the upper veranda; arches bordered the lower level. Fringed by elm trees, the branches leafy and the thick trunks covered in moss, the mansion looked disused: vines hung from the upper level trailing to the ground. It sat above the river, which was a loud rumble as it flowed fast and swollen below. I parked the TT and pushed open the heavy timber door, my boots echoing on the slate floor.

'Hello!' I called. There was no reply, and I walked down a wide corridor in search of a toilet. I found a door with a female figure and pushed it open, the stench of stale urine rising to meet me. I held my breath.

'Hello!' I called as I walked down the corridor passing a large kitchen. Two dumpy women stared at me from the dimness.

'Hello,' I said, and one of them beckoned me to follow her through the dining room opposite. It too was dark and disused, tables and chairs were pushed up against the walls. I heard voices. The woman walked through an open double doorway to the arched veranda. Five men sat in high-backed timber chairs around a table made of the same dark wood. The furniture was like relics from medieval times. The men had just shared a meal. The left-overs—bones and crusts of bread littered their plates. Three empty bottles of vodka sat between them. As I approached, they stopped talking instantly and stared. The two women stood behind me.

'Hello. I come from Australia,' I said nervously.

Two of the men laughed as though sensing my fear. '*Da Da*,' said an overweight man with a mop of scruffy black hair and a ruddy unshaven face. He waved a chubby arm for me to join them. Another man, tall and thin, quickly stood up and offered his chair.

'Sit,' he said. Almost immediately, an extra chair was placed at the table by one of the women who hovered nearby. A glass was placed before me and filled from a large bottle of Coca-Cola. One of the men said a few words and the two women disappeared.

I asked about camping using hand signals for a tent and for sleep.

'*Da Da*,' said the fat man, who I assumed was in charge, possibly the manager. The men were all quite drunk, and the evidence indicated their drinking and feasting was a marathon that had started at lunch. I suddenly felt uncomfortable. The warnings from Alan and the Turks suddenly had real meaning. As I was about to thank them for the Coke and say I must leave, the two women returned. One carried a plate of white cheese cut into thick round slices and a plate of the same kind of oblong bread I'd eaten earlier. It was all I'd eaten since breakfast. My stomach rumbled. The other woman carried a pan sizzling with pieces of fried meat and a large plate filled with quarters of tomatoes, slices of cucumber and spring onions.

'Eat,' said the man with a long bony face.

'Thank you.' I pierced a lump of meat with a fork and popped it in my mouth.

A small glass of cognac was poured from a fresh bottle placed on the table.

'Georgia good. Georgia no problem,' said the fat man holding up his glass ready to toast. He was the only one who could speak a little English. I raised my glass. The other men did too. The straight alcohol made me gag, but I swallowed and immediately my glass was refilled. We toasted again. I refused the third time and felt relief they were not insulted and did not insist. The bottle of cognac was emptied and replaced with another.

'Eat. Eat,' insisted the long-faced man and I filled my plate with more meat, salad and cheese, which was like feta, but not as salty. One of the women returned with a jug of green sauce, which was absolutely delicious. It tasted unlike anything I've ever eaten before. Aromatic and slightly tangy. The fat man told me it was *themali*. I later found out it was a Georgian speciality made from wild green plums, herbs and garlic. We then toasted thanks for the sauce, but I sipped the tiniest amount of cognac already feeling the effects of the two previous toasts. My glass was topped up. The second cognac bottle was emptied, and a bottle of vodka appeared. In several rounds of toasts in quick succession, it too was soon emptied. Since I'd arrived, they'd drunk two bottles of cognac and were now on their second bottle of vodka.

The rain continued to fall as a slow drizzle.

'*Motosiklet*,' the fat man said. The women had told him about my motorcycle, which was parked in the rain at the front of the building. The long-faced man opposite rose and beckoned me to follow. To reach the side veranda, we had to push the TT through the front entrance and through the dining room. When they saw the TT and studied the map on its side cover, they were impressed and insisted I join them in one last toast to praise my achievement. My world began to spin, I reached for the bread and another piece of meat to soak up the alcohol before it reached my brain. The men thought I was still hungry, shouted a few words and a few minutes later, one of the women placed a plate of stir-fried mung beans and omelette in front of me.

A long day on a tough road, a belly full of hearty food and too much alcohol; I struggled to stay awake. Propping my elbows on the table to hold my head upright, I asked again about a room. Camping was out of the question. Not only was it still raining, but I suddenly felt very vulnerable.

'*Da Da*,' said the fat man who was now rolling drunk and falling back into his chair when he attempted to stand. The oldest of the men, who had been quiet, almost invisible until now, stood and began pushing the TT back through the dining room. I trailed after him.

'Good night,' I called to the remaining four men, who waved drunkenly.

Beside the grand old mansion was a bungalow. The old man pushed open the heavy double doors, and I pushed the TT inside. A single bed was against one of the walls of the spacious room. There was a large fireplace. The windows, framed by solid wooden shutters, overlooked the river.

The old man pointed to the heavy beam that secured the front door. He crossed his arms and shook his head indicating I was to keep it closed. When he left, I quickly bolted the door and closed the shutters. It was still daylight, but I kicked off my boots and changed into leggings and a clean T-shirt and climbed into my sleeping bag, which I'd placed on the lumpy mattress. I soon fell into an exhausted sleep, but later in darkness, was woken by repeated loud knocking on the door. '*Heda!*' a man called. The knock turned to banging of fists and then kicking. I curled up thankful that the double door was solid and nothing but a battering ram would penetrate it.

'Hello,' the fat man called when I emerged the next morning into bright sunlight. I pushed the TT through the doorway, and a moment later three of the men came out from the house, followed by the elderly man. They stood pointing at the bike and discussing its merits as if nothing had happened and there was no need to apologise.

'Thank you so much for the room and food,' I said, and offered my hand to show my gratitude despite what could have happened if the door had not held under their barrage of thumps and kicks. I cast a look at the old man and hoped he understood how grateful I was for his warning.

'Georgia good. Georgia no problem,' the fat man said, shaking my hand. The others did the same. I started the TT, pulled on my helmet and gloves and under a clear blue sky warmed by the morning sun, headed towards Tbilisi.

The road I followed was a series of sweeping bends through a range of hills, and I could open the throttle. As I approached Tbilisi, the road emerged to gently undulating fields where robed men herded dreadlocked sheep. I passed the majestic Caucasus mountains, the peaks still heavy with snow. I took the bypass around Tbilisi and prayed my Russian visa would give me entry into Azerbaijan.

13

FLOATING IN OIL

Azerbaijan

The closer I neared the oil fields of the Caspian Sea, the more the price of fuel dropped. Mid-afternoon, just before the Georgia-Azerbaijan border, I asked a truck driver, a Turk, his rig broken down on the side of the road, about a petrol station. I had not seen any since leaving the outskirts of Tbilisi about an hour earlier, not even a roadside shack with a bowser. I had fuel for another fifty kilometres, about the distance to the Georgia-Azerbaijan border, but did not want to risk running out.

'*Benzin*, Azerbaijan. Much cheaper,' he called and waved me on.

I passed quickly through Georgian immigration and rode over an impressive bridge, to cross the Matsimus Tskali River and into Azerbaijan where I was promptly stopped. A group of Azeri border officials, four stern-faced men in military uniform, waved me down. One demanded my passport. Another poked my shoulder and pointed to where I must park: next to the immigration post, a small cement block building with a pitched rusting tin roof. The official with my passport disappeared inside. I followed. He was seated at a large wooden desk, flicking through my passport, studying each page in detail. Opposite, on a faded red couch, sat two men scruffy from days on the road. They looked Turkish and fed up—the drivers of the two rigs parked outside. I wondered how long they'd been there. Their enforced wait was just part of the ongoing contempt between the two nationalities.

'Visa!' bellowed an official.

'The Russian visa is my transit visa for Azerbaijan,' I politely replied, pointing to the folded piece of paper inside my passport. Luckily, it was 15 May. I smiled at how events landed me here on the very day my Russian visa became valid. He read it, stamped my passport and without another word handed it back. Before any further questions could be asked, I turned on my heel and was gone.

Azerbaijan was formerly part of the Soviet Union, and following the dissolution of the USSR in December 1991, there was much confusion over whether or not a Russian visa still gained entry into these former Soviet states.

A few kilometres after the border, I approached a petrol station. Just as the Turkish truck driver said, fuel was much cheaper. Several kilometres after that I approached a truck park. As I passed, a red truck with a refrigerated trailer pulled out, then suddenly hit the brakes. It was Alan Kendall.

'Fancy seeing you here,' I called up as he leaned out the window, a wide grin braking across the grey stubble of his unshaven face.

He flung open the door and climbed down. 'I was worried about you.'

'The Georgians told me the road was closed with snow,' I replied.

Even though I'd only met Alan two days ago, an overwhelming sense of happiness welled inside me.

'Bullshit. Was all clear,' he said.

'It's great to see you,' I grinned back. It felt like I'd been reunited with a favourite uncle after a long absence, but then realised I'd never felt this way for any relative, let alone my four uncles whom I vaguely remembered from childhood. We were a detached, distant extended family, often with thousands of kilometres separating us. Understandable due to Australia's enormous size and the need for families to move for work, leaving members scattered across vast distances. Before I turned thirteen, two of my four uncles shot themselves—both were alcoholics. The first turned to alcohol after a back injury from a horse riding accident. The second was a Vietnam War veteran unable to come to terms with the horrors he'd seen. The third lived overseas, and the fourth, while in the same state, had always been absent from my life.

A lot like my father too, in a way. He was there in person of course, but mostly absent as a father, especially in my teenage years when he worked long hours to provide for his family. Instead of offering guidance and encouragement, he doled out criticism that undermined my self-confidence and left me very unsure of myself. I like to believe it was unintentional, the result of 'his generation of men'. Like most fathers who grew up in the 1950s and 1960s, he probably thought these mental attacks would toughen me up; make me stronger. Maybe this was why I had thought I could ride a motorcycle alone to some of the most dangerous and isolated parts of the world?

'Stick behind me, and we'll travel for a few hours and then pull up for a cuppa,' Alan said. It was 500 kilometres to Baku, Azerbaijan's capital, where I'd take the ferry to Turkmenistan.

The road improved a little, but I still dodged the occasional pot-hole. Alan drove much slower than I, and I'd wait for him at a roadside tea shop, conveniently spaced at regular intervals. I accepted gratefully the tea offered. Payment was always refused. At one checkpoint, while two policemen attempted to extort a bribe from Alan, who refused to pay, I was invited for lunch, but declined out of respect for Alan.

We soon left the low rolling hills behind, and the road to Baku opened to grassy plains that became more arid the further east we travelled. I passed through decrepit towns and villages. Enormous rusting factories sat derelict on the outskirts, abandoned since the breakup of the Soviet Union. Under communism, the factories meant everyone had a job, but now I just saw poverty.

When day turned to night, the road stretched out over desert-like saltpans, and I rode beside Alan's rig using the full beam of his powerful headlights to light my way, grateful the tarmac was wide and smooth. There was something 'David and Goliath' about the two of us rumbling east, the flat expanse disappearing into an infinite blackness while the sun dropped off the edge of the earth behind us.

It was nearly midnight when we pulled into a truck depot on the outskirts of Baku run by the Azerbaijan International Operating Company (AIOC), a consortium of ten oil companies set up to drill the Caspian Basin. Amongst the rows of parked trucks was another from the UK. Alan introduced Tom from Scotland—a small stocky man with elfin ears and wiry red hair.

While I set up my tent between the two trucks, Alan and Tom got to work on frying up a feast of bacon and eggs, which we washed down with cold tins of Fosters beer.

'You'll find Mobil at AIOC's office in Baku,' Alan said scribbling, an address on a scrap of paper. 'They'll put you up in the contractors' camp. It's off the highway heading south. You can't miss it.' It was just after sunrise. He'd shaken my tent and handed me a steaming mug of tea as I emerged bleary-eyed after only a few hours' sleep. 'I'm up for unloading shortly,' he added.

'So this is the end of the road,' I said folding the paper and tucking it into a jacket pocket. 'Thanks for the tea and food and everything. I'll never forget that cuppa and the cambozola… and that view over the Black Sea. It's a pity I missed the ride over the mountains,' I babbled as I tried to find the words to show my appreciation. I felt we were kindred spirits, and was eternally grateful for our chance encounter.

'Keep in touch. I want to know you made it home,' he said and gave me a hug.

When we'd sat drinking tea overlooking the Black Sea, he'd told me how my father must be so proud to have a daughter like me. I didn't respond. The awkward moment soon passed, and words and laughter came easily once again. We'd swapped addresses on that day. That was when he told me I was street smart. I was strong: a survivor who would always come out on top. 'I've been around, you know. And you're one of those people nothing will stop,' he said as though he sensed the darkness in my eyes.

After leaving Alan, I rode through poverty-stricken townships and past the gloomy stares of villagers and into central Baku, which was unlike anything I expected. I rode along wide boulevards with monolithic Russian buildings, past four-storey apartment buildings, grandiose and Parisian. Baku appeared to rival any European city except here modern architecture had not quite made it, although several buildings were under construction, and cranes dotted the skyline. This was the first sign of the oil industry, fuelled by foreign investment, about to boom a second time. In future years, Baku would become a utopian city built on the nation's immense oil wealth. Its foundation though, came from the Swedish-Russian Nobel brothers Ludwig and Robert, older siblings of famous inventor Alfred Nobel, who a year before his death in 1896, established the Nobel Prizes. Alfred bequeathed nearly US$200 million or 94 per cent of his assets to the fund, because he did not want to be remembered as 'the merchant of death', having made a fortune as the inventor of dynamite. But in the late 1800s, Ludwig and Robert saw the potential of oil. By the early 1900s, Baku was the 'black gold' capital of the world, until the Russian revolution in 1917 when the Nobel brothers, along with the Rothschild family, Shell and number of other western oil companies sold up, and shipped out.

I soon found my way to the Mobil office at the AIOC headquarters in central Baku, a sprawling 1920s Art Deco mansion. There was no real need for me to seek Mobil's help. I still had four litres of oil I'd collected from the Mobil depot in Istanbul. I'd collect more from the Mobil office in Almaty, Kazakhstan. I certainly didn't need a rest. But still, there I was standing in the grand foyer with my letter of introduction from Mobil UK and a Mobil staffer advising he'd phone the AIOC camp to expect me. 'I've booked you in for a week,' he'd said and wrote down the address and explained the directions. 'Just follow the highway south. You can't miss it.'

It was late evening, my third night as a guest at the AIOC camp, and I lay in bed staring at the ceiling. My room had space for a single bed, side-table and narrow wardrobe. It was a donga—a demountable commonly used in mining and construction camps for fly-in-fly-out workers.

Over beers at dinner earlier, I'd asked the oil contractors about the vast oil fields that stretched along the fringe of the Caspian Sea—a mishmash of rusting pump jacks and triangular steel frames standing on crude-blackened soil. It was environmental degradation on an enormous scale, and I witnessed only a fraction of it.

'The Russians did it,' I was told.

'But what about the Nobel brothers and the other western oil companies? They were here before the Russians,' I'd shot back.

'Russians did most of it,' was the reply.

'Doesn't really matter who did it. What about the clean-up? Who's doing that?' I asked, the beer making me forget my manners amongst my pro-oil hosts.

'The Caspian is swimming in oil. It's the second richest field after Saudi Arabia. There'll be enough money for the clean-up. And once the pipeline is finished, this place is going to be swimming in money too,' said a burly Brit. He was referring to the Main Export Pipeline, which would run from Baku through Georgia to the Mediterranean. But construction was still years away.

The contractors, mostly British oil workers, who I drank beers with before dinner each evening had welcomed me, praising my achievement. Each evening, as I recounted my adventures through Africa and more recently through Turkey and Georgia, more joined our table. 'Millions dream of doing what you're doing, but few do it,' I was told on many occasions.

'Thanks,' I replied and thought: 'If only they knew the truth.'

Over the past three days at AIOC, I'd serviced the TT utilising their well-equipped workshop. I'd eaten my fill of bacon and eggs, fresh fruit, salads, smoked salmon, prawns and rump steak. I'd even become a minor celebrity after being interviewed on Azeri television and was featured in one of Azerbaijan's leading newspapers. I'd become so much part of the 'team' at AIOC that Mobil offered me a job as a data processor. It would be a twelve-month contract. The first AIOC oil rig was about to start drilling.

The job offer came after I'd told a Mobil staffer that I'd worked as a radiation safety technician for six years at the Ranger uranium mine in Australia's Northern Territory. Of course, I could not accept it. 'It's fantastic money,' the staffer said in disbelief when I politely turned down the offer. The money made no difference. 'I'm on a journey,' I said, hoping this would need no further explanation. While I knew the job offer was the financial opportunity of a lifetime, and in all likelihood would propel me into the oil industry, where there are no limits to career advancement and earning potential, I could not accept it.

As I lay staring at the ceiling, tears rolled from my eyes, wetting my hair and pillow. I could not accept it because what would happen in the middle of winter when temperatures dropped to below freezing, and I lost the fight? With weakened immunity, what if PCP struck me down again? I still had a six-month supply of Bactrim and was taking it as a prophylactic to keep this most virulent pneumonia under check. Recently, my body was coping better with the side-effects, and my face was just a rosy pink; easily covered with a light layer of foundation. What would happen when I got sick? I knew the virus was growing stronger. I could feel it. Despite the good food and rest, the heaviness of fatigue was slowly seeping into my body. How could I take this job knowing I was dying? How could I keep my secret if I had to be medically evacuated to Europe, to a western hospital, at their expense?

I felt engulfed by a deep sadness that threatened to suffocate me. The job offer reinforced my regret for the life I would never have. On that day when I'd been diagnosed in London, I had cried a flood of tears. On that day, aged thirty-one, my life would soon be over: there would be no marriage, children... no white picket fence. But on that day, the life that would never be mine was still distant with or without HIV. The Mobil job offer was here now. It taunted me, reminded me that I was no longer part of this journey called life: a life of infinite possibilities based on the choices we make when opportunities come our way. It drove home that such choices were closed to me. My only option was the road heading east, then south. The road was where I could escape from being found out; it was also where I still held hope.

How different my life could have been if I'd taken that job. Most importantly, I'd have had instant access to the internet and news of the discovery of HIV medications that were proving to be as good as a cure, even in May 1997. Of course, I knew none of this as I lay crying on that night.

It was late afternoon and I was waiting at the famous Baku Boulevard that runs parallel for several kilometres around the bay and lined with the nineteenth-century mansions of Baku's oil barons. I'd left the AIOC camp that morning, saying goodbye to the oil contractors at breakfast. Earlier I'd gone swimming in the calm waters of the almost saltless Caspian at a beach near the AIOC camp. It was Tuesday, and I had the beach to myself until a group of three young men and their father arrived to celebrate his fiftieth birthday. They had a picnic of kebabs, beer, vodka and champagne and invited me to join them. Their sense of celebration was contagious spilling over with the effervescence of the delicious champagne they continuously poured into my glass. I overindulged to forget the deep sadness I'd felt yesterday and gave no thought to the fact that I needed to ride a motorcycle through Baku's chaotic rush hour traffic. Somehow, I'd arrived at the boulevard unscathed.

The TT was parked nearby, and I sat eating an ice-cream, watching the afternoon promenade. It's what everyone did in Baku at the end of the day. Parents ambled past while their excitable children dashed around them. Couples, both young and old, walked arm-in-arm cooled by a gentle sea breeze. The city's office workers, on their way home, stopped to chat with friends. Old men played chess. The Baku Boulevard had become my favourite place, and it was here that I had arranged to meet Ramiza, an Azeri woman who rented out a room in her apartment to foreign visitors. Staying at the AIOC camp, I'd felt isolated from Baku with its slow-paced Parisian ambience and architecture: a Paris of 200 years ago. When I asked about a place to stay in Baku's city centre, a Mobil staffer suggested Ramiza, who worked as an advisor to the cultural minister, and also at times, for Mobil.

'Hello. Welcome to Baku. I am Ramiza,' said the Azeri woman who'd approached from behind. I turned to see a softly wrinkled face creased into a warm smile as the sun highlighted the red in her rich brown hair tied in a bun. She was short, about five foot, and aged about sixty, I guessed. She carried a large canvas shopping bag and wore a brown dress.

'I shop for our dinner. Please, we go to my apartment. It is not far.'

'Thank you,' I said and introduced myself. 'Where will I store my *mototsikl*?' and pointed to where it was parked loaded with my gear.

'Please bring. It is safe outside my apartment.' And with that, we headed off along the Boulevard and I wheeled the TT beside her.

Ramiza's apartment was on the second floor of a building along a narrow cobblestone lane a short distance from where we'd met. As we walked, I told her I'd been staying at the AIOC camp for the past three days and planned to leave Baku for Turkmenistan the day after tomorrow.

'Oh, no. You must stay longer in Baku. You have seen nothing,'

'I've seen the old city and the Maiden Tower and the prehistoric rock art at Gobustan,' I said. Before arriving in Baku, I'd expected a shanty town, but instead found a city and its surrounds full of history dating back to the Stone Age and the Persian Empire. Baku had been a vital link on the Silk Road. Later, the immense wealth from the oil boom changed it into a mini-Paris. The Russians also left their mark with wide boulevards, fountains and monolithic buildings.

'Yes, Baku is very old. There is much history here, but you see nothing of the Azeri people,' she huffed as though chastising me for my neglect in staying at the AIOC camp.

Ramiza lived alone in a two-bedroom apartment and rented her second room for the equivalent of US$5 a night including meals. 'I love to cook,' she said when I told her I was happy to pay more for food.

'It is good to meet foreigners. It is interesting to hear their stories,' she told me and explained later as we ate dinner that she had never married and did not have children. 'This did not happen for me,' she said, and her jovialness was suddenly replaced with a look of sadness as she handed me a pear-shaped glass of black tea. 'What of you? When will you marry?'

'Maybe this will not happen for me either,' I said picking up a lump of sugar and biting it before taking a sip of the tea.

'Oh. You must make it happen. It is my greatest regret not having children. Maybe not so much the husband,' she laughed. 'You don't want to end up like me, an old woman living alone.'

I spooned a piece of chicken drenched in a dark purple sauce onto my plate. 'This is delicious. What is this?' I asked moving the conversation to the feast laid out between us. On a small dining table cramped into her tiny apartment were plates of sliced tomatoes and cucumbers sprinkled with fresh tarragon, small chunks of white feta-like cheese, a fragrant rice pilaf, freshly baked flatbread, and a potato salad covered with bright red seeds—the colour of jewels.

'It is *fesenjan*,' she smiled. 'It is made from pomegranate juice, plums, ground walnuts and molasses. It is a favourite Azeri dish. Those are the seeds,' she said pointing to the potato salad. The seeds burst a sweet tanginess into my mouth and I scooped another spoonful onto my plate. 'Delicious. I've heard of pomegranate, but never eaten one,' I said, and ate another mouthful, my body responding to its goodness with a hedonistic abandon. There was something in the fruit that my defences deemed absolutely vital.

'You like?' Ramiza smiled and then disappeared into her tiny kitchen, returning with a large hard-skinned pinkish-red fruit. 'Pomegranate is the national fruit of Azerbaijan. It is the king of fruits. See—it even has a little crown,' she said cupping the fruit in both her hands and offering it to me as though it was a precious jewel.

And yes, it did have a crown-shaped protrusion. Pomegranates were an uncommon fruit in Australia, particularly in regional areas where I'd grown up. But in future years, we would be a major exporter.

'Pomegranates have been grown in Azerbaijan since ancient times. It is very good for you and gives strong health. We eat the fruit and drink its juice and use it in our cooking.' I later read that pomegranates are loaded with vitamins, minerals and antioxidants.

'The season is finished, but I still have a box of fruit that will last a few more months. Maybe till September when we can feast again,' she said.

I stayed three days in Baku city wandering its streets, breathing in its vibrancy, and always drinking tea with Azeris when I stopped to rest. On my last night with Ramiza, I bought a bottle of champagne and a 125gm tin of black Beluga caviar for US$25. It was an expensive indulgence, but a fraction of what it would cost in the west. I had always liked the salty burst of flavour from caviar. But I'd only ever eaten fish roe purchased in tiny jars from supermarkets, not this exquisite delight harvested from sturgeon, the fish that produce the world's most expensive caviar. Ramiza had one small spoonful, refusing to eat more. What I'd spent was equivalent to two weeks wages for the average Azeri. While money was flowing into Baku from foreign oil companies, local people were yet to benefit.

'Only the oil executives and the foreigners benefit,' Ramiza said when I commented how the oil would bring jobs and prosperity. 'Azeris work as cleaners and labourers. Soon there will be no more caviar. The oil is polluting the Caspian, and the sturgeon are dying. Every year there are less fish and nothing is being done,' she said.

Other Azeri locals I'd shared tea with had also told me, with anger, how the oil pollution and river inflows laden with toxic chemicals from Russia were killing the Sturgeon and many other fish species too. The centuries-old fishing industries of several countries fringing the Caspian would soon be gone if the pollution was not stopped and cleaned up.

'The oil companies say it is not them and blame it on the past, on the Russians. They are just interested in taking our oil and making money, leaving us with nothing,' she added.

The next morning, I said goodbye to Ramiza.

'You have been like my mother,' I said and gave her a hug.

'You are like my daughter,' she replied. In the space of just over a week two people had come into my life, one like a father, the other like a mother. Both left an indelible mark on my soul.

I rode down the cobblestone street toward the port where I'd board the rusting hulk of a ferry to cross the Caspian, to Turkmenistan.

Part 3

TURKMENISTAN TO KYRGYZSTAN

14

THE CALL OF THE DESERT

Turkmenistan

'Visa!' boomed the Azeri immigration official resplendent in military uniform.

'I have a Russian visa,' I shot back, pointing to it glued in my passport. Whether or not my Russian visa would gain entry into Turkmenistan was up to the discretion of whoever was on duty at the time. As a former Soviet state, Turkmenistan still had many Russians in government positions, such as in immigration, and some did not yet accept Russia was no longer the ruling power. But this official clearly showed no such loyalty.

'Turkmenistan visa,' he hissed.

It was a stalemate. And no amount of feigned innocence on my part would change the situation. My mind raced as I calculated my options; there were none.

'*Televideniye, televideniye!*' yelled a man pushing his way through the crowd of onlookers. He was a colleague of the official who glared at me with narrowed eyes. An animated discussion followed. There was much arm waving, pointing at me, accompanied by nods of approval from the motley crowd of mostly dock workers who'd paused to witness the commotion. I understood that my celebrity status in that moment came from the publicity Mobil had garnered from my story. Some of the people must have seen me being interviewed on Azeri national television as well as being featured in one of its leading dailies. My story brought a touch of the outside world to the Azeri people—a touch of adventure that captured the innate human spirit to explore. This sense of exploration was perfectly aligned with Mobil's winged horse.

'You go,' said the first official handing over my passport, his defiance replaced with acquiescence.

I kicked the TT into life, and in my nervousness opened the throttle. The bike lurched forward, the front wheel was slightly airborne. It was a freakish rendition of Mobil's trademark when I clanked it into first gear. I regained control and rode sedately along the pier and into the ferry, a rusting hulk of a freighter that appeared unlikely to make the fifteen hour, 240-kilometre voyage. It was mid-morning and once loaded, it would chug its way across the Caspian towards Turkmenbashi. I was told we would depart late afternoon, but it could be tomorrow or even the day after that. My ticket was US$80 and included a bed in a four-bunk cabin and all meals. I and a posse of Turkish and Iranian truck drivers were the only passengers. They were transporting goods to Central Asia as just about everything consumable is imported from Turkey, Iran and Europe, but mostly from China. Trucks were what plied the Silk Roads today, not the camel trains of antiquity that once numbered nearly a thousand strong. No fee was demanded for my motorcycle. Maybe my notoriety as a minor television celebrity had followed me!

After orientating myself—exploring the engine room, the mess and the bridge, where an officer showed me our plotted course—I settled into my cabin, reading and soon sleeping until the engines fired, thankfully, into life late afternoon.

From the deck, Baku slowly disappeared, and we glided over a dead calm sea. As day turned to night the silhouettes of oil rigs dotted the horizon framed against the sun, a giant orb, that cast the scene in gradients of crimson, burnt orange and touches of mauve. The Caspian was so still, it felt as though we were not moving at all and only the ripples at the bow proved otherwise.

Just before the sun disappeared, the sea and sky melted into one, awash in ever-darkening orange hues. The ferry seemed suspended in time adrift. I gripped the railing, overwhelmed by this other-world immensity, as though we were gliding through deep space washed in the glow of an enormous sun. Likewise, I could have been witnessing a scene from earth's creation when it was a gaseous ball of fire. It was a surreal moment of absolute purity.

The smells of frying meat reached me as I entered the mess a few moments later. About a dozen men, the officers and crew, sat waiting for dinner. A group beckoned me to join them, and vodka was poured into the sort of glass commonly used for a café latte. Theirs were refilled to the brim, and another toast was shared, the empty glasses clanked in unison on the table. I'd taken only a sip, and questioning eyes turned to my mostly undrunk vodka as though this was the greatest insult. Another round was poured. As I knocked it back, the straight alcohol burnt down my throat and my face screwed in repulsion. All cheered. Another round quickly followed. 'Who's steering the ship?' I thought, reaching for a shashlik from the pile on a tray as it was placed on the table. But then remembered nothing except a vast inland sea surrounded us, until we reached Turkmenbashi mid-morning tomorrow. Yet another round of vodka followed. I declined and asked for a beer, advising my hosts it was the national drink of Australia. A can of chilled Azeri beer appeared.

My Russian visa was not accepted in Turkmenistan and the Turkmen immigration official demanded I pay US$20 for the visa and US$20 for my motorcycle. I happily handed over the cash, grateful I was allowed into this reclusive desert country that even after the downfall of the Soviet Union was still difficult to enter for the independent traveller. Within the space of twenty-four hours, I knew I'd struck it lucky again.

It was mid-morning and already too hot to venture into the Karakum desert on the straight black line of tarmac that stretched east to Uzbekistan, a three-day ride across a flat expanse of sun-scorched earth. Turkmenistan was eighty per cent desert, much of it the Karakum, which means 'black sands', although here it appeared a faded ochre. Even now in early summer, daytime temperatures soared to nearly 50°C, which would cook both me and the TT if I pushed through it. I could probably fry an egg for my lunch by cracking it into my cooking pot and leaving it in the sun for a few minutes. I would only be able to ride from early morning till about 11.00 a.m. and then again from 4.00 p.m. till dark at around 8.00 p.m. During the heat of the day, I'd seek shade, food and water at a village café or roadside truckers' stop.

Now that I'd reached Turkmenistan, the Lonely Planet's *Central Asia* guidebook I'd bought in London was at last useful. I'd stop briefly at the underground thermal pool at Köw Ata on the way to the capital Ashgabat, where I'd visit its famous market. Then overnight in Mary, to wander amongst the ancient ruins of nearby Merv.

Since leaving London, I'd not used a guidebook (nor the internet, which was still embryonic in 1997), and yes, I'd undoubtedly missed out on some not-to-be-missed fascinating sights, but other opportunities had spontaneously materialised. But my guidebook was now a valuable source of information as it gave an insight into the political and cultural history of places to be visited. Thanks to Lonely Planet, I had an overview of the five Central Asian Soviet Republics, artificially created by Stalin in the 1920s and 1930s— and an understanding of Soviet collectivisation. It was a policy that displaced millions to work on collective farms designed to boost crop yields, but ended nomadic lifestyles and family-owned farms, and squashed religious beliefs. In mostly Islamic Turkmenistan alone, over 400 ancient mosques were destroyed. This unwanted control understandably caused resistance fuelled by ongoing skirmishes of guerrilla warfare.

As well as Turkmenistan, I'd cross Uzbekistan, Kyrgyzstan and Kazakhstan, and very briefly into Tajikistan, transitting a narrow finger of its territory that poked in between Uzbekistan and Kyrgyzstan. It epitomised Stalin's thoughtlessness in carving up the borders of a region that was formerly a patchwork of nomadic tribes and chiefdoms until annexed, without consultation, by the Soviets. These details would have been lost to me without a guidebook as I spoke no Russian and few spoke English well enough to explain.

I was reading my guidebook in the cafeteria of the gleaming newly constructed ferry terminal. I was the only diner and was yet to order lunch. It would be a long afternoon, and I needed to stagger the hours before it would be cool enough to cross the desert. The Baku to Turkmenbashi ferry route across the Caspian was the new

Silk Road linking Central Asia to Europe, and Europe to China. In ancient times, the Silk Road traversed from Baku around the Caspian and through Iran, but trucks and trains had replaced camels. And ships, including a rail-ferry link, provided a more direct route across the sea.

'Hello, I am Ali,' said a handsome, well-dressed man aged about thirty. He was dark-haired with high cheekbones and a regal straight nose. 'Can I sit with you? I invite you to lunch.'

I nodded and closed my guidebook.

'Thank you,' I smiled at both the welcome offer of lunch and conversation with an English speaker—somewhat rare in these parts. I introduced myself, and we told our stories. Ali was from Iran and worked as a liaison officer overseeing the shift change for the fly-in-fly-out workers on the oil rigs.

'The shift change is this afternoon. I must wait many hours, so I am honoured you will have lunch with me, and I can learn of your travels.' He waved a manicured hand to a waiter, a glimmer of gold flashed as his watch caught a stray beam of sunlight streaming through the cafeteria windows. Two plates of pan-fried sturgeon fillets, chips and salad soon appeared along with two bottles of chilled Georgian mineral water. The fish was stiff like mackerel and slightly oily. When I took a bite, it felt wrong to eat fish more precious alive for its caviar, than dead on my plate, and one that was so endangered due to pollution.

'Delicious,' I lied not wanting to voice my trepidation nor insult Ali's hospitality.

'Do you like the new ferry terminal?' Ali asked. 'It has only just opened.'

'It is very grand, but very quiet.' I cast a glance around the empty cafeteria with its rows of shiny metal tables and chairs. 'Where are all the people?' The ferry terminal, in all its steel and glass glory, sat waiting for emerging economies to boom and the new Silk Road to bustle with traffic and people.

'They will soon come. Turkmenistan has much gas and oil. This country is going to be very rich once we have our own pipelines to

Europe, India and China. Ali was referring to a series of pipelines planned for Turkmenistan, as it sat on the world's fourth largest reserve of natural gas and a significant amount of oil. In the meantime, its oil was shipped, and its gas piped to Europe via Russia.

'Let's hope these riches also flow to the Turkmen people,' I said.

'Ah, Niyazov is already bleeding Turkmenistan, even before the real money makes it here,' he whispered, leaning forward even though we were alone and out of earshot of the two waiters idly chatting near the kitchen. Ali was referring to Saparmurat Niyazov, Turkmenistan's self-appointed president 'for life' who had ruled the country from when it was a Soviet state, since 1985. He also called himself Turkmenbashi, head of the Turkmen, and renamed this port city, formerly Krasnovodsk, in his own honour.

'Most of the people are illiterate. The schools are old, and falling down. Much needs to be done so he needs to spend a lot of money for things to improve. And not just in Ashgabat. With the wealth here, Turkmenistan could be like Iran,' he said and sat back in his chair running a hand through his smooth black hair, and I thought it rather strange he should care about the poor of this country he called a nation of nomads.

'How much money does one man need? Surely there will be enough to spend on the people as well,' I said. 'Happiness comes from helping one another. Not from greed and gluttony.'

A smile washed over his handsome face. 'Ah... I see you are enlightened. A pilgrim travelling the Silk Road?' His tone was playful as though he was relieved we had moved away from the touchy subject of government corruption.

'Yes, I think. Sort of. I've found that things happen on the road, strange things. Everything seems to always work out. Like it is destiny or something,' And so as not to jinx the fortuitous unfolding of these events, I added, 'Well so far things have worked out.'

'This is what you believe! Interesting. Allah has answered my prayers too. Things have worked out for me, but I have worked hard. I have a good job. Next is a wife and children,' he said spreading his arms wide to thank God for the unfolding of his life just as he desired.

Time passed, and at around 2.00 p.m. Ali said goodbye.

'You will see many trucks taking cotton to China and bringing cheap vodka back to the Stans. Everyone drinks too much vodka here, and they will want you to drink it too. Tell them it makes you sick. Say 'bol'noy, bol'noy'. They will understand; otherwise, you will become very drunk.'

'I don't understand this when these are Muslim countries.'

'Islam was suppressed for too long. They grew up with Russian ways, and I don't think they will give up their beloved vodka,' he laughed. 'Good luck on your journey.' Then he strode out of the cafeteria, leaving me alone.

It was still too hot to ride into the Karakum, so I waited until about 4.00 p.m. in the cafeteria, reading my guidebook and writing my diary, but when I pushed the doors open, I walked into an oven. The heat was unrelenting even this late in the day. There was only one main road out of Turkmenbashi, and I followed this straight, smooth line of tarmac leaving all traces of civilisation behind. The landscape was flat and shimmered with heat haze. It was so vast, it felt as though I was not moving at all. Every hundred kilometres ticked over agonisingly slow. My only reprieve was a brief stop to guzzle tepid water from the four one-litre bottles I carried. I planned to spend the night camped in the desert. Alone in this vastness, I could watch the sun slowly sink below a flat horizon, lay under a blanket of stars, and then watch the sun rise again.

As the sky darkened, I turned off the highway and rode over a hardened crust of sand as though the sun's heat had fused the minerals to a molten mass. The expanse was endless, devoid of all life and as I rode with the sun on my left, I realised I could ride into this void and never be found. I could respectfully disappear. The report would read: 'Australian woman travelling by motorcycle last seen in Turkmenbashi'. It would be an honourable end: clean and shameless. Not the death of emaciation from AIDS that awaited me. The report would say how in the intense heat, I must have fallen victim to hallucinations and veered off the road and into the desert. With an almost, full tank of fuel hand-pumped from a bowser at a roadside shack earlier, I could ride 400 kilometres or more. This would take me far into the night under the bright glow of a full moon. It would be a fitting last ride, and I would wish it to go forever, the bike's engine a deep rumble under me. Hours later, exhaustion would force me to stop. I would lay down in the sand until the sun rose out of the desert. Under a scorching sun, death by dehydration would be quick and painless. With two litres of water, it would take a few days, maybe less. In Africa, I'd experienced the first stage of dehydration in northern Kenya, when I'd gone on a fool hardy detour in search of sapphires with a Somali guide. Rather than pain, I'd felt a slow fading into blackness as if I'd soon fall asleep and never wake up.

After just five kilometres, I stopped, turned off the engine and sat frozen with fear by these suicidal thoughts, which had risen so intensely, so unexpectedly. It was as though such thoughts had been brewing in my sub-conscious, waiting for the right moment to strike. A moment when I was vulnerable; when everything was perfectly aligned for optimal success.

I gripped the handlebars. 'I'm not giving up. Why should I give up? I'm not sick. I may never get sick. I'm not giving up!' I shouted into the desert's endless void, making a stand against the constant repetition since my diagnosis. 'I'm going to die, I'm going to die,' the voice of doom had boomed. At first, it had been deafening, a constant pounding, but lately I didn't even hear it, or I'd become used to it. But this voice had found a collaborator in the depths of my subconscious and together they had devised a sinister plan.

Maybe it was the heat that caused me to have those thoughts. Maybe I'd fallen into a sense of timelessness from riding across a desert when the sun had lost its sting, and this harsh, unforgiving land was bathed in a soft, almost cool light. But I did not want to die, not yet, not when there was still hope.

There was no need to set up my tent. I'd sleep under a clear night sky, a billion stars above me and a cool breeze to blow away the day's heat. I spread out my groundsheet, camping mattress and sleeping bag. I'd need its warmth against the early morning desert chill. I ate a tin of sardines, and bread I'd saved from yesterday's breakfast on the ferry. After lunch with Ali, I didn't feel hungry but ate anyway. The suicidal thoughts had pumped my body with adrenalin, a survival response to threat.

My sleep was troubled. Several times I woke from a nightmare where I was falling into a pit of tortured souls, their bony hands reaching to pull me down, long fingernails brushing against my skin and making it crawl as if giant insects walked over me.

As the first rays of sun appeared over the desert horizon, I quickly packed the TT to gain some distance before the heat would force me to stop.

For the long-distance motorcycle traveller, there are moments on a ride when time stands still. When you wish the road would go forever: when everything is in perfect harmony. The road is smooth, ideally with sweeping bends; the wind on your face is a gentle caress. The temperature not too hot and not too cold, just right. And your motorcycle and all its machinations purr blissfully under you as though you've become one—part human, part machine. This was one of those moments as I rode on the straight black line of smooth tarmac across the desert towards Ashgabat, Turkmenistan's capital.

The first hundred kilometres was a blur, but the next I felt I was about to pass out. The sun, still several hours from its zenith, beat down with growing intensity. Mid-morning, I rode through a village and spotted a rusted sign depicting a bowl and spoon. I turned off the highway to follow a dirt road that ended at a ramshackle café overlooking a canal filled with muddy water. It was the narrower end of the enormous 1400-kilometre-long Karakum Canal, which snakes its way across the desert to end at Bereket where it then flows through a pipeline to Turkmenbashi.

Built by the Soviets in the 1950s, the canal diverts water from the Amu Darya, Central Asia's largest river, fed by snow and glacier melt from the Pamir Mountains. Its purpose: to bring life and prosperity to the desert by irrigating huge collective cotton farms, wheat fields and fodder for livestock as well as providing water to towns and villages along its length. They did the same in Uzbekistan with the Syr Darya, but diverting a significant amount of water from these two major rivers reduced the Aral Sea to a puddle. In 1990, the Aral split in two, with the southern sea becoming a dusty salt flat, its thriving villages abandoned and rusting hulks of fishing boats littering its shores.

I'd crossed over the Karakum Canal several kilometres back and was impressed by how the landscape had changed from dry, lifeless desert to swathes of green plots. When the Soviet Union collapsed in 1991 so did large-scale collectivised farms, but this didn't end cotton farming. Instead, families leased plots of state-owned land, selling the cotton they grew to the government. While the Karakum Canal opened up a million hectares of desert to commercial agriculture and provided life-giving water to towns and villages, its poor construction meant that nearly half of the water was lost to evaporation and to seepage causing salination as groundwater levels rose at seepage points. Was it too high a price to pay? The environmental disaster of the Aral Sea for the benefit of thousands of people who relied on the Karakum Canal for their livelihoods, water to irrigate crops, water for their animals and for their very survival?

I pulled up at the front of the restaurant, which comprised of a few rickety wooden tables and chairs on a cement slab under a corrugated iron roof with open sides. As I took off my helmet, I was greeted by a man who beamed a broad smile from his round, slightly Mongoloid face. He babbled a few words in Russian, the *lingua franca* of Central Asia. English, I was to discover, was hardly spoken.

I'd purchased a Russian-English dictionary in Istanbul and quickly retrieved it before following the man.

I was seated at a table overlooking the muddy canal. There was an ever-so-slight breeze, and under the shade, it felt comfortable. Two middle-aged plumpish women approached; each carried two large bowls filled with noodles. Pieces of meat and vegetables floated in a clear broth. The man who greeted me, the owner of the restaurant I presumed, sat down with me and two other men joined us. A bottle of vodka and four glasses appeared, and a toast was shared.

The soup was slightly spicy and absolutely delicious. It was called *lagman* and was a staple food of the Silk Road. This dish originated in China thousands of years ago, making it as far as Russia. It had also become a staple food of Central Asia today, and I was to eat many bowls of it over the coming weeks.

'*Eto ochen khorosho*,' I said stumbling over the Russian words for 'This is very good,' as I read from my phrase book. I finished the last of the broth, and as I rested the spoon in my bowl, it was quickly whisked away to be replaced by another full bowl of the delicious noodle soup. As I'd not had breakfast, I welcomed seconds. Another glass of vodka was poured. Another toast was shared, and as I slurped up the last of the noodles and broth, the restaurant owner called to one of the women. It was then I realized that finishing all I'd been served meant I was still hungry.

'No more,' I said placing my hand over the bowl and shaking my head. '*Nyet Spasiba*. No thank you. No more,' I repeated, and the men laughed. The woman retreated to the kitchen with my empty bowl, and another round of vodka was poured before I could say *nyet* to that too. I'd learnt my first lesson in Turkmen dining etiquette, but had not yet grasped control of what seemed an unstoppable flow of vodka. Another round was poured, and thankfully this emptied the bottle. The TT was parked in the sun, slowly cooking and I staggered towards it to push it under the shelter and shade. The men seeing my intentions, quickly followed, going into lengthy discussion when they saw the map on the side-cover.

After we'd pushed my motorcycle undercover, I told them I needed to rest and placed my hands against my head. They nodded and disappeared probably to do the same. I rolled out my camping mattress and lay down just as the vodka buckled my knees and I fell in a heap. With diary and pen in hand, I propped myself against the TT's front wheel and feigned that I was in complete control and not, in fact, blind rotten drunk. It did not last, and a moment later I was asleep.

I woke several hours later vowing this would never happen again. I cursed myself for leaving myself vulnerable, though I'd felt no threat from the men. There was no indication that my personal safety was at risk. What were the Russian words that Ali had told me to tell my hosts that vodka made me sick? I looked it up in my phrase book.

When I woke several hours later, the restaurant owner and his two friends were sipping tea from small bowls and waved me over. As I approached, I pulled a bundle of Turkmanistan manat notes from the pouch attached to my belt to pay for my lunch. My host shook his head repeating *nyet nyet* and poured me a bowl of tea. I thanked him for his generosity.

It was nearly 5.00 p.m. when I said goodbye, but the coolness of late afternoon had not yet descended over the desert. I rode just fifty kilometres before I had to stop and guzzled nearly half a litre of water. Being hungover, but not yet sober, did not help. I refilled my water bottle from a narrow pipe where fresh water trickled forth. I was at a rest stop, and before long an army truck pulled in and several soldiers spilled out. They were young men in their twenties, new recruits by the look, on a training exercise. As they filled their water bottles, they peppered me with questions, and I was grateful they spoke a little English. Pointing to the TT's side-cover answered most of their queries.

'Where you sleep tonight?' one asked.

'At Köw Ata, the underground cave lake.'

'Yes, this is a good place,' another said and then gave detailed directions so I would not miss the turnoff. The soldiers piled back into the truck and waved goodbye. It was still another hundred kilometres to Köw Ata, and I'd easily make it before dark.

Just as the sun sank below the Kopet Dag mountains that divided Turkmenistan and Iran, I rode into a fenced compound that enclosed the underground lake nestled below the Kopet Dag's lower slopes. A sign advertised it opened at 9.30 a.m. Two men, both of a thickset stature, in trousers and shirts, more dirty rags than clothes, emerged from a small cement block house. They approached, but both stopped gaping in disbelief when I pulled off my helmet.

'Hi. Can I camp here?' I called as I walked towards them, making the symbol of a tent with my hands.

They waved me over, and I pushed the TT to the front of the house. They then beckoned me to follow them inside and pointed to a room with a single bed covered with a worn lumpy horse-hair type mattress. Other than the foyer, there were only two rooms in the house, and the reality of my situation suddenly dawned on me. In the room opposite were two single beds. A large blackened pot sat on a small table between the beds. One of the men sat down and reached into the pot with his overly large hand and pulled out a handful of meat and rice shoving it into his cavernous mouth. The second man, his broad shoulders filling most of the doorway, motioned me to sit on the bed then sat down beside me and began eating from the pot. He insisted I do the same.

I was still full from lunch and hung over from the vodka, but out of politeness, I picked a smallish piece of meat, squashing it together with some rice. Neither spices nor oil had been used. There were no vegetables. It was just meat, which tasted like goat, and boiled rice.

The men continued to eat and insisted I eat more. As we ate in silence, I nervously wondered what would become of me once the meal was over. Despite their brute-like appearance, the fact that I was a woman alone with no means of escape, and no other people for miles, certainly not within shouting distance, the men gave me no reason to feel threatened. I snatched quick sideways glances as they ate with a kind of ravenous hunger. Their arms were thick. The muscles as hard and coiled as wire rope. As they sat hunched over the pot, it appeared they had no necks. Their large heads, with broad flat noses, sat on broad shoulders. Their black hair was coarse and matted. And their skin was darkened by the sun to resemble the toughest leather. They looked nothing like the fine-boned Turkmen with their slightly Mongol features that I had encountered so far. I assumed by their dirty clothes that they were the groundsmen, the labourers, at the underground lake compound, which was a popular day trip for families and tourists from Ashgabat.

As I sat with the men, I felt a sense of shared humanity. We had a common bond that reached far back into the mists of time before civilisation existed some 250,000 years ago when Neanderthals first hunted animals that grazed the steppes to the north. In fact, the remains of a Neanderthal child were found in a cave just a thousand kilometres northeast of here, in Uzbekistan. And some anthropologists say that Turkmenistan was the last stronghold of the Neanderthals. It made sense as its deserts and dry hills were inhospitable for all but the hardiest of people. This is where the Neanderthals would have found refuge from the humanoid tribes intent on slaughtering them on the grounds they appeared scarcely human, or trapping them as slaves, which would invariably have resulted in some interbreeding. I sensed these men were the lost descendants of those last Neanderthals. And according to my father, we shared a common bond, because he'd advised over beers one night before my world motorcycle travels, that he was a 'throwback', which apparently, made me a descendant too! I'd read up on Neanderthals after he'd told me this and discovered they were stronger, lived longer and could resist disease better than homo-sapiens. Would my Neanderthal genes be my salvation against HIV? In me, would the virus meet its match? It was in Africa while fighting a bout of malaria that I began to question where my resilience and man-like physical strength came from.

It was far too hot to sleep in the stuffy room as the men had offered. Instead, I pointed outside, indicating I'd sleep next to my motorcycle. And when they'd attempted to move a foot-high rough-cut wood frame shaped like a small single bed from the side of the house, I declined that too. With my hands, I showed them I'd sleep in my tent, but even though there was a slight breeze, it was too hot for that. There was no shower, but I was shown a tap and a hole-in-the-ground toilet. I rolled out my ground sheet and mattress and spent an uncomfortable night with the wind blowing fine dust on my face while enduring the feeling of things crawling over me.

I woke at daylight, packed the bike and waited for the caretaker to arrive and open the gate to the lake and a swim. As the sun rose over the desert, the two men appeared and waved for me to join them for breakfast of stale bread and tea. We said goodbye, and they wandered off to do whatever it was they did maintaining the compound.

I'd lost three hours of riding in morning coolness before the caretaker arrived. He introduced himself as Shari, a Turkman who was of slight build and in complete contrast to the two brutish groundsmen. I paid my US$5 entrance fee and Shari, who was enthused to have a foreign tourist, guided me down the sixty metres of steps. The first ten metres were lit by electric light, and after that, I used my torch as we descended into the darkness to the cavernous depths of the lake, which is seventy metres long and thirty wide and smelt of rotten eggs from the sulphur that infused the water. Shari spoke some English and explained that the lake water, which contained a number of minerals, had been revered for its healing properties for thousands of years, dating back to the Persians, when people lowered themselves down from the surface with ropes and held burning torches to light their way. 'Several men die building these steps. They carry the cement by hand,' Shari added in reverence as we descended into the darkness; a minute of silence followed for their loss.

While I swam in the warm waters tinged a blue-green, Shari held my torch, and I tried not disturbing the silt on the bottom after he told me the cave was home to a huge bat colony that hung from the ceiling above me.

When we returned to the surface, I was impatient to reach Ashgabat before the heat forced me off the road. But Shari insisted I stay for lunch and we sat on the shaded veranda of the tourist office with a meal of flatbread, beef stew, Pepsi and vodka. As we waited for the stew to warm, I shared one toast, but refused a second and was grateful he understood I had to ride my motorcycle.

'You must visit the gas crater at Darvaza,' he said. 'It is a burning fire rising out of the earth. I have never seen it, but I hear it is a sight to behold.' I retrieved my map and Shari pointed to its location. Darvaza was 300 kilometres north of Ashgabat, in the middle of the Karakum desert.

'Too far. I'll have to pass on it,' I said. A two-day round trip in this torturous heat was out of the question.

'Yes, it is very far,' he agreed.

It was around 1.00 p.m. when I rode away from Köw Ata, grateful the sky was overcast as a storm brewed over the Kopet Dag mountains.

I reached Ashgabat two hours later but only stopped to refuel. This dusty city with its Soviet-era blocks of apartments fringing its outskirts depicted an uninviting urban sprawl. With the description from my Lonely Planet guidebook: 'it has a dust-blown, shutter-banging-in-the-wind quality, and on a sun-scorched afternoon all that's missing are vultures wheeling in the burning blue sky,' sealed my decision. Other than the market, which was on a Sunday, and today was Wednesday, there was nothing of interest to hold me.

Late afternoon, the storm that brewed earlier, moved across the desert, blackening the sky, and I rode through patches of rain. With my jacket unzipped, I reveled in the coolness as it soaked through my shirt. I crossed a wide section of the Karakum Canal just before nightfall and pulled up at a roadside café. I was welcomed by the owner, a jolly well-dressed Turkman in his sixties sporting an impressive moustache. He directed me to park the bike inside one of the buildings, a private dining room. It was hot and stuffy, and when I advised I wanted to camp outside, he looked horrified and began pushing the bike into the room himself, so I had no choice but to comply. I was then ushered towards the café where I was served tea, a glass of Coke and a plate of sweets and half-melted chocolate bars. When I did not help myself to the sweets, the man selected one and unwrapped it for me. He then returned with a plate of fried fish, bread and salad of tomatoes and shallots.

Despite the heat, I slept soundly. I was exhausted from the day's riding and the little sleep of the previous night. At daylight, I washed in the canal, and when I returned, the owner of the café was waiting with a bowl of *lagman*. I produced a handful of manat notes to pay, and he refused. In the three days I'd been in Turkmenistan other than fuel and the entry fee to the underground lake, I'd spent no money; such was the hospitality of the Turkmen people.

Due to a late start, I'd only ridden about a hundred kilometres before the heat forced me to stop where a roadside café bordered the canal. Somehow, I'd taken a wrong turn, and this was confirmed when I showed my map to the owner. He ushered me to a table and soon a bowl of *lagman* and plate of *pirozhki*, small fried Russian potato pies with spring onions, was served. Three local men at a nearby table, all drunk at only 11.00 a.m., insisted I join them until the owner yelled a few words to leave me alone. He poured me a glass of vodka and one for himself. I refused pointing to the bike saying I had to ride. He downed both and then returned with a bottle of cognac, which I was not allowed to refuse. When I emptied my glass, it was immediately refilled. My protests were ignored, and after the third shot, I needed an alcohol-induced afternoon nap.

On waking two hours later, two more shots of cognac were poured, and my offer to pay for lunch refused. As I was about to leave, I was offered a large glass of sour milk. I think it may have been a Turkmen home remedy for sobriety, especially as the very thought of it nearly made me vomit. In the coolness of late afternoon, I rode away from the café and did not realise how drunk I was until two hours later; I had a sobering close call with a truck as I rode up over an embankment to reach the road after stopping to wander amongst the ancient ruins at Merv. With all the best intentions not to drink alcohol even when my hosts ignored my refusal, I had failed miserably. While the Turkmen people are undoubtedly the world's most hospitable, they are also the most persuasive!

I'd made it to the ruins of Merv after riding surprisingly unscathed, with a blood alcohol level far exceeding the limit, through the depressing industrial city of Mary.

Built by the Soviets, Mary sat on the Murghab River and was surrounded by a patchwork of cotton fields. Its economy also benefited from a vast nearby gas field. Merv, a short ride from Mary, was established at the site of a large oasis as far back as about 3000BC. At its height in the twelfth century, it was the second most fabulous city in the Islamic world; Merv was 'Queen of the World' while

Baghdad was 'King'. This walled metropolis was the intersection of a number of trading routes on the Silk Road. It was the mid-point for merchants from the south, east, west and north and, at its height, was home to a million people who lived surrounded by palaces filled with treasures. It was also a city of learning with enormous libraries and lush gardens in which its citizens could seek reflection and relaxation. I imagined these gardens awash with colour as the finest of brightly coloured silks worn by groups of women were blown by a gentle desert breeze. Their laughter joining the chatter of children who played chasing games around them.

At the time, a complex system of irrigation canals diverted water from the Murghab River to fields of wheat and crops of fruits and vegetables. Camel caravans arrived and departed, bringing goods from the far reaches of the civilised world. Merv was also an export hub and was famous for its steel, pottery and cotton as well as its artisans, musicians and scholars. Trading was brisk; fortunes were made, and life was good in this city of riches. I imagined the wealth, culture and learning that circulated inside its walls was the envy of many.

But peace and prosperity ended in 1221 when Genghis Khan's army slaughtered all its inhabitants after the rulers of Merv refused to surrender and pay the taxes the Mongols demanded. Death was by decapitation as the Mongols swung their metre-long razor-sharp swords. No one was spared except for 400 artisans taken prisoner and a few survivors who escaped. The ground I stood on was once soaked with the blood of over 700,000 men, women and children (historians write that the Mongols counted the bodies).

After the slaughter, the city was burnt and most buildings were demolished, leaving just the shell of Merv's outer walls and several of its more massive fortress palaces. As I sat alone on a dirt mound that was once possibly a family home, I shuddered at what one group of humans had done to another. In a day, it had gone from paradise to a bloodbath of terror: a mad frenzy of killing. And humanity was still killing each other; nothing had changed. There had been massacre after massacre over the 800 years since this glorious time.

As I headed across the Karakum towards Uzbekistan, the desert changed from flat pale-brown crusted expanse to golden sand dunes that reminded me of the shifting dunes of the Sahara. In the cool of late afternoon, I leaned back into the Gearsack, the TT purred in rhythmic contentment. The kind of contentment that engines exude when its components move in blissful harmony. I still basked in the warm glow of the cognac, and I gave no thought to where I'd sleep, other than knowing that just as the sun began to sink below the horizon, something would turn up. It was liberating to be free of worry about such simple necessities. It was a liberation that was a deeply ingrained habit having slowly developed since my travels in Africa and it made me wonder where worry came from. Just when did humanity begin to worry? Did worry come from having possessions, which lead to thoughts of losing possessions? In their shining city of abundance, safe behind the city's walls with the sultan's army ready to fend off any attack, the people of Merv had no cause to worry—until it was too late. But what of family? Parents worry about the safety of their children as mine did for me—and with good cause. Is this a modern dilemma? When we lived as a tribe, a village, we lived together; we protected one another, we shared our possessions. Is this where communism evolved?

As I travelled through the former USSR, I now questioned why the west was so against communism. Since Georgia, I'd heard the same complaints. 'Arrh Perestroika,' they'd say when I asked how things were after the collapse of the Soviet Union. 'Life was good before Gorbachev ruined it. Everyone had jobs,' they'd lament.

As the sun sank below the horizon, I approached a cluster of flat-roofed cement buildings. It was Repetek, a small village with a truck stop and restaurant surrounded by dunes that were ever-changing by the restless winds. Russian scientists, discovering the complex ecosystem of plants, rodents, snakes, lizards and insects living in a 346 km² area of dunes and dry scrub, lobbied the Soviet government to protect the area. The Repetek Desert Reserve was set up in 1928. I later read that in the height of summer Repetek was the hottest place on earth, with temperatures in this part of the Karakum reaching above a scorching 50°C.

Three rigs were parked at the truck stop, and when I pulled up at a terracotta-tiled veranda shaded by a tin roof, four men waved me over. They sat around a table drinking vodka. A glass was offered, and I surprised even myself by knocking it back without flinching. Probably, because I'd not yet sobered up from the cognac. In three days, I'd gone from teetotaller to old pro. The owner came out, and I asked to camp, but was shown a stuffy room that looked like it was crawling with all manner of insects. I pointed to the flat roof of a cement-block building behind the restaurant and asked about sleeping there because this is what people did in the deserts of North Africa, where they'd be cooled by a gentle night breeze.

'There's a ladder,' I said pointing to it against the wall and beaming at the prospect of peace, privacy and a comfortable night's sleep. The man reluctantly nodded.

'Shower?' I asked expectantly.

'*Da.*'

And I followed him outside to the small cement structure.

Later, I sat alone in the restaurant, opened my diary and for the first time since Turkmenbashi, began to write, but my solitude was short-lived. A truck driver, a big-boned tall man with an overly large belly, staggered towards me.

'You sleep with me,' he demanded. 'Come.'

He was drunk and was convinced I was a Natasha, a prostitute who moved from one truck stop to the other, back and forth along the Karakum Highway. Prostitutes had always moved back and forth along the Silk Road. Only the means of transport had changed. Instead of camel caravans, it was now trucks.

'No thank you.'

'Come,' he demanded.

I ignored him but could feel his anger burning into me. He would not accept my refusal as he was convinced I was a Natasha. As a woman alone on the Karakum, what else could I be?

'Heda, over here,' called one of the Turkmen truck drivers I'd spoken to earlier. I quickly gathered my things and joined them.

'He is Iranian. They like Natasha, and you are a woman so for him you are Natasha,' said one of the young Turkmen. 'Stay here, and he will not trouble you.'

'Spider!' I screamed, and the men laughed. A large spider. The largest I'd ever seen—as big as my hand with extremely long legs—ran across the tiled floor. One of the men stood up and squashed it under his boot.

'There are many spiders in the desert,' the man said as he sat down.

'That spider lives out there in the desert?' I asked, pointing, my hand shaking.

'Yes, there are many. They hunt at night when it is cool.'

'I've been sleeping in the desert. On the ground,' I stammered as I recalled the past two nights when I'd dreamed 'things' crawling over me, and those 'things' had been the most horrendous and largest of spiders plus all sorts of other insects. I later read that there are over 1500 species of insects including 335 species of spiders living in the Karakum with the highest concentration at Repeket. The four men looked at each other, shaking their heads in disbelief, and I got the feeling this was both at my stupidity and in awe that I'd survived the experience.

'In Karakum, never sleep on the ground.' He held his hand a few feet above the tiled floor. 'Some spiders are very poisonous. If they bite, you will die. You are very brave.'

And a toast was poured. Then another.

I later learned that the Karakurt spider common in these parts (a type of black widow) was the deadliest spider on earth, with its venom ten times stronger than that of a cobra, which was also common in these parts.

It was a surreal evening with the four Turkmen truck drivers. The vodka flowed, plates of shashlik, salad, bread and pumpkin seeds were served. I insisted on a pot of tea, and that was served as well. And with their limited English, the men shared stories until the early hours. I told of my travels, and they spoke of their hopes and dreams for Turkmenistan. Everyone knew of its wealth; of the gas and oil pipelines planned. But they were sceptical the ordinary Turkmen people would reap any benefit.

'Niyazov takes everything for himself and for Ashgabat,' I was told and after so much vodka, they no longer cared who overheard them.

The party ended when the Iranian truck driver staggered towards our table, yelling 'Natasha' and kicking over the teapot I'd placed on the floor. The four Turkmen threatened to beat him, and he retreated to his truck. One of the Turkmen was wearing a watch, and I read it was 3.00 a.m. I said goodnight, but they insisted on one more round and gave me two parting gifts: a tin of bully beef and a Turkmen knife, a bone-handled dagger with a sharp nine-inch blade that came with a stiff-hide sheath. It looked ancient, and a prized possession, and I refused to take it, saying it was very special to the man who offered it.

'You must have this. Maybe the Iranian come back for you,' he said and pushed it back into my hands.

They returned to their trucks and I to the roof, pulling the ladder up behind me. Holding the dagger tight across my chest, I quickly fell into a deep alcohol-induced sleep only to be woken at daylight, about two hours later. The restaurant owner, a jovial shortish round man who'd been so helpful earlier, sat beside me groping for my breasts.

'Nyet, Natasha, Nyet Natasha,' I screamed as I staggered to my feet, pushing him away with one hand and brandishing the dagger with the other. He retreated and climbed down the second ladder he'd placed against the wall. I quickly packed my things, and as the sun rose up over the dunes, I rode toward Uzbekistan. Soon the harsh beauty of the desert was behind me, and as I neared the Amu Darya river, I passed through a patchwork of farms growing cotton, wheat and animal fodder.

15

A MOMENT OF MADNESS

Uzbekistan

I crossed the Amu Darya riding on a series of barges strung together to form a bridge. Swollen with snow and glacier melt from the high peaks of the Pamir and Tian Shan mountain ranges, this wide brown river flowed deceptively fast as it entered the lowlands. But soon its waters would be stolen by the vast array of Soviet-built irrigation canals, the largest being the Karakum, which I'd ridden over and bathed in for the past four days. By the time the Amu Darya reached the Aral Sea, it would be a mere trickle compared to the expanse of water I now crossed.

I was grateful for the TT's high clearance and enduro capabilities as several trucks also traversed the barge bridge as I did. The weight of each truck pushed the barges out of alignment by thirty centimetres or more, and I had to wait for just the right moment to open the throttle and jump my motorcycle onto the next barge—a split-second maneuver before the gap widened again.

Once on the other side, I passed through Uzbek immigration without even a raised eyebrow over my one-month Russian visa with only two weeks remaining on its validity. Although it was just a two-hour ride along broken tarmac to Bukhara, it was nearly mid-day, and I could not travel any further in the heat so pulled up at a roadside café until late afternoon. The Uzbeks welcomed me as warmly as the Turkmen, and I was treated as an honoured guest. Lunch was a large bowl of soup, the pieces of mutton and vegetables floating in a thick layer of melted fat. To honour the café owner's hospitality, I accepted the glass of vodka but adamantly refused a second, grateful he was not as insistent as the Turkmen over the river.

I approached Bukhara as the last of the sun lit up its turquoise-domed mosques with the Kalyan minaret standing tall like a beacon guiding those who had trekked across the desert to reach this ancient Silk Road city. I was greeted with the same vista that the merchants, travellers and pilgrims had witnessed since medieval times. While Merv lay in ruins, Bukhara had been spared by the Mongols. Although not entirely, as they had ransacked its treasures and massacred much of its population as they'd also done in Samarkand, 200 kilometres to the east—another ancient Silk Road metropolis I'd visit after Bukhara.

When I asked about a '*deshevo*' (cheap) hotel at a petrol station, I was directed to the city's outskirts, to a run-down Soviet-era apartment block that partially operated as a hotel. A room was 500 Uzbekistan som, (about US$4), but I'd have to leave the TT outside as it would not fit in the small lift that rattled to the rooms on the fourth floor. As I perused the recommendations in my guidebook, a neatly dressed young man, his black hair stylishly cropped short, approached. He introduced himself as Ahmed, a student from Pakistan. I told him I was looking for accommodation that cost little money and he suggested the Bukhara State University.

'You can stay at the language faculty. There is a student hostel,' he said.

'Can you lead the way?' I asked, and after moving the Gearsack to the back rack on the TT, he climbed on as my pillion. Ahmed was studying Islamic history, he told me as we bounced over the pot-holed road past Bukhara's ancient madrassas to the university compound. Bukhara, he advised, was once one of the most important sites for learning in the Islamic world.

The university was a four-storey run-down cement building with a number of smaller buildings in a similar state of decay. As we climbed the front steps to the administration office, I was introduced to the vice chancellor. He'd just finished for the day, but was so intrigued by my journey that he invited me to stay as a guest of the university in exchange for giving a talk to the fourth-year English students on Monday morning. It was Friday, and I had the luxury of a private room with shower and flush toilet. These were amenities I desperately needed as I'd come down with diarrhoea. At first, I'd thought it was a symptom of my body purging the alcohol consumed in Turkmenstan, but quickly realised it was something more sinister and started a course of Flagyl, a powerful antibiotic effective against most stomach bugs. I'd most likely picked up giardia from filling my water bottle whenever I'd come across a water tap just as the locals did.

The giardia was a setback that my body could ill afford. It was a detrimental blow to my battle-weary immune system. I vowed not to be so careless again. But despite the heat and the diarrhoea, I refused to let it dampen my enthusiasm to explore Bukhara. It would be an enormous effort, but I would not be beaten.

Early Saturday morning, before the heat, I took that first step—and then another, to gaze in wonder at Bukhara's mud-walled Ark, a massive fifth-century fortress and royal palace that was home to the emirs until 1920 when Bukhara was overthrown by the Russian-led Bolsheviks. From the top of its high steps, I looked out over an expanse of packed earth, its main square (the Registan), just as the emirs once did. From this vantage point they'd oversee public gatherings of thousands of people. Public executions, apparently, were a real crowd pleaser.

Bukhara was the centre of Islamic academia during medieval times, with over one hundred madrassas (Islamic schools) scattered throughout the city, educating more than 10,000 students. The faithful worshipped in over 300 mosques, and the townspeople shopped in a multitude of covered bazaars, while travellers rested in numerous *caravanserais*. But its madrassas had long since closed; its *caravanserais* were in ruins; and its bazaars were filled with stalls selling crafts and carpets to the few tourists, that like me, wandered its streets bewildered to have stumbled across this living museum.

Outwardly, not much had changed over the past thousand years or so, but while Bukhara appeared a sleepy town with no real purpose in the modern world, authorities were preparing for its next renaissance. Signs of restoration work were everywhere: lost and loose tiles being replaced on the blue-domed mosques; men pushing wheelbarrows; chisels banging on stone; and clouds of dust rising up from the restoration of a ruin.

During the heat of mid-afternoon, I sought refuge at the Lyabi Hauz, writing and sipping tea, my table shaded by an old mulberry tree, its leaves once feeding a farm of silk worms. It grew next to a large man-made pool of uninviting green water. Surrounded on three sides by enormous madrassas and fringed by a wide limestone piazza, the pool, built in 1620, was the centrepiece of Bukhara. It was the only pool that remained of many that once existed throughout the city. These stagnant pools were sources of water-borne disease and had been filled in by the Russians.

In the cool of late afternoon, as I ambled back to the university, I came across three heavily laden motorcycles: two Honda XL600s and a Suzuki DR650. Each bike carried two tyres strapped on top of a mountain of luggage. All were off-road Dunlops, and as most riding in Central Asia is on tarmac, would wear in no time. The dual-purpose Metzler tyres I'd bought in Istanbul still looked new. The riders, three men, aged about thirty, sat at a nearby café. As I inspected their motorcycles, one called me over.

'I'm travelling by motorcycle too,' I said and introduced myself as I sat down at their table littered the remnants of a meal and half-drunk bottles of Coke.

'We are from Paris. We are Patrick, Frédéric and Fabrice.' Two of the men nodded as they were introduced by the man who was Fabrice. 'They speak only a little English,' he said.

Fabrice was dark-haired and olive-skinned. He had an air of abundant confidence and was the leader of the trio. A handsome man with broad shoulders who beamed with that sense of freedom: an expectation of adventure, of being on the road, that all motorcycle travellers share. Despite the other two men being brothers, Patrick was tall with thinning sandy brown hair, while Fredrick was stocky with a mop of thick brown hair. Both just looked exhausted—a little shell-shocked about what they'd gotten themselves into.

'We ride through the desert from the Aral Sea. It was a hard journey. Very hot. The sand was tough,' Fabrice said as if to explain.

They were from Paris, and this motorcycle journey had been twelve months in the planning. While Fabrice was an experienced motorcyclist, Patrick and Frédéric were new to the tribe, having learnt to ride for their adventure along the Silk Road.

'They have many falls in the sand,' Fabrice said, and his two friends looked at him questioningly.

As we chatted, I learnt that they were on a trip of a lifetime to Mongolia, to the centuries-old Naadam festival in Ulaanbaatar. Held in early July each year, it was famous for its horse racing, and games and displays of wrestling and archery. During the Naadam, the grassy plains would be awash with the colour of thousands of nomads in traditional dress who descend on the city from across the steppe. It was early June, and they had a month to get there.

Fabrice asked me where I was staying, and I told him the student hostel at the university. We bid each other *bonne journee* for the road ahead, and I'd thought that would be the last I would see of them.

When I returned to the university, Ahmed and another young man were waiting for me.

Ahmed stood as I approached: 'We invite you to dinner at the house of our teacher.' His friend was Saad, also from Pakistan, and just as neatly dressed as Ahmed. He too was studying Islamic history. And after I'd showered, grateful the Flagyl had settled my bowels, we strolled along Bukhara's narrow mud-walled streets dotted at regular intervals with a simple door made of wood and covered in rusted studs. We stopped at one, and it was opened by a middle-aged man who was introduced to me as Ali. Inside, a small open courtyard was covered with reddish-brown intricately woven carpets for which Bukhara is famous.

We kicked off our shoes and sat down on soft cushions, and Ali's wife brought out a feast of shashlik, salad, bread and *palov*, a rice dish with pieces of mutton, carrot, raisins and onions. She did not join us. I was grateful no vodka was offered in this strictly Islamic home, and we sipped tea. For my benefit, all spoke English. Our chatter was light and punctuated with laughter that rose up into the clear warm night filled with bright stars. Time seemed irrelevant. We shared a meal, stories and ideas just as people had always done as they bought and sold goods, exchanged theories, philosophies and religious beliefs along the Silk Road. As students of Islam, Ahmed and Saad told me they're focus was on Sufism, which they explained was the study of Islamic mysticism.

'Sufism is about absolute trust in God and how you are guided to enlightenment,' Saad said.

'We aim to achieve illumination,' Ahmed added, explaining that he and Saad had come from Pakistan to study in Bukhara because it is the centre of Naqshbandi Sufism, established by the twelfth-century Islamic mystic Naqshband, who is buried at a village, his birthplace, near Bukhara.

'Pilgrims once travelled from all over Central Asia to seek his advice or to study Sufism at his school, and thousands continue to visit his tomb. Naqshbandi Sufi groups are all over the world, and there are many followers in Pakistan,' Saad explained.

At first, I found it challenging to understand Sufism, but as I revealed my own thoughts on spirituality, I realised it was not dissimilar to my own understanding—my own theorising as to what it all meant. The closer I came to my death, the closer I reached out to what awaited me. Intuitively, I felt there was something there other than the finality of blackness.

'As a Sufi, you search for enlightenment with God and part of this search is experiencing visions through *hurqalya*. This is a place between the real world and heaven. It is the place where God can communicate with us,' Ahmed said.

'Have you had one of these visions?' I asked, suddenly feeling energised my own memory of what happened in Mauritania, when another dimension of colour, light and energy had revealed itself to me. I was about to share what I'd seen when Saad leaned forward and whispered: 'Such visions will be shown when Allah wishes it. But we do not discuss these experiences. Allah knows what is in our hearts.'

'Such visions come when the student has reached spiritual ability,'

Ali interrupted. He'd been quietly listening to our conversation like a wise old sage. 'This takes much inner reflection and trust in God. At first, these visions may come as simple flashes of light, but as our spirituality grows, these can last longer, are brighter and more colourful. This is God speaking to you.'

I stared open-mouthed for Ali's explanation confirmed that my vision was real and was not a hallucination after all. I had not tipped over into madness on that night in the desert. Ali smiled back knowingly.

A quietness hung over the four of us as we reflected on Ali's words. The evening was over, and we thanked him for the meal.

As we walked back to the university, Bukhara was dark and eerily quiet, with only the barking of a dog here and there in the distance. Occasionally, a mysterious shadowy figure passed us on the narrow streets. All were men, and it suddenly occurred to me that the last woman I conversed with was Ramiza in Baku. Of course, I'd seen plenty of women in the villages I'd ridden through in Turkmenistan. There were even a few women at some of the roadside cafés although most patrons were men. In Bukhara, I'd also seen plenty of women in their colourful long floral dresses and headscarves, either selling their wares and produce or as customers at the bazaars. I'd even seen plenty of young women at the university when I'd arrived, but I'd spoken to none of them. I'd not even questioned why Ali's wife did not join us and only said a brief hello and thankyou when she'd served the meal and cleared our plates. I didn't even ask her name. Through habit, because it was always men who approached me, I'd fallen into a quiet acceptance that my world was male, absent of all females, except for myself.

As we walked into the university compound, I was surprised to see the three motorcycles belonging to the Frenchmen, parked next to mine. The next morning, I joined them for breakfast and told them I'd give a talk about my travels to an English class on Monday morning and then ride to Samarkand.

'We too will give a talk to the French students,' Fabrice announced. I spent the day with them exploring more of Bukhara and enjoying their company, but mostly I sat with them at a number of the city's cafés and restaurants. They'd finish one meal, and an hour later it was time to eat again. Patrick and Frédéric, at times, joined the conversation between me and Fabrice, adding a word here and there and at one point told me, it was terrific to meet me because they could practice their English. I apologised for my lack of French, the words I'd learnt in Francophone Africa now mostly forgotten.

Monday morning arrived, and I was taken to the English class where it was standing room only. Later, I along with the Frenchmen, after they'd given their talk, were all invited to a special lunch organised by the university language faculty. As it was nearly 3.00 p.m. by the time lunch finished, we asked if we could stay another night and would be on our way early the next morning. 'You are welcome,' we were told.

As the Frenchmen were also heading to Samarkand, I asked to join them. I had travelled alone for so long, that their company was a welcome change and Fabrice had a great sense of humour. I found myself laughing continuously at his antics. It was the kind of carefree, silly laughter that I'd not enjoyed since my diagnosis when my world had dimmed, and all sense of fun had disappeared. Without hesitation, they unanimously agreed.

I was awake at daylight, and after I'd packed the TT and saw no sign of the Frenchmen, I woke them about 6.00 a.m. as they'd agreed the night before we'd leave early to avoid riding in the heat. It was mid-morning when we rode out of Bukhara, but stopped after only an hour for lunch at a roadside café.

With four of us, I experienced none of the hospitality while travelling alone and could only assume, that four people (three being men with hearty appetites), would have pushed the limits of the owner's generosity. Instead, we were treated as customers like any other.

We arrived at Samarkand late afternoon pulling up at the magnificent Registan Square bordered by three enormous blue-domed madrassas built over 200 years from the fourteenth to the sixteenth centuries. It also housed a mausoleum, the tomb of Amir Timur, founder of the Timurid Empire. During the fourteenth century, this empire under the brutal rule of Timur, who was set to rival Genghis Khan until his death in 1405, stretched across Central Asia to Turkey and the Caucasus; modern-day Iran and parts of Syria and Pakistan. The facades, covered in mosaics of every shade of azure with touches of yellow, towered above us as we walked through the grandiose paved square. Even the domes were covered in tiny tiles painstakingly laid in intricate patterns. It was a stunning spectacle of medieval Islamic grandeur. But the madrassas were no longer places of Islamic academia. Instead, the carpet and craft sellers had moved in, selling souvenirs to the tourists who'd mostly left for the day.

'We should go to the university. We can offer to do talks for the French and English students in exchange for accommodation,' Fabrice announced as I opened my guide book to read the list of budget hotels.

'Staying at the student hostel in Bukhara in exchange for my talk happened by chance,' I said.

'We do not require a hotel. The university will be pleased. This is a wonderful opportunity for their students. Very few motorcycle adventurers make it to Central Asia. We are pioneers,' he replied.

And so it was settled we would turn up at the Samarkand University and convince them to host us 'the intrepid adventurers' as special guests in exchange for giving talks to their English and French language students. But Fabrice was right; I'd not come across any others on motorcycles since Turkey. In fact, I'd seen no independent tourists travelling by any means at all in Central Asia.

When we put our offer to give talks to the vice chancellor, he accepted readily, saying it was such an honour. When Fabrice asked about accommodation in their student hostel, he did not hesitate, and we were directed to a ground-floor three-room apartment with a foyer large enough for all four motorcycles to be securely parked overnight. Once again it was standing room in the English class the next morning, and Fabrice told me it was the same with the French students. After our talks and a lengthy question and answer session, we were invited by the language faculty to a special lunch held in our honour—a spread of delicious Uzbek dishes and plates of apricots and the fattest, juiciest cherries I'd ever seen. At the mere sight of this fruit, my body tingled with anticipation.

'It is excellent you think of giving talks,' Fabrice said as he chewed on a piece of mutton and filled his plate with more pilaf.

'It happened by chance,' I said, feeling a little uncomfortable that we'd somewhat duped the Samarkand University for free board and lodgings.

'Yes, yes. It is *bon chance*,' he smiled mischievously.

It was mid-afternoon when we rode away from Samarkand heading towards Tajikistan where we would cross the narrow finger of land as a shortcut into Kyrgyzstan. Two hours into our ride, we pulled up to refuel with 76 octane, which was all that was available in Uzbekistan and my 21-litre petrol tank gave a range of a mere 250 kilometres instead of 400. As I refuelled, a small four-wheel drive pulled up behind me. Its driver was a dark-haired young man, his glasses giving him that scholarly appearance.

'I see you are Australian,' he said, reading the bike's rear number plate.

He told me he was from Turkey and worked for a German pharmaceutical company studying natural remedies used by villagers across Central Asia.

'In remote communities, there is no western medicine, or the people have no money to pay for a doctor, so they use herbs. But many of these remedies have powerful healing properties that can be used to develop pharmaceuticals for new treatments,' he explained.

'What sort of new treatments?' I asked.

'My focus is arthritis and the immune system.'

'Like for people with HIV?'

'Could be,' he said looking at me questioningly. To avoid his gaze, I looked down and double checked I'd tightened the fuel cap.

'Unfortunately, the knowledge could soon be lost as it's the old people who know these remedies. Young people mostly move to the cities and use western medicine,' he said.

'Do you photograph the plants? Do you use slide film?' I asked, wanting to both change the subject and realising photographs would be a vital part of his research. 'I'm down to one roll and can't buy it anywhere.'

'Ah, yes. Of course,' he said and returned with a roll of 50ASA Fuji Sensia slide film, refusing the money I offered.

We moved on, passing through a patchwork of vast cotton fields irrigated by a network of Soviet-built canals fed by the third largest of Central Asia's mighty rivers, the Zeravshan, which also flowed down from the Pamirs. The young cotton plants were covered in tiny green bolls that would be a blaze of white fluffiness by August. As well as farm labourers and the unemployed, thousands of government workers and university students would then be press-ganged into picking the crop over the two-month harvest and paid a pittance for their labour. I'd read children as young as nine were also part of this country-wide labour mobilisation.

While at the university hostel in Samarkand, I'd stuck up a conversation with one of the English language students, a girl aged about twenty. She'd been keen to practice her English, and when I'd asked about this forced labour, and questioned her about children picking cotton too, she'd been coy at first, saying it was the duty of every Uzbek to help their country.

'We are proud to do this,' she'd said but quickly added with a sigh: 'It is only for two weeks'.

I got the feeling it was nothing like a summer holiday camp aimed at team building and evening singalongs, but rather an exhausting two weeks where students slept in barracks with poor sanitation, had little to eat and worked twelve hours a day picking up to a hundred kilos of cotton bolls each. With an abundance of labour, the government, under the dictator Islam Karimov, a Soviet official who moved into the job after independence, preferred hand-picked cotton, which fetched higher prices. Machines picked indiscriminately, and such cotton was poor quality.

Moreover, the profits from hand-picked cotton were creamed

off by the government, and none of it flowed down to farmers and pickers, who worked in fields drenched in pesticides. The government bought the cotton at a state-fixed price and sold it on the world market, pocketing the profits. Uzbekistan was the world's sixth largest producer of cotton, much of it trucked to China where it was turned into clothes worn by just about every person on the planet. Being hand-picked, bolts of cloth made from the softer, silkier Uzbek cotton was mostly purchased by the top fashion houses. Although, when I asked about value adding, I'd been told by one of the English teachers at lunch in Bukhara, that there were plans to set up a textile industry in Uzbekistan. He'd explained there were plans to repair and better maintain the canals, which had steadily fallen into disrepair since the Soviets left in 1991. 'Without the canals, there is no cotton, and without cotton, there are no jobs. Uzbekistan needs cotton,' he'd said.

As we neared Tajikistan, we left the dry desert heat behind and a cool afternoon breeze blew through my open jacket. We'd been riding for about two hours when Fabrice pulled over where a roadside café hugged the broken stretch of tarmac. I was behind him with Frédéric and Patrick following me. The line-up changed between the three of us, but Fabrice was always in the lead.

Everything took so much longer as a group. Waiting for each rider to be ready; to start their bike; to wait for a rider if they fell behind just in case they'd broken down. Fabrice announced he was hungry and we waited on the edge of the road near Shirin for the other two to catch up before parking our bikes at the café. The Frenchmen ordered a late lunch of shashlik, salad, bread and bottles of Coke. I declined as I was still full from the lunch laid on at the university, and ordered tea. With only about two hours of daylight, I suggested we camp there for the night. I'd noticed a group of tin shacks in a high-fenced compound at the back of the café and had already asked the owner if we could store our motorcycles and pitch our tents.

Like me, the trio was also travelling on a budget and after speaking amongst themselves, agreed. It was a warm evening, and I set up my mosquito net just as the mosquitos descended with a vengeance. With so many open canals, they bred to plague proportions; I wondered about malaria. Fabrice and Patrick quickly retreated to their tent advising they were exhausted and after a spray with repellent, Frédéric and I returned to the café and were invited to join four Uzbek men who were dining on shashlik and drinking vodka with the wanton abandon of those celebrating. They spoke no English or French, and we were unable to find out the source of their merriment. Maybe a birthday, perhaps the birth of a child, or maybe they'd received a down payment from several wealthy Uzbek government employees who had no intentions of picking cotton in the upcoming harvest and paid the men to pick their quota instead.

It was mid-morning when we left the roadside café but stopped an hour later for a late breakfast of pilaf. I was shocked when Fabrice told me that they had not paid for the meal yesterday afternoon.

'Why didn't you pay?' I screeched unable to control my anger.

'I thought we had paid,' he replied hurtful, I'd wrongfully reprimanded him.

Maybe it was an honest mistake. Perhaps, he thought Frédéric had paid being the last man standing. But it was an oversight that annoyed me so much I sat fuming as they scoffed into plates of pilaf.

As Fabrice had told me, we were pioneers. The first of a trickle of motorcycle travellers that would one day turn into a flood as word filtered back to Europe that the once-closed, former-Soviet Central Asia was motorcycle adventure nirvana. In a bid to recoup our unpaid bill, I'm sure there was one roadside restaurant in Uzbekistan that would inflate their prices for the next group of motorcycle adventurers that stopped for shashlik. On this journey along the Silk Road, I was unique as a traveller from the outside world, and the people had welcomed me. They had shown me unfathomable hospitality. I felt a sense of responsibility to protect this yet untouched, uncorrupted world. Yes, we were pioneers, but we and the other travellers that followed us, were caretakers too.

From Shirin, we followed a dirt road to reach one of the many small border crossings between Uzbekistan and Tajikistan. We'd planned to cross at Bekobod, but when we refuelled, the man at the petrol station advised we pass at a point he marked on my map.

Together, the four of us walked into the Tajik border post, a small tin shack where it was standing room only. In the cramped confines, the heat was oppressive; none of the Frenchmen wore deodorant. A middle-aged man in a sweat-stained grey military uniform, the buttons straining across his round belly, sat behind the desk. Two other younger men in the same grey fatigues stood beside him. The only other item of furniture was a tall wooden cabinet. Behind the official was an open window, which framed a spindly tree. A small bird sat on a branch tilting its head inquisitively.

'Passeports,' he demanded, the sweat beading on his brow framed by a stock of thick greasy black hair.

'You no cross. Pay one hundred dollar!' he boomed.

'We are transiting to Kyrgyzstan,' Fabrice replied while Patrick and Frédéric vocalised their objection in French with a few phaws.

An evil smirk spread across the guard's face that dropped as a series of folded bristly jowls onto his collar. 'You pay. No cross.'

Fabrice stood his ground. Hands on hips. 'We have permission to transit. We have a Russian visa.' As if anything to do with Russia was still held in high esteem in this backwater of the former Soviet Union.

I kicked his foot and leaned close to whisper: 'We must pretend we don't understand.'

At this point, a vehicle pulled up outside in a cloud of dust. The Tajik border official and his two off-siders pushed Fabrice aside as they headed towards the door. We filed out behind them. The vehicle was a four-wheel drive with UNHCR emblazoned across its side. A huge man unfolded from the vehicle. He stretched to well over six foot and was enormous both in height and body width. Not obese, but his sheer size demanded instant respect. Proclaiming his support for refugees, he wore a black T-shirt printed with the words in white, 'Einstein was a refugee'.

'Where you from?' he asked. We pointed to our motorcycles parked opposite saying France and Australia. 'Long journey,' he said nodding to me when I said I'd ridden through Africa. 'I was in Rwanda. Very bad what happened there,' he added and told us he was from Bosnia and stationed at Osh in Kyrgyzstan.

Since Soviet independence, Tajikistan had been gripped by civil war from infighting amongst its various clan groups, but foreigners were allowed to transit the stretch between Bekobod and Kulundu, a distance of about fifty kilometres. But we were not at this 'official crossing' for foreigners. Instead, we'd ridden over a narrow bridge to cross the Syr Darya and across a semi-arid plain; it was as if a finger of the Karakum desert had followed me all the way from Turkmenistan. I'd read that nearly 50,000 Tajik villagers had died from the fighting between the clan groups, leaving more than half a million refugees. Russia had stepped in, and around 25,000 of its troops were stationed in Tajikistan, effectively making it a Russian protectorate. This peacekeeping force also made it safe to transit into Kyrgyzstan as long as we kept away from the Afghan border where there were still skirmishes between the faction groups.

It made little sense as to why Stalin, back in the 1920s, had so unreasonably carved up the borders where three Central Asian nations met: Uzbekistan, Tajikistan and Kyrgyzstan. I could only assume it was to ensure the countries remained linked like the entwined fingers of lovers so they would forever retain a close and loyal bond.

'Is there problem?' the UN official asked the Tajik border guards.

'*Nyet. Nyet* problem,' the man in charge replied meekly.

'It's alright guys. You can cross.' The Bosnian climbed back into his vehicle and with a wave, was gone just as suddenly as he had appeared. We all watched speechless as the vehicle disappeared in a trail of dust.

'You pay,' the lead official boomed from behind us. Then the three officials marched back to the tin shack. We followed.

'Can you stamp our passports please,' I asked in demure politeness pointing to our passports stacked on the desk.

'No. You must pay five dollar.'

'Okay,' I said. At least the Bosnian's arrival had saved us each US$95. The Frenchmen nodded, and we filed out of the hut to retrieve the money from our money belts so their prying eyes would not see our booty, especially Frédéric. He had told me he carried US$5000 in cash strapped to his belly. Fabrice and Patrick, I imagined, carried the same. 'Aren't you worried you'll get robbed?' I asked in disbelief when he'd told me. 'This never leaves me,' Frédéric had said patting his round stomach, his money belt hidden under his T-shirt with it all held in place by a wide kidney belt. It not only protected his kidneys and vulnerable insides should he crash, but also gave no indication that he carried a small fortune in a country where the annual salary was US$600.

Knowing you are going to die does strange things to your way of thinking, namely in the risks that you'd otherwise never consider taking. In the weeks that followed my diagnosis, I rode around London with no regard for speed limits, road rules and consideration of other road users. Perhaps those vodka-infused days in Turkmenistan where I'd nearly come to grief several times while riding inebriated were also part of this disregard for my own safety. This wasn't a conscious decision. It was just what happened. I was beyond thinking I might get hurt or I might die. What happened next at that Tajik border post, I can only think, had something to do with this unconscious death wish that occasionally took control of my behaviour.

But it was also a desire to seek approval, seek forgiveness from my father. The offer of a gift that would please him. A parting gift that was so significant that it may even go so far as to nullify the perceived shame I'd brought on my family. These were my distorted thoughts on that day.

When I'd walked into the hut, a grey Russian army cap lay on the desk. I'd picked it up, saying, 'I give you ten dollar.' The official sitting at the desk snatched it from me and threw it behind the cabinet. When he'd gone outside as the UN vehicle pulled up, I'd quickly retrieved it and stuffed it under my kidney belt and zipped up my jacket.

We paid our five dollars and with our passports stamped, were about to file out the hut, when the border official in charge pulled out his revolver and pointed it at Fabrice's head. I held my breath thinking he'd thought Fabrice had stolen the cap. Patrick and Frédéric stood motionless beside me. Fabrice turned white. The two other guards smiled as if they shared a private joke. The Tajik with the gun flashed a demented grin, his finger on the trigger. Then he turned and fired the gun through the open window at a small bird sitting on the branch. It looked like the same bird as before. Unbelievably, it did not fly away. Like us, I expect, it was too shocked to move. The Tajik fired off another four shots, deafening us all in the tin shack, and still, the bird did not move. Only when it was quiet, and the Tajik had returned the gun to its holster, did the bird fly away. Without a word, we slowly filed out of the hut then ran towards our bikes.

Just as I was about to hoist my leg over the TT, the Tajik in charge stormed out of the hut, pointing to his head, his two assistants closely behind. I knew exactly what he meant, but the Frenchmen looked at him dumbfounded. I rushed back inside the hut, the Tajiks following close behind, but I reached the doorway first and knelt down near the cabinet and pulled the cap from under my kidney belt dropping it on the floor. The Tajik in charge grabbed my arm lifting me off the ground and shoved me against the wall.

'Your cap. There it is. Remember, you threw it behind the cabinet.'

'*Duzd, Duzd*,' he repeated his face contorted in anger as he squeezed my arm. I assumed this was Tajik for thief.

'Fuck off, you bastards!' I screamed pulling my arm away and pushing past the three men like a deranged woman. 'Go! Go!' I yelled at the Frenchmen who sat astride their idling motorcycles.

The TT fired first kick. Pumped with adrenalin, I dropped the clutch and opened the throttle. The bike launched itself and me to freedom leaving the three Tajiks standing in a cloud of dust. I fully expected a bullet to lodge into my back, but no shot was fired, and yet again I'd escaped a respectable death. As I followed the Frenchmen, I realised I risked pulling them down with me. For their own safety, it was time I moved on.

16

THE LAND OF THE NOMADS

Kyrgyzstan

Kyrgyzstan was refreshingly cool after the baking heat of Turkmenistan and Uzbekistan. Snow-capped mountains, the Pamirs, towered in the distance: a massive wall of white-tipped bare rock that divided one world from another. It must have seemed an insurmountable feat for those who travelled on the Silk Road crossing from east to west with their wares strapped to their camels as they lumbered from Samarkand up the Ferghana Valley. They were heading toward Osh and would pass over the Tian Shan to reach Kashgar in China.

From the Tajik border, we'd found ourselves on a minor road to Isfana at the southern end of the valley. The narrow gravel track was lined with poplar trees and littered with pot-holes. It made for a slow ride, and included several stops for tea and snacks, and a long lunch. We only covered about 150 kilometres on that first day. Lunch had been exorbitantly expensive at nearly US$20 in Kyrgyzstan som, but we ate our way through a volume of shashlik that amounted to a small sheep. I remembered my lesson from Turkmenistan: to always leave something in my bowl otherwise it would be repeatedly refilled as it would be assumed I was still hungry. I'd mentioned this to the Frenchmen, but they had enormous appetites for meat and *phew-pharred* me when I tried to explain. The café owner may also have seen an opportunity and adjusted the price to reflect our status as 'rich western tourists'.

We reached Isfana late afternoon. It sat in a valley fringed by a range of bare brown hills, the edge of the Alai mountains with the peaks of the Pamirs looming as a jagged line beyond. We passed ramshackle wooden houses where every available piece of land was growing various kinds of vegetables, but mostly potatoes, a legacy left by the Russians. There was no space for something as frivolous as a lawn. Every family had an orchard, the trees loaded with fruits: apples, apricots, plums and cherries. Probably almonds and walnuts too; I'd read that the world's largest walnut forest was in Kyrgyzstan, 11,000 hectares on the lower slopes of the Ferghana range to the north. The home-grown fruits we passed would soon be harvested, dried and bottled for the long, bitterly cold winter. Climate and low wages had forced the Kyrgyz people to be resourceful. The average monthly wage (if one had a job) was about US$40 per month. While summer in the western world was a time for holidays, here it was a time for work, for reaping the harvest to fend off starvation in the winter. As we passed, villagers tending their gardens stopped momentarily to stare in disbelief.

Isfana appeared deserted, and I could only assume people turned in early in these parts. We found a local hotel, and after repeatedly banging on the door, an elderly man eventually opened it, and we paid in som, the equivalent of about US$2 per room, which was clean with crisp white sheets. We shared a squat toilet and shower down the hall and had space in the foyer for our motorcycles. At dinner, the only dish being served was soup: lumps of gristly mutton and cabbage floating in a layer of melted sheep's fat. Not long after my body purged the lot.

All day, I'd been trying to broach the subject of leaving the trio, of doing my own thing, but couldn't do it. Despite the minor annoyances of travelling as a group, I enjoyed travelling with the Frenchmen. For my benefit, they spoke English. And Patrick and Frédéric's ability to hold a conversation was improving daily to reveal personalities that were filled with just as much humour as Fabrice. They constantly made me laugh, and in their company, life was as it should be: fun, carefree and filled with a sense of child-like wonder. The repeated drum roll of 'I'm going to die' had increasingly grown fainter the deeper I'd immersed myself into the adventure that was Central Asia, and even more so since travelling with the trio.

My reluctance to leave them was also due to an unfounded sense of fear of travelling alone as a woman. When on my own, I'd never given this another thought as everything always worked out. Yes, there had been minor threats, but no harm ever came to me. But travelling with the security of three men, this habit was no longer being reinforced and I increasingly dwelled on what might happen to me without their protection. While past experience told me that once I took that first step, everything would fall into place, I found a myriad of excuses to stay with the Frenchmen. They had suggested I accompany them to Ulaanbaatar for the Naadam festival in July, still a month away. From there I could cross into China and down to South East Asia. It was a long detour from my loosely aimed destination, Darwin in northern Australia. But if I stayed, to protect them from my 'death wish', I vowed there would be no more risk-taking.

Before meeting the Frenchmen, I hadn't decided exactly how I would traverse the Central Asian sub-continent to reach South East Asia, and then Australia. I had several options; my preferred was the Torugart Pass to Kashgar and into Tibet. I could get the visa at the Chinese embassy in Bishkek, Kyrgyzstan's capital, and take a chance sneaking my motorcycle through the border hidden in one of the many trucks carting bails of raw cotton into China. But would a truck driver risk everything for the US$100 I planned to offer? I'd met an English backpacker while working at the hostel in Istanbul who told me if I managed to travel halfway into Tibet undetected, the Chinese police, if I were apprehended, would probably let me continue all the way through to Nepal rather than send me back to Kyrgyzstan. But he did not mention anything about fines, imprisonment and deportation, which other travellers had warned me about.

My second option was to take a flight, with my motorcycle, from Kazakhstan to Pakistan then ride overland through India, Bangladesh and into South East Asia.

The third, recently emerged, option was staying with the Frenchmen until Ulaanbaatar, but my rear tyre would be worn to the canvas after riding over 4000 kilometres of tarmac that stretched as a straight black line across the Russian steppe. It would be a week of mostly endless flat grassland. The Frenchmen each carried a spare set of tyres for their return trip as, apparently, none could be bought in Ulaanbaatar. But my one-month Russian visa was due to expire in a week. With the date neatly printed in red ink and an extension unlikely to be granted, I would need to make a decision on one of these options very soon.

After our first day in Kyrgyzstan, it was clear this was the land time forgot. Untouched by tourism, it was a magical place with its narrow dirt roads that meandered through quaint villages of wooden cottages; a mountainous land with the ever-present snow-capped Pamirs towering in the distance. In the height of summer, the fields were iridescent green. Purple and yellow wildflowers grew everywhere.

We travelled a mere 140 kilometres on that second day, reaching the township of Khaidarkan, which housed the workers of a nearby mercury mine set up in the 1940s by the Soviets. In an otherwise hidden world of pristine beauty, it was a blot on the landscape, the environment and the long-term health of its residents. Plumes of mercury-laden dust from the uncovered tailings mounds would be carried for miles by the winds, and mine water was pumped directly into a river that flowed fast and swollen with snowmelt all the way to the Ferghana valley in Uzbekistan.

As we rode into the township of stark Soviet-style cement buildings surrounded by denuded brown hills, I wondered about the health of its inhabitants after nearly fifty years of mining. We pulled up in what looked like the centre of town and were immediately surrounded. Men in traditional *kalpaks*, elongated black-and-white felt hats; women in floral dresses and bright scarves tied tightly around their heads; and groups of inquisitive bare-foot children, all stood gazing at us with dark almond eyes that hinted of their Mongol ancestry. Some could speak a little English, and we heard a chorus of invitations: 'I invite you to my house'. I looked questioningly at the Frenchmen, but the decision on whose offer we should accept was made by a girl aged about fifteen. Her thick black hair was tied in a ponytail falling to her hips, and as we looked undecided from one offer to the next, she burst into tears. I had never experienced such open competitiveness to offer hospitality, and feeding us would be a financial burden on these people, who lived on the brink of poverty.

We introduced ourselves. Her name was Susanna. She then beckoned us to follow, and we slowly rode our motorcycles behind as she trotted ahead to a house down a narrow street.

As the road we travelled was not the usual route to Osh, we were probably the first independent tourists to pass through their village. I had brought potatoes, tomatoes and two loaves of round flatbread from a roadside stall earlier in the day. I'd hoped we might camp beside one of the many mountain streams we'd crossed and this food would be enough as we'd had an enormous amount of shashlik for lunch.

When we arrived at the family's house, a square double-storey cement structure, I gave all my supplies to the girl's mother, which she accepted graciously. At the door, I took off my boots and nudged the trio to do the same. Susanna was beside herself with happiness and bounded up the stairs leading us to the lounge room where we were seated on a couch covered with a length of bright patterned fabric to hide its faded and threadbare exterior. She returned a moment later with a tray laden with a pot of tea, cups and a plate of flatbread broken into pieces. Susanna poured the tea before disappearing down the stairs.

A moment later her father arrived. His name was Roman, and he spoke some French and Fabrice told me that he would go with him to buy drinks. About an hour later they returned with several litre-bottles of soft drink and a large bottle of vodka. 'I'll give you money later,' I whispered to Fabrice wanting to pay my share. But then I worried, what if Fabrice had not paid? The drinks were a huge expense the family could ill afford.

The vodka was quickly opened, and after several toasts and another hour, the special feast for the visiting foreign guests was laid on the low table in front of the couch. Its centrepiece was a large plate of *plov* (spiced rice covered with pieces of mutton, carrots and onion), a plate of shashlik, salad, something that looked like samosas and a plate of large steamed wontons. Roman and Susanna ate with us, but we never saw her mother again.

Fabrice translated the conversation. Roman worked in the mine as a labourer and Susanna's mother was a cleaner. There was an older brother who worked in a tanning factory near Bishkek. Susanna hoped to become a school teacher. It was unusual for a family to have only two children, but high levels of mercury had the worst impact on the developing fetus. I wondered how many miscarriages and stillbirths Susanna's mother had endured and whether or not the Soviet doctors explained the connection to mercury.

Roman told Fabrice that everyone still had jobs, but there was talk that the mine will soon close. 'Now the Soviets are gone, the west wants Russia to close the mine.' Fabrice translated. 'The world can recycle mercury, so there is no need to mine it anymore.'

'What will the people do for work?' I asked.

'This town will die, but today, life is good. They have jobs and money.' Fabrice spread his arms wide over the table. 'And we have this feast.'

It had been a bitterly cold day, the grey skies heavy with rain as we rode into Osh late the following afternoon. We'd left Khaidarkan mid-morning. We'd slept in the lounge room, our camping mattresses and sleeping bags spread over the carpeted floor. After a late breakfast of freshly baked bread, thick cream and black tea, we'd thanked the family and followed a dirt track through a range of low hills to reach Osh. Patrick had fallen off many times. Frédéric also struggled with riding his heavily laden bike across the many washouts as the track, covered in loose scree, followed an undulating path through a low range of bare hills.

All day the Frenchmen had argued about taking this backroad and blamed Fabrice, who like me, relished the challenge of off-road riding. He had a GPS, which I'd never seen before. It allowed him to find minor roads not even marked on either of our maps.

This technology, like the internet, had emerged virtually unbeknown to me. In London, I'd lived on a narrowboat sheltered from this new world order. And before that I was in Africa, where such technology was still years away. The Frenchmen were from that technological world, and they found it rather odd that I knew nothing about it.

'With the GPS, we never get lost,' Fabrice had told me as I'd held the gadget as if it was the most precious thing.

As I looked at the screen, which showed our position, I felt trepidation over exchanging it for my map, which had brought me closer to the local people and their culture. There had been many times on my travels when I had been forced to stop and ask for directions. A GPS would take that all away as it would tell me exactly where I was and the road I needed to follow. It would isolate me from the experience of travel.

Fabrice was in the lead when we reached the outskirts of Osh. He pulled off the road and I stopped beside him.

'A family will invite us,' he shouted through his helmet. 'We wait here.'

'These people are very poor, and there are four of us. We are a burden,' I shouted back.

'No, no, no. It is good,' he replied, his helmet now perched on his mirror, and the bike's engine silenced.

A short time later, Patrick and Frédéric pulled up behind us. Within a few minutes, a middle-aged man walked towards us probably on his way home after a long day at work. He stopped and immediately invited us to stay with him. He lived about 200 metres up ahead and off the main road. His name was Markus, and his family's humble home was made up of two ramshackle timber and brick bungalows surrounded by a rusted corrugated iron fence. They had a vegetable garden and several fruit trees heavy with apples, apricots and plums. We were welcomed by his wife, Julia. Both Julia and Markus could speak a little English.

Later she asked me how old I was and when I told her I was thirty-three, she said I looked much younger. She was twenty-two and had two children, a boy aged five and a girl aged two years. Life had been hard on her as she looked closer to forty and a little undernourished, as did her two children. Her arms were covered with scabs, which looked like mosquito bites. Both her children's heads were shaved, probably to stop an infestation of head lice. We had no food to give her as I'd expected we'd stay in a hotel in Osh.

Markus and Julia and their two children lived with her parents. Her brother and sister and their three children also lived with them in the second bungalow. They were all Russians originally from Ukraine. After independence, they'd stayed in Osh as they did not have the money to return to Russia. Markus worked as a driver for the American Medical Corps, but while his wages were above average, he was the only one with a full-time job. His brother-in-law worked in the Osh bazaar unloading bales of Chinese clothes that were trucked through the Talydy Pass to Irkeshtan. I'd read the bazaar was massive and sold everything from cheap Chinese clothes and merchandise to car parts, furniture, fruits, nuts and vegetables. Julia also worked there on a stall, and we'd meet her tomorrow.

There was no offer to cook us a feast like the one we'd received last night, and I caught snippets of a growing argument between the trio. Patrick and Frédéric were tired and hungry and wanted to stay at a hotel and eat a decent meal as we'd only found a roadside stand selling shashlik for lunch. As the trio had a petrol stove and pot, I offered to cook dinner of a packet of pasta and the tin of bully beef given to me by the Turkmen truck drivers. Julia gave me three potatoes, and I gave her a tube of Betadine ointment for her scabs. I also noticed a large clump of garlic chives in her garden and asked if I could pick some. She nodded.

As we ate, Frédéric and Patrick continued grumbling at Fabrice, and I couldn't blame them. We'd been offered the outside raised timber platform, its corrugated iron roof sheltering us if it should rain. But they could easily be sleeping in a hotel room with crisp white sheets, a hot meal and no mosquitos.

Julia left early the next morning refusing the hundred som, (about US$6), I offered. I later put this in an envelope and gave it to her mother. Julia's pride had made her refuse, but the money would be a big help for this obviously impoverished family, who'd asked nothing from us.

Before leaving Osh, we stopped at its famous bazaar for breakfast. It is a kaleidoscope of colour and activity with different ethnic groups from all over Central Asia. As well as clothes and shoes, there was kitchenware and furniture, tools and car parts, and vast amounts of fruits and vegetables. I was mesmerised by the displays of the biggest fattest cherries, I'd ever seen, even bigger than those I'd eaten in Uzbekistan. We emerged from the covered bazaar to row upon row of tea shops, huge woks of *plov* and stalls selling beautifully iced cakes. Julia had given me directions to the stall where she worked selling soap and when we arrived, she took a break to join us. Fabrice brought a cake and we had morning tea scoffing the treat, giggling at the indulgence. 'Thank you for having us at your house,' I said and pushed a box containing a whole cake into her hands. I'd bought it while she was saying goodbye to the trio. 'For your family,' I said.

The road from Osh over the Talas Ala-Too mountains to Bishkek is surely on the list of the world's most spectacular mountain roads. It was our fourth day in this fabled land, and it began in a torrential downpour not long after leaving the hotel we'd found overlooking a lake at the base of the mountains. As the day wore on, we climbed over 3000 metres and emerged into sunshine as we rode over the Ala-Bel Pass. We started this ride on smooth tarmac, but the narrow road soon turned to dirt as it climbed higher. I rode in front and stopped many times to take photographs, but the Frenchmen soon grew impatient.

'You keep going. I'll catch up!' I yelled as they pulled up beside me. It was just too beautiful to rush, and I wanted to savour every part of this eighty kilometres of twists and turns where snow-capped mountains towered all around us.

At the height of the pass, we rested in a wide meadow dotted with bright orange and purple wildflowers. The sun was warm, and in the clean, crisp air, the sky was a deep blue. I did not want to leave, and it was only when the trio had mounted their bikes that I reluctantly followed. I let them ride ahead so I could stop and admire the views as the road, a series of sharp switchbacks and loose scree, descended to a wide sweeping valley lush with thick green grass and dotted with cream-coloured yurts, the felt pulled taut over a round frame.

These were the traditional summer tents of the Kyrgyz nomad families who grazed their sheep, goats, yaks and horses on the lush grass of these high-altitude valleys. In the distance, the snow-capped peaks of the Tian Shan rose like a giant wave; a tsunami of grey rock and snow, an impenetrable line dividing west from east. It was an imposing natural barrier that would have deterred all but the hardiest of early explorers and would-be invaders. But they would not be defeated and had marched on and found the narrow passes through the Tian Shan. Trade, ideas, religions and even diseases flourished as these passes linked the Silk Roads. These were the world's first superhighways. After the collapse of the Soviet Union, the newly independent Central Asian nations were rediscovering these highways and a new era of prosperity. Kyrgyzstan, in particular, embraced free trade, and China was only too happy to truck its mass-produced goods into these new markets.

The road levelled into the valley, and the Kyrgyz nomads stared at us as we rumbled past. Herds of horses galloped beside us in fright. We pulled up at a yurt close to the road, and a teenage boy immediately called us over, insisting we sit down on two lengths of logs either side of a low table covered with a floral cloth. An elderly man and woman appeared, each carrying two bowls of *kumis*, fermented mares milk. It was slightly fizzy and a little sour with the consistency of skim milk. It was also slightly alcoholic, about two per cent alcohol. The rest of the family had stopped whatever it was they were doing to stare at us.

Even though Kyrgyzstan and the other Central Asian countries had been free from the shackles of the Soviet Union for six years, few independent travellers, and especially those on motorcycles, were yet to venture here. And in the far reaches of Central Asia, in this magical mountain kingdom, we were a novelty. So unique, we might as well have been aliens from another planet.

As well as the elderly couple, who I assumed were the grandparents of the several children ranging from toddlers to teenagers, there was also a husband and wife aged about forty. They all smiled at us from round faces framed with black hair, their skin tanned a deep rich brown from many summers under a high-altitude sun. A boy aged about twelve could speak a little English and told me they would stay in the valley all summer to fatten their animals. In winter, they'd pack up their yurt and move their herds back to their farm on the lowlands. There was no school over summer, he told me when I asked. 'We go *Jailoo*,' he said, and I understood that this was the word for their time in the valley over the summer and was the very essence of Kyrgyz nomadic culture, which had gone unchanged for thousands of years.

It was nearly dark and bitterly cold when we reached the township of Kara-Balta, which was only sixty kilometres from Bishkek. I refused to ride any further saying it was too dangerous with my dim six-volt headlight, besides I was exhausted from riding down the range and its many tight switchbacks where a moment's loss of concentration would have seen me and the TT hurtling down a drop of hundreds of metres.

'You keep going. I'll catch you in Bishkek,' I said, but Fabrice said they'd stay too. Wise choice, I thought. It's when you're tired and riding a motorcycle at night on unfamiliar roads littered with pot-holes and other debris that serious accidents happen. We pulled up outside a café. Opposite sat the police station. On seeing our motorcycles, the two officers on duty came out and insisted it was safer we store our bikes in their compound rather than the Soviet-style hotel next door, where a room was US$2 in som. Dinner was a bowl of onion-filled boiled wontons, and I could see the trio regretted their decision to stay.

We reached Bishkek mid-morning and found a budget hotel, but it was clean and spacious. More importantly, there was hot water, and the beds were comfortable. It was here that I'd planned to say goodbye to the Frenchmen, who would be leaving the next day for Almaty where they'd get their Mongolian visas. We were sitting at an outdoor café drinking beer and eating shashlik, which the trio seemed never to tire of.

'You should come with us to Mongolia,' Fabrice said as if reading my thoughts that I was about to announce my departure. While they'd already asked me to join them, I was still unsure about what route I'd take to reach South East Asia.

'I'd like to try Kashgar,' I replied.

'It is impossible. You have no permit for your motorcycle. You never make it,' he added, dismissing my idea.

'I think you're right. The Chinese are not easily fooled,' I replied after the stupidity of this option dawned on me. This was not Africa, where remote borders can occasionally be crossed undetected.

'Good. It is settled. You come with us to Mongolia,' Fabrice said.

'Okay,' I said avoiding the gaze of Patrick and Frédéric who I knew would've preferred just the three of them.

Ordinarily, I would not have given up so easily, but lately, I felt tired. It was a tiredness that had seeped into my muscles right down to the bone. Everything was such an effort: getting up, packing the bike, even staying awake while riding. It felt like my limbs had been dipped in lead and the air had turned to the dense consistency of mud. I now welcomed the Frenchmen's many stops to eat throughout the day.

But despite these frequent stops, I still fought to stay awake when riding. I'd be continually shaking my head encased in its helmet: shaking off the sleep that pushed at my consciousness. In such a state of sheer exhaustion, my mind teetered on the brink of a black abyss called a microsleep. A microsleep can sneak up on a motorcyclist just as easily as it does a driver. It happens when you're so fatigued that the brain takes over and momentarily shuts down for several seconds.

Somehow, I managed to hold back the blackness, but when we'd finally stop for the day and soon after our dinner, I'd fall into bed into a void; a vacuum no dream could penetrate.

With the onset of this crushing fatigue, I embraced the comfortable sense of security that travelling with the Frenchmen provided. While I'd only been with them a week, those days of travelling alone seemed so distant, so not me, and I doubted if I would ever have the courage, the strength, to go it alone again.

After a late breakfast of pastries and coffee we rode away from Bishkek towards Almaty. It was an anxious four-hour ride as my Russian visa expired on 15 June, the very day we would cross into Kazakhstan, but the three border guards, all Russians, gave our passports no more than a cursory glance. Kazakhstan was the most Russian-ified of the former Soviet Central Asian nations and had not yet fully embraced its independence from the 'motherland' after Perestroika.

'Welcome to Kazakhstan,' said the young Russian official beaming a smile from rosy pink cheeks as he handed back my passport.

'*Spasiba*,' I said thanking him most graciously.

17

STEPPELANDS

Kazakhstan

We were in Almaty, Kazakhstan's capital. Nestled in the foothills of the Trans-Ili Alatau mountains, the northern edge of the mighty Tian Shan, snow-capped peaks rose nearly 5000 metres before us. Drenched in warm sunshine under a cloudless blue sky, the Frenchmen and I were enjoying this vista from an outdoor café as we sipped sweet milky coffee. Our late breakfast was a plate of *baursaki*, delicious doughnut-like pastries, which the Frenchmen dropped into their coffee, slurping the soggy mess from a spoon.

The trio and I had just collected our Mongolian visas issued on the spot for US$50. Intuition told me I'd just wasted a significant amount of my travelling funds—US$50 would easily last a week or more. Since leaving St Johann nearly four months ago, I'd spent about US$1500, all the result of cheap fuel and the generous hospitality that had been bestowed upon me since Greece.

Even though I'd accepted the trio's invitation to ride with them to Ulaanbaatar, I felt uncomfortable with my decision. My Russian visa had expired the day before, and my guidebook advised an extension was not possible. In fact, if I turned up at the Russian consulate, I would most likely be deported at my cost plus issued with a hefty fine. And what of the TT? Would I be allowed to take it with me? Even if I could get an extension, I would need to contact Lena, the Russian girl in London who'd given me a letter of support. Preoccupied with my diagnosis, I did not plan for such contingencies and failed to make a copy. I had no means of contacting her. My only option was to convince the Frenchmen to take a backroad into Siberia to reach Ulaanbaatar. My guidebook mentioned that the border between Kazakhstan and Russia was 'fairly porous' and a backroad, would mean an even more flimsily manned border post if one existed at all.

What if I could not cross from Mongolia into China with the TT? Where would I go then? Would I be able to replace my rear tyre worn to the canvas after 4000 kilometres of steppe? But I ignored all these very real scenarios in favour of staying in the safe embrace of the Frenchmen, who were ignorant of my conniving ways.

The only other diners at the café were a hip young Kazakh couple. They looked to be professionals. Possibly meeting for coffee before heading into Almaty's city centre where ultra-modern offices rose up from the monolithic buildings of the Soviet past. Dark-haired and fashionably dressed, they were the 'beautiful people' of the new Kazakhstan. I'd only noticed them as Fabrice had been staring at the woman, who was stunningly beautiful with golden brown skin, long legs and a mane of hair the colour of dark chocolate. She flashed elongated dark almond eyes demurely towards Fabrice. She was the perfect mix of genes from Russian and Kazakh heritage that stretched back thousands of years to the Mongols, with a touch of Persian and Chinese too. The height and svelteness of the Russian, the high cheekbones of the Kazakh and the skin tone and elongated eyes of the Mongols.

'I have never seen more beautiful women than here in Kazakhstan,' Fabrice crooned as he slurped another piece of soggy pastry from his coffee.

'What are you doing?' I asked Fabrice as he wrote a note then handed it to the waiter, pointing to the woman.

'I ask her to join us. I would like to meet her. She is beautiful, yes.'

I nodded. 'But you can't do that. She is with her boyfriend. Maybe it is her husband.' The waiter gave the note to the woman, and she looked over at us and smiled from full luscious lips.

'If she does not want to meet with me, she will ignore my note. This is what we do in France. Why not take a chance? What is there to lose?

'You'll make the man feel uncomfortable. How can he compete with a foreigner?' I shot back.

'Ah. You see this is the problem with you English. You make so many complications. You need to see things as they are, not what you think they are.'

'I'm Australian,' I huffed.

'It is all the same. Australian, English, American *phar*. Don't make a big deal of it,' Fabrice said and stood up as the woman approached, leaving her partner sitting alone and looking decidedly uncomfortable. She wore tailored pants and a floral blouse that emphasised the absolute perfectness of her lithe body and full breasts. Fabrice quickly pulled over a chair and crooned a welcome. She beamed a smile. I could understand enough French to understand the flirtatiousness of their exchange. I could even feel the sexual tension that filled the narrowing space between them as they leaned closer to each other. Patrick and Frédéric gave their apologies and moved to their motorcycles parked nearby. I had no choice but to do the same, leaving Fabrice to do what generations of Frenchmen do best—flirt with another man's woman! As I walked away, I realised how neutral I'd become towards my own sexuality. Before my diagnosis, there were often times when I'd meet a man, and there would be those fleeting thoughts as to his suitability. Thoughts that were innate, instinctual, unavoidable—the drive to procreate. It was an urge that was now completely devoid in me. Survival had replaced procreation as my body's purpose in its final days.

As Patrick and Frédéric looked at their map, they asked me where I thought we might stay that night.

'I don't know, but something will turn up. It always does.' But my whimsicality did nothing to reassure them.

They returned their gaze to the map, muttering something in French; an insult confirming my madness, I expect. Ahead of us, we had several long gruelling days of riding over undulating grassland, the beginning of the steppe that stretched across Kazakhstan and into the vastness of Russia. There would be no hotels on the open plains, parched brown in the height of summer. Instead, we would sleep at a roadside café that would conveniently appear at day's end in favour of stopping early or riding dangerously into the night to reach a town and a non-descript Soviet-era hotel, that while clean would shield us from all contact with the Kazakh people and its culture.

More than half the population of Kazakhstan was Russian and most lived in its cities and towns while the Kazakh people, once proud nomads possessing vast herds of sheep, cattle and horses, mostly lived in the smaller towns and hamlets scattered across the steppe and fringing the Altai Mountains that bordered Russia and Kazakhstan. But the Soviet's policy of collective farming had destroyed all this. The herds were gone and with them the Kazakh nomad culture. What remained were families with a few animals struggling to survive hot summers and harsh winters growing potatoes in poor soils surrounding their dilapidated timber houses.

I opened my map, spreading it across the top of the Gearsack on the TT. Patrick and Frédéric turned, but I had nothing to reassure them—no place name to uphold their ill-conceived notion that there would be a hotel with comfortable beds and a hot meal. Instead, I scanned the map where villages were closest along the Kazakh-Russian border for a backroad linking the two through the Altai Mountains. While my map indicated no such backroad, it would have been used by nomads, traders and hunters for centuries and Fabrice's GPS would tell us where.

As late afternoon approached, my attention turned to somewhere to stay before day turned to night. And with this thought, a cluster of tin shacks appeared in the distance. It was nearly mid-day when we left Almaty, and fortunately, the trio were happy to push on, and we'd ridden nearly 400 kilometres, our only stop was fuel and a soft drink. I opened the throttle to pass Fabrice and pulled up at the shacks. The family's yurt was set up at the back and was probably the kitchen for the roadside café. Before the Soviets, this family would have grazed their animals across the steppe moving with the seasons. Home was now in the middle of nowhere; a lone beacon of civilisation on the endless steppe still tinged green from a recent downpour. This may have been their winter refuge, but with their livestock gone they eked out a living selling food and vodka to passing truck drivers.

As the trio pulled up behind me, two Kazakh men approached, beaming broad smiles of welcome from round brown faces. 'Can we camp? We have a tent.' I asked, making the universal sign for sleep.

'*Da, da*,' said the older and larger of the two men, whom I assumed was the patriarch and owner. He pointed to the yurt.

'*Nyet*,' I replied placing my hands together to form the shape of a tent then pointed to our motorcycles. The man ushered me to follow him to the back of the yurt where we would not be seen from the road nor disturbed late into the night. Nearby was an outdoor toilet. Along with a hot meal and vodka, what more could we need? After thanking the man, I returned to the trio.

'We cannot sleep here,' Frédéric said, snorting his disgust.

'We need a hotel,' Patrick added.

'This isn't so bad. They are cooking shashlik,' Fabrice said breathing in the aroma of roasting meat. My stomach rumbled in support.

'The next major town is over 100 kilometres. It'll be dark soon,' I said and swung my leg over the TT to ride behind the yurt and set up my tent. The trio followed.

Marijuana grew wild, as prevalent as summer weeds, around the yurt and cluster of shacks. All day, I'd noticed it growing here and there along the road verge. With a constant supply of nitrogen from urine, it grew particularly vigorously around the outhouse as men drunk on vodka had peed around it instead of the hole-in-the-ground toilet.

But these plants were a distant cousin of the marijuana used to get high or used medicinally. Instead, this variety, while covered in seeds, lacked the sticky residue and overpowering smell that indicated THC.

I reached to pick a seed-laden bud, crushing it in my palms and sniffing its aroma. Nothing. This was hemp, and it was a remnant from an ancient past when its seeds were either crushed for oil, roasted, ground as flour or cooked as gruel, a high protein and nutrient-rich food of the peasants. The whole of Russia used hemp back then, as did the world. In fact, wars were fought over controlling Russia's export of hemp: the French, under Napoleon, invaded Russia for its hemp, and in 1812 America and Britain also fought to control its supply.

Hemp was also a significant crop in ancient China. Hemp fibre is strong as well as soft to touch and is ideal as both rope and sails for ships and for clothes and paper. Its leaves were used as a nutrient-rich fodder for animals during the long Russian winters, and its oil was cold pressed from seeds for lamps said to burn the longest and brightest of all the oils. It was this same oil, I'd read, that was used as a pollution-free fuel in the first automobiles until petroleum was refined from crude oil and pushed as the preferred fuel by those set to profit. It is also a strong and viable alternative to plastic.

All that was left of Russia's massive hemp plantations (and China's, too I expect) were scatterings of weeds. Such plantations never had a chance to thrive elsewhere in the world. What happened? How could humanity be robbed of a crop that proliferated so vigorously without pesticides and chemical-based fertilisers, and with little water in arid conditions and poor soil? This was a crop that had so many beneficial uses, but the greed of the powerful elite had robbed humanity of its gift.

Instead, we have petroleum, petrochemical plastics, synthetic fibres, cotton, timber-based paper and all the chemicals and excessive water use that goes with these industries. All are linked to powerful industrial companies initially owned by a smattering of individuals who profit enormously from such products at the expense of the planet and all living things. Our world could have been so very different after the 1930s when the campaign to demonise hemp as a recreational drug began. It was about the same time significant advances in hemp processing technology were discovered.

'You druggie.'

I turned, the hemp still in my hand. It was Frédéric, who sneered at me as he pushed past to reach the toilet.

'It's hemp,' I said, but he'd closed the door.

The dislike I'd felt from Frédéric and Patrick had intensified since Almaty where they'd assumed we would go our separate ways. They wanted me gone and Fabrice back. They wanted their old dynamic, not what had emerged when our paths had crossed in Bukhara. Their lack of English had isolated them from the easy banter, Fabrice and I enjoyed. Yes, the original plan was for me to ride with them to Almaty then go our separate ways, but I had not resisted Fabrice's offer to continue to Ulaanbaatar. While my task to convince Fabrice to take a backroad over the Altai Mountains and deviate from the 'planned route' would be without resistance, Frédéric and Patrick would take some persuading.

'We have shashlik,' Fabrice called as I rounded the back of the yurt after setting up my tent, map in hand. He sat alone at a rough-cut timber table outside the yurt, which was like a large dirty igloo. Inside were a few tables and chairs for diners, a wood stove, bench and pots and pans hanging nearby. Today was warm, so the shashlik was roasted on a coal fire outside.

'From here, it's over 2600 kilometres of straight road going through Novosibirsk to Ulaanbaatar,' I said, pointing to the route on my map spread out on the table. 'That's four days. Even if we ride 700 kilometres a day, which is too much, we can't keep that up. But there's a shortcut. It will save us 1000 kilometres, and it'll be far more interesting than nearly 3000 kilometres of steppe.' I added another 400 kilometres onto my argument for effect.

As I picked up a shashlik, the sparkle for adventure brightened Frabrice's eyes. One of the Kazakhs placed the bottle of vodka and four glasses on the table, which I'd just ordered.

'Spasiba,' I said and poured two glasses grateful that Frédéric and Patrick were still battling with their tent.

'Ridder,' I said pointing to the town near the Kazakh-Russia border. 'I'm sure there'll be a backroad that'll take us across the border and into Russia. Your GPS will tell us. We can cross into Mongolia at Tashanta. We'll get to see the real Mongolia rather than 4000 kilometres of boring steppe,' I crooned as I popped in another thousand kilometres. 'If we go through Ridder it'll only be 2500 kilometres and a lot more fun. It'll be an adventure.' I leaned forward, picking up my glass to make a toast. 'To adventure,' I said. Our glasses touched, and in unison, we downed the vodka. As Fabrice pulled the GPS from his daypack, I refilled the glasses.

Fabrice looked up from the GPS, beaming a wide smile. 'There's a road. From Ridder to Karagay and then Yustik. All up it's 155 kilometres, about three hours.'

'We're about 700 kilometres from Ridder. If we start early, we could make it by tomorrow afternoon,' I said smiling back.

With head down and brow creased, Fabrice's focus on the GPS was intense. 'The road passes through the Altai Mountains. It's dirt, but it should be easy enough on the bikes,' he added.

It was a good twenty minutes before the other two joined us. As they sat down, I poured each a glass of vodka and another two for Fabrice and I. '*Nostrovia*,' I said raising my glass.

'Ah, Frédéric and Patrick. There is a change of plan,' Fabrice said in French, though I understood. 'We will take a shortcut to Ulaanbaatar. It will be boring to ride 4000 kilometres of steppe. Instead, we take a backroad to Russia. We ride through the Altai Mountains. Then we see the real Mongolia. This way is 2000 kilometres shorter.'

They looked at Fabrice in disbelief, then glared at me. To escape their gaze, I looked down, pretending to study my map.

Under a rapidly darkening sky, we reached Ridder late the next day. Since daylight we'd covered more than 700 kilometres crossing a vast swathe of Kazakhstan's steppe on an unrelenting straight line of tarmac. I had battled fatigue all day, and felt a great sense of relief when we approached the low ranges of the Altai and the road wound through birch forest and green fields and past hamlets of small timber houses where every available space of garden was lush with potato plants. We pulled up in front of an imposing building in the sprawling town square. Immaculately litter-free, I guessed it was the town's administrative centre. The square was eerily quiet and devoid of people and traffic until a moment later, a police car screeched to a stop beside us. Two uniformed men in peaked caps climbed out.

'*Passeports*,' one of them demanded. We obeyed, and I prayed my lack of a Kazakhstan visa and expired Russian visa would be overlooked in the bundle of four passports the officer held.

'We are looking for the road to Karagay,' I said, unfolding my map.

'No road. Is not possible. You go back,' he said and with no more than a cursory glance at our passports, handed the bundle to me. I retrieved mine and gave the rest to Fabrice.

'Is there a hotel?' Fabrice asked.

'*Nyet* hotel. You leave now,' the second officer boomed.

They wanted us out of their town immediately, and the terms for our departure were non-negotiable.

As we rode away, they followed until we were a good five kilometres from Ridder. When they'd done a U-turn, we rode on another few kilometres then stopped to discuss our next move.

Frédéric and Patrick wanted to continue with the original 'sensible' plan and ride the long way round to Novosibirsk and across the Russian steppe to Ulaanbaatar. Fabrice was still dazzled with the idea of an adventure through the Altai Mountains to reach Russia and then into Mongolia. My expired Russian visa left me no choice but to enthusiastically side with Fabrice. Although, I too was excited by this adventure as it was a far more enticing option than boring Russian steppe. My anticipation for it was so great that the reality of my situation, was entirely forgotten, and this alone was a driver to continue despite the risks.

As the three argued in French, I scanned the area for somewhere to camp. It was nearly dark and the next town likely to have a hotel was two hours away and would mean backtracking around fifty kilometres. On a low rise, a short distance from us, I spied a cluster of timber houses.

'Look, a farm. Let's ask if we can camp,' I interrupted, and before they could respond, I'd shoved on my helmet and was riding toward the dirt road leading to it.

The farm consisted of a few shacks of rough-cut dark timber with steep pitched iron-clad roofs. Nearby, were several lean-to sheds used to house livestock during the harsh winters.

'*Dobryy den,*' I called the Russian greeting for good afternoon. A man with a stock of thick golden blond hair aged in his thirties stood perplexed, staring with bright blue eyes. A woman aged about the same, with short, blond hair stood, at the doorway of the main shack and four girls also with fair hair, aged from about ten to fifteen years stood, around her. One of the older girls held a toddler, a boy, who clung to his sister tightly.

'*Bonjour, madame,*' I heard from behind as Fabrice approached. A wide smile broke across the woman's face, and Fabrice launched into a conversation with her and the man. 'Ah, this is very good. They speak French. And yes, we can camp. We are their guests.'

We set up our tents at the back of the shack. Then the man, whose name was Alexia, ushered us inside, where we sat at a rough-cut timber table. His wife, Elena, served us steaming bowls of potato soup with stale bread.

As we ate, Fabrice told me that the cluster of timber bungalows, shacks and animal sheds were all that remained of a farm from the Soviet-era of collectivisation. Stalin introduced the policy in the late 1920s to increase agricultural production and industrialise the Soviet Union. Produce from collective farms fed the people in the cities as well as providing exports with which to buy farm and mining machinery. There were only three families left barely surviving with their few animals and sustaining themselves on mostly potatoes grown over the summer. All were Russian, their grandparents most likely forced to move here under Stalin's grand plan of cultural assimilation of the entire USSR including countries of Central Asia. Alexia and Elena's family came from Latvia, which explained their blond appearance. Fabrice said the other two families originally came from Ukraine. Their grandparents were probably caught up in Stalin's policy to purge Ukraine of wealthy peasants, or *kulaks*, who were accused of hoarding grain, which was needed to buy foreign currency. This was in turn used by the government to purchase machinery from the west to industrialise the Soviet Union. In 1932, when unrealistic quotas from the grain harvest were not filled Stalin confiscated what was left of the harvest and peasants found hiding even the tiniest amount of grain were either executed or sent to prison and labour camps: the gulags. Many of these gulags were in Central Asia. This purge lead to an artificial famine, the *Holodomor*, in which more than five million people starved to death.

As we ate, Alexia and Elena chatted in French with the trio. Fabrice occasionally translated, when I pestered him to do so. Before the Soviet Union, French was the preferred language of the nobility, and this love of French continued well into the 1960s when French was taught in secondary schools. I understood snippets of the conversation from the French I'd picked up during my travels across Zaire and West Africa, and more recently from the trio. 'Ask about the road to Russia,' I said, nudging Fabrice.

'Yes. I have asked. And yes there is a road. There is a rail bridge nearby. We can cross the river there to reach this road,' he said, annoyed I had interrupted him.

Unable to join the conversation, I had no choice but to observe. The four girls sat nearby and when the meal was over, the older two cleared the table. This family was very poor. As poor as many of those families in Africa, who had offered their hospitality when I had unexpectedly turned up on their door step. Poorer still than those who had taken me into their homes more recently along the Silk Road. With their blond hair, blue eyes and creamy skin tanned a smooth caramel, they did not belong in this scene of abject poverty. With a jolt, I suddenly realised as a white person, I viewed the world through a culturally conditioned lens tainted with subconscious racial bias. It lay coiled deep inside my psyche. Its foundation came from my parents who grew up in the era of Australia's white-only immigration policy. I was not alone; subconscious racial bias is pervasive for many people from a white-majority culture. The solution to purging it comes first from awareness.

18

THE LAST NOMADS

Kazakhstan

After a breakfast of thick cream and crusts of stale bread, we thanked Alexia and Elena for letting us camp and feeding us. Earlier, I'd spoken to Fabrice about offering the family some money, but he insisted we would insult their hospitality.

'We ate potatoes, cream and stale bread. This is nothing,' he'd said. But I replied, 'There are four of us. It is a lot of potatoes, cream and bread.'

Alexia assured Fabrice that the road into Siberia over the south-eastern edge of the vast Altai Mountain range was easily passable on our motorcycles. We would reach Russia and the village of Karagay that evening, after all, it was only 100 kilometres according to Fabrice's GPS. I hoped so because between us we had very little food. Fortunately, we had refuelled in Ridder before the police had hunted us out. I'd intended but not managed to stock up on supplies there too, just in case it took longer than planned to reach Karagay. On this backroad through the Altai Mountains there would be no roadside cafés grilling shashlik. My only food was my emergency rations: two tins of sardines I'd carried since Turkey.

As we could not ride through Ridder to reach the road to Karagay, Alexia gave Fabrice directions to ride around the town by following a railway line that crossed a river. We easily managed the bridge and after several kilometres found the road as Alexia promised, and which Fabrice confirmed on his GPS. It was then easy riding, first along a narrow dirt road that wound through a thick birch forest, then over a range of low-forested hills and down into a green valley lush with summer grass, but unusually devoid of livestock like we'd seen in abundance in Kyrgyzstan.

Around mid-afternoon, we came across a small farm where a

Kazakh family was enjoying a late lunch outside their bungalow. Fabrice rode over and pulled up to ask about road conditions ahead. We'd had a late start, around 9.00 a.m. but had only travelled about thirty kilometres. And while it was just another seventy kilometres to Karagay, it appeared we wouldn't make it before nightfall. Their farm was comprised of two bungalows made of the same dark rough-cut timber and steep, rusted iron-clad roofs as Alexia and Elena's. There were several pens made from birch branches; these housed pigs, a cow and a mare with a newborn foal. Chickens foraged in and around the enclosures.

As Kazakhs, these people were nomads, and for generations, each summer would have grazed their animals: sheep, horses and cattle, on the Altai's mountain pastures. But collectivisation robbed them of their traditional nomadic lifestyle when their animals were confiscated by the Soviets, which started in the 1930s. The livestock was either packed live into carriages or slaughtered in the winter. A network of railways transported the animals live or as meat to Moscow and other cities to feed millions of factory workers building a powerful industrial Soviet Union. Many of the nomads, I'd read, also killed their own animals rather than hand them over to the Russians.

The old man, who smiled a toothless welcome from a grey-bristled, creased face, must have experienced this. A boy at the time, his family would have lost most of their herds, and unable to feed themselves had no choice but to move to collective farms or starve to death. About a third of the Kazakh nomads, an estimated two million people, had suffered this fate. With the dissolution of the Soviet Union in 1991, the collective farms had collapsed, and the Kazakh nomads returned to their traditional winter homes where families such as these sustained themselves from a vegetable patch, filled mostly with potatoes, and a few animals: sheep and goats for meat, a cow for milk and cream, and chickens for eggs.

The younger man, aged about forty, with his brown skin, elongated dark eyes, and black hair tied in a kind of top-knot, looked as though he was a direct descendant from Genghis Khan's hordes. The Mongol armies travelled through this region during the thirteenth century to conquer all in their path as they advanced across Eurasia. The three women and their children (three boys and a girl aged about eight to twelve), stared wide-eyed at us from a doorway. They all appeared to have the same Mongol heritage, and I wondered how they were related to the old man who looked more Russian than Kazakh. Maybe he was a visiting relative, the owner of the farm, or a passer-by like us? Unable to speak Kazakh or Russian, I would never know.

The younger man rose from the table laid with a lunch of unleavened bread, a bowl of sliced tomatoes and cucumbers and a plate piled with meat on bones; probably mutton. He beckoned us to join them. It appeared to be some kind of celebration as it looked rather extravagant for a simple lunch. Fabrice spoke a few words of French, but they didn't understand and spoke no English either. We would have to manage with my Russian dictionary. I retrieved it, and my map, from the Gearsack. We sat down to eat as the family insisted and I translated that we were riding to Karagay.

'Nyet problema na mototsikl,' the younger man said, as I pointed to it on the map. With the meal done, a cake lavishly iced with thick cream and wild strawberries was placed on the table, and it was then I realised the significance of the day. Since we arrived one of the boys had sulked nearby, and it dawned on me why. It was his birthday. This lunch, and more importantly, this cake, was his much-anticipated birthday treat and four foreigners were about to devour the lot.

'I think it's the boy's birthday,' I whispered to Fabrice, casting a glance towards the boy, who looked away embarrassed. 'Don't eat the cake,' I begged.

'It is rude to refuse their hospitality,' Fabrice replied, accepting the large slice offered. Frédéric and Patrick did the same, and before I could raise my fingers to show just a little slice, a plate with the same generous portion was placed before me.

'Don't eat any more,' I said to all three. 'It's the boy's birthday cake, and we've eaten half already.'

'Ah, it's just a cake,' Fabrice said, then complimented the woman on her cooking. As he ate the last mouthful, the woman offered us all another slice, and in unison, the trio said: 'Da.'

'*Nyet*,' I said, a little too severely when the woman was about to serve me a second slice.

'You've eaten nearly all of it,' I hissed, kicking Fabrice under the table.

'They offer. What we do?'

'Refuse,' I shot back. Just a few pieces of the cake remained, and my heart reached out to the boy. My eyes were saying sorry we'd spoiled his special day. I wished we had arrived much later when the celebrations were over, if in fact, I'd read the signs correctly and that was the situation. Maybe I was wrong and Fabrice was right in saying I jumped to conclusions too quickly.

Using my Russian dictionary, Fabrice asked the family if we could stay the night.

'What? It's only 4.00 p.m.' I said, glancing at his watch. 'We can ride another three hours before dark. Then camp somewhere. 'We may even make it to Karagay.'

'We do not want to camp. The family has offered us a bungalow,' Fabrice said pointing to the smaller house about fifty metres away.

'Someone must sleep there. We are taking their beds,' I said.

Fabrice was now as pissed at me as the other two and strode over to his bike getting on to ride to the second bungalow. The children followed as the pen next to it contained the mare and newborn foal. The birthday boy climbed through the fence wrapping his arms around the foal's neck. It stood complacently. The boy beckoned me, and I ran my hand over the smooth softness of its brown coat. I smiled at the boy, and he smiled back.

Outside the bungalow, the trio tinkered with their motorcycles. I lay on top of my sleeping bag on one of the four spring beds starring up at the inside of the rusted iron-clad roof. I now welcomed this reprieve to rest and write my diary. I'd not written anything since Almaty three days ago. Travelling alone, I always had time to write, but travelling with the Frenchmen, those moments of solitude were rare. There was also the deep tiredness that weighed me down, and I was now grateful for this afternoon rest.

We rose at daylight, packed and thanked the family for their hospitality. But the trio were angry that breakfast was not offered, and we'd ridden away from the farm with grumbling tummies. By early afternoon, it was clear we would not make Karagay that day. We'd travelled only about twenty kilometres on a narrow dirt road that wound through low hills and through several rocky mountain streams to reach the foothills of the Altai Mountains. The route had been easy for our off-road motorcycles. Fabrice, like me, was experienced both on and off-road, but Frédéric and Patrick had found the riding difficult.

We'd also crossed a river swollen and fast flowing with snowmelt and summer rains. But the bridge made of rough cut timbers had mostly collapsed from the weight of trucks, and we'd had to help each other push our bikes across the broken timbers. The effort had exhausted us and having not eaten since the meal with the Kazakh family the day before, we were also weak with hunger. When we came across a deserted log cabin, I could not believe our luck. Inside was a large vat containing about ten litres of honey, the leftovers from last summer. Dead flies floated on the surface, and I hauled out a dead mouse, or a small rat!

Our only food, until this windfall, was the two tins of sardines, which I was saving for our evening meal. The trio had nothing. Not even a packet of sweets or bar of French chocolate between them. 'Why would we carry food? There is always a café or someone roasting shashlik,' Fabrice told me when I asked what food they carried.

The cabin was the base for an apiary of hives transported to the area over the summer, allowing the bees to feed on the wildflowers that grew in abundance in the birch forest and grassy meadows. But we'd seen no hives when we approached.

I'd read that honey found in Egyptian tombs was still edible after thousands of years. Being virtually waterless, acidic and containing hydrogen peroxide, honey was a hostile environment for bacteria even when a rodent had fallen in it. I dipped my finger into the vat.

'Delicious. Nothing wrong with it,' I said and stuck my finger in again.

'I'm not eating that,' Frédéric snorted, casting a glance of disgust at the dead mouse lying on the dirt floor and then at me.

'Please yourself,' I said and returned to my bike to retrieve a half-litre plastic bottle that still carried the remnants of milk powder left over from Africa. I tipped the milk powder into a plastic bag, then washed the bottle and dried it. Using a spoon, I gently filled the bottle, taking care to avoid scooping up any dead flies and bugs.

'You're crazy,' Patrick said as he stood watching me in disbelief.

'Wait till you're hungry. You'll savour it,' I said swallowing another spoonful and feeling its energy pour through my body. They had not yet experienced real hunger as I had in northern Kenya. This honey was energy that would sustain me, and the trio too, if they wished, until we reached Karagay.

After crossing the collapsed bridge, Patrick and Frédéric had told Fabrice they wanted to turn back, but he assured them the road was clearly marked on the GPS and we were nearly there. They were hungry, they replied. They'd expected this ride to be easy. I too was concerned about what lay ahead. What rivers we'd have to cross. Whether there would be a bridge and whether or not it would be more damaged than what we'd just crossed. And what of the mountains? We had just reached the foothills, and the GPS signalled the village was still about fifty kilometres.

But like Fabrice, I wanted to push on. I wanted to trust that we'd make it. That nothing would go wrong, and if it did, something would turn up and save us.

19

THE RESCUE

Kazakhstan

A brilliant rainbow arched across the horizon as though guiding us on this last stretch to Karagay. It ended where the two-wheeled track dropped sharply from the plateau into a vast bowl-shaped valley. We stopped to gaze in awe at this magical scene of wild splendour. Yellow and purple wildflowers dotted the lush grass and snow lay in drifts in the shadows of the rounded peaks behind us. The Altai stretched for over 2000 kilometres from China's Gobi Desert into Mongolia and Siberia, and across the top of Kazakhstan. The mountains rolled endlessly into the distance to disappear amongst storm clouds that darkened the sky. The view was a brief respite from all we'd endured since leaving the bee-keepers' cabin yesterday.

It started as a pleasurable ride through a birch forest, but the smooth two-wheeled track had quickly deteriorated to rocks, loose scree, washouts and a shingled river, wide and fast flowing. The ice-cold water rushed past my thighs as I'd struggled to hold my footing in bare feet on the slippery rocks. We'd taken off our jeans and boots to push the motorcycles across, a process that took us more than two hours. We spent the night on the side of a steep hill where the track took us higher into the Altai. With spectacular views across the mountains, a steady trickle of spring water to quench our thirst and two tins of sardines for our dinner, it was a welcome reward for an exhausting day's ride.

I'd woken to catch the first rays of sun fall on the distant snow-capped peaks, casting the scene in delicate shades of pink and mauve. While the track was often covered in loose scree and crossed rocky streams, it was terrain our off-road motorcycles were designed for, but Frédéric and Patrick struggled. At first, I reminded them it would not be long before their clutch plates would be worn beyond adjustment. Fabrice too had tried his best to explain the damage they were doing by riding the clutch, mostly in first gear, but this always turned into a diatribe of abuse in French, with frequent glances and pointing at me. Since the bee-keepers' hut, Frédéric and Patrick now openly blamed me for taking this backroad, and Fabrice too, had sided with them. 'We should never have listened to you,' he'd said before falling into an exhausted sleep last night.

'You all could have said no,' I scoffed, but secretly I was sorry I'd deceived them and caused such undue suffering and loss.

But we'd come too far to turn back. From where we were parked at the top of the valley, the GPS indicated it was just another twenty-three kilometres to Karagay: the village would be over the next range of low hills. We'd crossed into Siberia yesterday, but there was no border saying we were now in Russia. It was the end of our third day riding to Karagay, a ride of 100 kilometres that should have taken us several hours. An hour earlier, we'd stopped at a cattlemen's hut asking the three wild and bearded Russian men who greeted us, if we were in fact, heading the right way.

Their hut was made of rough-cut timber with a precarious lean looking as though it might topple in a strong wind. Three bedraggled horses were tied up nearby.

'Da, da. Karagay,' they said, their rough hands with blackened nails pointing to the track that climbed steeply to traverse a forested hill. Fabrice had asked the men for food, and we'd been invited into the hut, the seven of us squeezing inside. One of the men had retrieved a large glass jar of thick cream from a shelf and placed it on the table of rough-cut timber. Another grabbed a cloth bag that hung on a rusted hook; a few pieces of stale bread rolled out. 'Echt,' he said. The men were Russian; the toughest of mountain men who grazed their cattle on the Altai's lush summer pastures.

When we first reached the plateau from where we watched the storm brew, the track forked, and the GPS gave no indication which one to follow. We chose the one that appeared most used, but within a kilometre, it deteriorated into no more than a goat track. As we rested after crossing a rocky stream, which had been the last straw for Patrick's clutch, three men riding horses approached. Armed with rifles and bags heavy with supplies, it appeared they were Russian marmot hunters. And with the supplies they carried, they could be gone for weeks hunting the elusive marmot that emerges from its burrow to feed on summer grasses.

The large brown rodent weighs up to seven kilos and is killed for its thick, dense fur, highly prized for its warmth when turned into an *ushanka*, that notable Russian fur hat with ear flaps. It is illegal to hunt marmots as the rodents can carry bubonic plague from fleas, but the ban is mostly ignored. Even today, there are occasional reports of infections, which are quickly contained before an outbreak can spread. The disease is transmitted from the bite of an infected flea and from contact with plague-infected tissue and bodily fluids. It is the same bubonic plague, the Black Death, that spread across Eurasia and Europe in the fourteenth century killing as many as 25 million people. It lasted for about ten years and is said to have originated from Kazakhstan's steppe.

When we asked the hunters about the road to Karagay, they pointed back the way we came. Fabrice asked for some food, rubbing his tummy. One of them reached into a bag tied to his saddle and tossed him a lump of smoke-cured pig fat, *salo*. They then moved on, their horses slowly ambling over the rocky trail, the men sharing a joke, no doubt, at the stupidity of four tourists without supplies lost in the Altai Mountains. As I'd watched them ride away, I pulled out my pocket knife and sliced off a strip of fat still attached to the rind covered in bristles. It was absolutely delicious. Hunger got the better of the trio, and they did the same.

'Come on then,' I said as the distant storm clouds blackened and moved towards us from where we watched from the plateau. I started the TT and rode in front and over the edge following the track, which dropped steeply into the valley. It soon disappeared into thick grass—and a bog. A wetter than usual summer meant the valley had not dried out after the spring thaw and it would be impossible to ride any further. As the valley was several kilometres wide, we could not push the bikes across either.

Fabrice stomped the squishy ground: 'Impossible. What we do?'

I looked up at the steep track we'd just descended. 'We go back.'

None of us would be able to ride our loaded motorcycles up it. Not even Fabrice. But it was too late in the day, and we'd have to camp on the squishy wet ground because the storm would soon be upon us. I asked Fabrice if I could sleep in their tent as my two-man tent of doubtful quality would not cope in the rapidly approaching downpour. And I didn't want to deal with a wet sleeping bag as well! I'd bought the tent cheap in Frankfurt as I thought I'd mostly be in hotels on this trip, which turned out the complete opposite: I'd mostly slept in my tent since leaving Europe. Rather than individual tents, the trio carried an excellent quality six-man that was easily big enough for us all. Just in time to escape the downpour that fell in great sheets as the storm passed and the temperature dropped, we were dry and snug inside.

'We are to die,' Patrick moaned as we huddled in our sleeping bags.

'I am so hungry,' Frédéric grumbled. Fabrice offered some pig fat, and his friend reluctantly accepted.

'I'll have some too,' I said and as I chewed a plan began to formulate. 'In the morning we unload the bikes and you three ride back to the cattlemen. Their horses can carry our gear. It is the only way.'

'Yes, you are right,' Fabrice said and despite the rain, the cold, our hunger and Patrick's conviction this was the end, we soon slept. Waking as the sun warmed our tent, we emerged to a clear blue sky.

Once we'd unloaded most of the luggage, leaving just the panniers, the three Frenchmen easily rode up the steep track to the plateau. We were only about five kilometres from the cattlemen's hut, and within an hour or two I assumed, one of the men would soon return with their horses. We'd packed away the tent, so I pulled out my groundsheet and lay on it to bask like a lizard, the morning sun warming my body still chilled from the cold night.

Two hours later, Fabrice appeared at the top of the valley. The cattlemen had trusted him with their horses, and he rode one leading another two.

'They gave you their horses!' I said in disbelief.

'It was no problem. They are good men,' he said, adding with a smile: 'I did not tell them, I never rode a horse before.'

'You ride very well,' and we both laughed at the unlikeliness of it all. As well as motorcycles, I'd also grown up riding horses and relished the chance to take the horses back over the plateau. Fabrice was only too happy to ride my TT.

The horses plodded up the steep slope undeterred by the weight of our luggage; the trio's spare tyres were tied precariously with bungee cords to the saddles. These were hardy, sure-footed, uncomplaining animals, bred with a toughness that came from a bloodline dating back thousands of years: from stock that had survived harsh winters with little to eat. Horses at home in the mountains.

Without its load, the TT easily climbed the steep track, and as Fabrice reached the plateau, he opened the throttle to enjoy the bike's enduro power. Holding tightly to the lead reigns, I kicked my mount, and the three horses quickened their pace eager to head home. As we reached the snow drifts, the blue sky darkened and a strong wind blew across the plateau. The storm appeared out of nowhere and came with a loud clap of thunder. I gripped the reins and pulled the two pack horses close, convinced they would spook, but all were steadfast as the storm moved over us and we were soon heading down the forested track towards the cattlemen's hut.

Oleg, Ivor and Vlad, the three cattlemen who'd so kindly fed us the day before and without question, had given us the use of their horses, gave us their sleeping area too. We'd settled into the mezzanine level of their small hut, while they slept downstairs spreading their bedding around the small table. 'Nyet problema', they said when we protested saying we would sleep in our tents. But we relented when Oleg pointed to his arm and then the narrow ladder.

Oleg had broken his arm when a young horse he'd been breaking bucked him off. This happened just before I rode back to the hut with the three horses and seeing he was in obvious pain, I gave him a strong codeine-based painkiller from my first-aid kit. That was three days ago, and I was down to my last packet. Oleg couldn't praise me enough, and at last, I could repay the kindness we'd been shown by the Kazakhs and the Russians of the Altai Mountains.

On that first day, when I returned on the horses, they advised we stay with them as a truck with supplies was due to arrive in one or two days, maybe three, and it would take Oleg and the four of us, and our bikes, back to Ridder. We could not believe our luck. And we had no choice as it was impossible for Patrick to ride with a worn clutch and retrace our route over the rough terrain.

The truck, we were told, came once a month to resupply the men with food, vodka and tobacco. We learnt all this from the little French they spoke, and the slow process of translation, using my Russian dictionary.

The cattlemen had been perfect hosts, sharing their small hut and meagre supplies. For the past three days we'd lived on a diet of thick cream and stale bread for breakfast and lunch, and pig fat and boiled potatoes for dinner, which they cooked into a delicious stir fry flavoured with spring onions growing wild in the mountain stream that flowed behind the hut. I added wild strawberries for dessert. It took hours to pick enough of the deliciously sweet tiny berries, each no bigger than my little fingernail, for the seven of us to enjoy with a dollop of thick cream.

But I had hours to fill so I enjoyed my time alone on the grassy meadows warmed by the morning sun after a cold night. The forced rest and abundance of nutrients from this wild food, cream and pig fat, energised my body with each day that passed. The impact was so miraculous that it could not be ignored and with this knowledge, I gorged on the wild strawberries, absorbing the vitamin C that would recharge my immune system.

While I quickly fell into the slow rhythm of mountain life and reinforcing my body's armoury, the trio grew more agitated with each passing day as we waited for the truck.

'We will miss the Naadam,' they moaned.

'It is because of you,' Frédéric and Patrick sneered, looking at me.

'We planned for two years for this trip,' Fabrice reminded me.

Yes, they would miss the Naadam festival that commenced on 11 July and celebrated Mongolia's nomadic culture dating back to Mongolia's warlords and Genghis Khan when soldiers tested their skills against each other.

It was the 6 July, and while the men told us, we'd be in Ridder tomorrow afternoon in time to catch the train to Novosibirsk, it was a two-day journey. Before they could leave Novosibirsk for the ride east, they would face another two day wait there for the courier, DHL, to fly new clutch plates for Patrick's bike, from Paris. Opening the engine, Fabrice had found the plates worn beyond adjustment. If the truck arrived today as the men had assured us, it would still be another week before the trio arrived in Ulaanbaatar. If they made good time, they might just catch the last day of the Naadam.

On our fourth day, we all sat outside the hut basking in the warm sunshine, and waited expectantly for the truck, our ears strained for the first sound of its arrival. At last, at about mid-day, an old Russian army truck rumbled up the low rise, its ancient gears crunching as its huge wheels rolled to a halt outside the hut.

The cattlemen exchanged a few words with the Russian driver and his off-sider, and it was agreed they would take us to Ridder, dropping us at the railway station outside the town for US$20 each. We happily agreed on the fee. With the bikes loaded onto the truck, we pooled our camping mattresses and made a soft bed for Oleg. Before leaving, we all had one last toast with Ivor and Vlad, who'd already opened the first bottle of vodka from their month's supply.

The truck took a shorter route back to Ridder, crossing several fast-flowing rivers, its large wheels easily climbing over the boulders. Several hours later we pulled up outside a farmhouse on the outskirts of Ridder and off-loaded Oleg.

'*Bolnitsa?*' I asked Oleg, wondering why we were not taking him to hospital.

'*Nyet deneg*,' he replied. Without money, he would have to rely on Russian home remedies to mend his broken arm. With few doctors and even fewer hospitals, Russians and the peoples of Central Asia alike, had developed very effective home remedies and used herbal medicines to cure a multitude of ailments. When Oleg was carefully off-loaded into the arms of his worried wife, I gave him the last of my painkillers and wished him well with his recovery.

An hour later, the truck was parked at the railway platform. With all day to dwell on the reality of missing the Naadam, Fabrice, Patrick and Frédéric became openly hostile towards me. With our motorcycles unloaded and the truck gone, I feared this anger would turn into a physical onslaught of punches. I had destroyed their once-in-a-lifetime trip to see the Naadam, a journey that had cost thousands of dollars and two years of planning, so their anger was entirely understandable.

'Sorry,' I said, quickly pulling on my helmet and gloves and kicking the TT to life to disappear from their lives.

A year later, I would receive a postcard from Paris signed from all three: 'We want to say to you the best in your life, and we are very sorry for the last day with you. There's no excuses! Please write to us because we miss you, really. You are welcome if you want to go to Paris.' I wrote back saying I was sorry too, and that I'd made it home to Australia and was at university studying journalism. A second postcard arrived late in 1998 wishing me a happy new year and asking me to join them on a second trip to Central Asia and Siberia during the summer of 1999 because their time in the Altai with me was the most exciting adventure of their trip in 1997. I'd always felt bad that my conniving ways had destroyed their dream, but all had been forgiven and as I read their correspondence, I wished that we would, one day, meet in Paris and drink red wind and eat cheese and laugh about our adventures together in the wilds of the Altai Mountains.

20

AT HOME WITH THE RUSSIANS

Siberia

After leaving the Frenchmen, I rode for two hours on smooth tarmac that wound through green hills. There were no villages, and I passed no shops or roadside stalls selling food or even snacks. Still worried about the police seeing me, I didn't dare ride back into Ridder. Here and there farmhouses dotted the lush countryside, and as the sun set over the distant steppe, I looked for refuge: a place to sleep. I hope this time, more than any other, I would be offered food. My last meal was a few morsels of pig fat and stale bread provided by the Russian truck driver, but despite eating little for the past week, I was not weak with hunger. A diet of pig fat, cream, potatoes, spring onions and wild strawberries had more than sustained me.

Up ahead a dirt track wound its way to a farm that sat on a low rise. I turned, and a moment later pulled up outside the timber house, the wood blackened with age. A young couple, hearing the deep rumble of my motorcycle, stood outside to greet me. They wore faded tracksuits, a little like pyjamas, as if they'd cleaned up for the night after a hard day's work and were ready for bed.

'Welcome, you stay,' said the man. The woman smiled warmly. With the sun behind her, the last rays highlighted her shoulder-length auburn hair in a golden halo.

'*Spasiba*,' I said. 'You speak English?'

'A little,' the woman replied. The man nodded. 'I am Heather,' I said.

'Niko and Karina,' the man said, his electric blue eyes shinning brightly from a gentle sun-weathered face framed with a stock of thick blond hair. While they were quite young, perhaps in their early thirties, they both looked weathered from a life lived outdoors.

When I told them my story, and that I was on my way to Mongolia,

I conveniently left out the ordeal in the Altai with the Frenchmen. Would they wonder where they were. Why I was not with them, and more importantly, why we had stupidly ridden through the Altai in the first place? It was better to keep things simple and more readily understandable—and acceptable.

Niko and Karina, I assumed, were European Russians, descendants from the Baltic states like the family the Frenchman and I had stayed with the night before we rode into the Altai. While that first farm with the three Russian families was all that was left of a collective from the Soviet era, Niko and Karina's farm stood on its own, surrounded by lush pasture where a few cattle grazed. I wondered how they came to be there. Were there some ageing parents inside? Had they inherited the farm? Where were their children? It seemed too early for them to be in bed. These were all questions that rushed through my mind, but questions too impolite to ask from an unexpected foreign visitor—a blow-in who came empty-handed. Maybe the lack of children was a sensitive subject and once asked would cause distress.

'Come,' Niko said, and I pushed the bike to the back of their farmhouse. Beside it sat a small square hut with a flat roof made of logs, the gaps sealed with mud.

Karina ushered me inside the house, and I sat down to a table laid with two bowls of soup and a plate of unleavened bread cut into thick chunks. Karina filled a third bowl, ladling the soup from a blackened pot on a wood stove. The thick potato and bacon soup was delicious, and as we ate, the couple asked me questions about my journey. Karina repeated over and over, 'Aren't you afraid? What of your mother? She worry for you?

'You sleep here,' Karina said showing me the small room behind a curtain next to the kitchen when we'd finished eating. 'You change. We have banya.'

'Banya?'

'Yes, bath.' And when I looked at her confused, she laughed. 'In small house outside. It is banya.'

I retrieved the Gearsack and changed into bathers and sarong and with my towel headed outside to the small log hut. The banya was their ingeniously home-made sauna. Inside, coals glowed red, heating a pile of stones, and Niko and Karina sat on a wooden bench, their towels wrapped around them. On the stone floor was a bundle of leafy birch branches tied with string. Niko picked it up, dipped it in a bucket of cold water and began briskly lashing Karina's back.

'It is *venik*. Good for blood. *Stimulirovat* blood,' Niko said handing me the *venik*.

The sauna and the lashing with the birch leaves were invigorating, but why use the fresh birch leaves? Why not use something more permanent like a few strips of leather tied to a stick? I later read that it was not just the lashing to stimulate the skin and blood, but the release of essential wood oils from the birch. The scientific name for these are phytoncides: substances emitted by plants to help protect themselves against attack by harmful insects, germs and decomposition. Exposure to phytoncides increases our immune cells; scientific studies have confirmed this. Even time spent in a forest has the same impact as lashing yourself with a *venik*.

As I sat back to relax into the heat, I realised my last shower was in Almaty, over a week ago. While staying with the mountain men, to ensure my privacy, I'd walk deep into the forest, following the icy stream that ran behind their hut to bath naked. Afterwards, I'd stand in the filtered sunlight to dry. It was a surreal, timeless moment and I'd breathe in the fresh, pure air mixed with the aroma of forest, enjoying the gentle song of birds that had quickly resumed their chatter after realising I was not a threat. In Japan, such walks in the forest are positively encouraged to improve health, and many people regularly engage in *shinrinyoko*, or forest bathing. Why didn't the west encourage this too? Why weren't we all lashing ourselves with a *venik* in a banya like the Russians do, I wondered.

'For you,' Niko said after he'd ladled warm water from a drum into a bucket. Next to it was a large bowl and bar of soap. Niko and Karina then left the room so I could wash. I later found out that the *banya* dates back centuries and is a tradition as old as Russia itself. Every family, no matter how poor, either has their own *banya* or go to a communal *banya*. As well as the social benefits of time spent together, the heat stimulates the immune system, relaxes the muscles and reduces stress while a good lashing increases blow flow and the phytoncides boosts T-cells, the immune cells we need to fight infection.

I don't know if any of this made a difference on a cellular level, but after I'd enjoyed several cycles of the *banya* ritual with Niko and Karina, I felt an intense sense of vigour as though every one of my thirty-seven trillion cells (the approximate amount scientists have calculated), were vibrating in some kind of harmonious splendour.

Farm life started early, and after breakfast of potato and bacon stew, I thanked Niko and Karina and headed towards Siberia, worried how I would be received: a tourist with an expired Russian visa. I followed a narrow strip of tarmac towards the Russian border and soon left the rolling green hills behind as the road opened to the vastness of the steppe. Unable to ride over the Altai Mountains, I was still determined to cross into Mongolia where its border met Russia and Kazakhstan in the far eastern reaches of the Altai.

An hour later, I approached a small timber guardhouse that stood solitary on the grassy plains. Unbelievably, the boom gate was up and not an immigration official in sight. I slowly rumbled past just in case a guard suddenly appeared, yelling 'stop!' Other than a rusted sign, there was nothing to indicate that this was, in fact, the border between two countries: one a superpower, the other the size of Europe. I could not believe my luck. 'Hello Russia,' I shouted and opened the throttle before anyone was the wiser.

It was 400 kilometres to the industrial city of Barnaul and regional centre of Siberia's Altai district. As I headed east, back towards the Altai Mountains, the landscape changed from open brown steppe to vast cultivated paddocks of cereal crops. Passing through a mostly deserted town, once the centre of some kind of factory, I changed US dollars for rubles at a petrol station, a shack with a bowser beside the road, and ate lunch at the cafeteria next door. It once provided hundreds of meals for Soviet workers. Now I, a truck driver, his rig parked outside, and an old couple were its only customers. The two *babushkas* in floral headscarves tied tightly under their rounded chins served me in silence, slopping the food—various incarnations of potato and a cabbage and beetroot dish—into thick white china bowls. They spoke no English and stared at me with expressionless eyes when I asked how much. I fished out some rubles from the wad I'd stuffed into my jacket pocket, handing over what amounted to about fifty cents.

As I ate alone at a formica table, I endured suspicious stares from the Russians. No one approached me, and I got the feeling that even though it had been six years since the end of the Soviet Union, nothing had really changed in these remote towns and villages. They had probably never seen a foreigner travelling independently by whatever means, let alone a single woman on a motorcycle. Who was I? What was I doing there? But more importantly, did I have permission and did the authorities know? I carried my tray and empty bowls back to the counter, thanked the women and left.

As I neared Barnaul, the endless crops gave way to forested hills, and I stopped to rest where two small children aged about seven were selling wild strawberries, their mother bent over the family's potato crop, which surrounded their quaint timber cottage.

Early afternoon, I reached its outskirts and pulled up next to a patch of birch forest to pee, my last opportunity before tackling a major city of half a million people at rush hour. I'd just returned to my bike when a police car approached and screeched to a halt. The two young officers unfolded themselves from the small car and stood before me. '*Passeport,*' one demanded. I reached into my jacket pocket.

'You follow,' the other boomed and I obeyed. It appeared the police had been alerted about me. I had raised the suspicions of so many Russians since I crossed from Kazakhstan that morning and one or more of them had phoned the police. Or the official at the border had seen me cross illegally, although I had not seen him.

The police car wove slowly through the wide streets lined with dull blockish Soviet buildings painted in various shades of grey with touches of beige and pastel pink. It eventually stopped outside the police station, an imposing building in the city centre. I followed through the gates and past the armed security guards. The two officers, one on either side, escorted me up the wide steps and down a long corridor to a large room, bare except for a wood desk, a chair behind it and a single chair in the middle. A naked light bulb hung from the high ceiling. I was told to sit. The two officers left and locked the door.

As I looked around the stark room with bars on the windows, I knew my run of good luck had ended. I was in Russia illegally. How many days, weeks or months would I linger in a Russian prison before being deported? What fine would be demanded? This was the end.

The reality of my situation dawned on me, and I kept thinking of the TT in a way one feels about the welfare of a beloved pet. He would be taken from me, and I was powerless to stop it. As I waited for what seemed like an hour, my attention turned to the room. It could have been a scene from a spy movie: James Bond perhaps. It was quite surreal. So those scenes depicting American spies being interrogated by the KGB, a single light bulb glaring into their eyes, are actually based on fact, I thought.

A key rattled in the door and three policemen filed in. One sat at the desk, while the others stood to attention, one either side. The man at the desk slowly flicked through my passport studying the multitude of visas. The page turning stopped, and he looked up with steely grey eyes. 'Russia visa expire 15 June. No entry stamp for Russia. You criminal.'

'I'm sorry,' I offered. 'I am going to Mongolia.'

'Three weeks you in Russia as criminal.' He leaned forward, his eyes narrowed. 'When you come here. Where you enter Russia?

'Today,' I said, my voice shaking. It was 10 July. 'From Kazakhstan. On the road from Shemonaikha. There was no border crossing. Just a boom gate. It was up, so I thought Russia and Kazakhstan were the same.' I hoped this would explain everything. 'I have a visa for Mongolia,' I added.

'We send you to Moscow,' he shot back, ignoring my explanation as totally irrelevant. 'You will be deported to Australia. You pay thousands of dollar.' And with that, he stood up, and the three men filed out locking the door behind them.

This latest development came as a shattering blow. I'd not only lose my beloved motorcycle that had been with me through so many adventures, that had been my trusty steed on our crusade, but I'd also lose my purpose. After my diagnosis, I'd gone back on the road because that was where things always worked out for me. It was on the road in Africa, and it was now turning out, on the Silk Road too, that I'd felt a guiding force. I feared once I stopped moving, once I arrived home, the magic would be gone. Reality would take over, and I would have nothing but death. I would have to face my parents, and as they watched me die, I would have to endure what I perceived, to be their shame.

Dejected by the inevitable, I let my body slump in the chair. There was no hope; no fight left in me; no chance of deviously scheming my way out of this one. With the Russians, I had met my match.

After what seemed like ages, an hour perhaps, the three officers returned. Two stood at the door, and the one who spoke earlier came towards me. I stood up, thinking I was to be escorted to a prison cell before being sent to Moscow.

'You go back to Kazakhstan,' he said, handing me my passport. 'They follow you out of Barnaul.' He cast a glance towards to the two officers, who stood expressionless. 'You keep going. You not come back,' he said.

'Yes,' was all I managed to say. I could only assume that sending me to Moscow would cause undue attention from the upper echelons of Russia's police: 'Just what were they doing in the provinces? Can't they control their borders?' It would highlight their incompetence purely through the fact that a tourist was travelling 'willy nilly' around Russia without a visa and had easily slipped through an unmanned border post. Or maybe they let me go because it was just easier. They couldn't be bothered with the paperwork. Let the Kazakhs deal with me instead.

The two officers followed behind as I rode out of Barnaul

towards Kazakhstan. I kept checking my mirror, but after about twenty kilometres they stopped and turned. I rode on for another five kilometres, and when I came to a deserted stretch of road, I pulled up, my hands shaking as I undid my helmet. I sat down on the grassy verge to assess my next move. Almost instantly, I decided I would not be going back to Kazakhstan, I'd ride on to Mongolia as planned.

The thought of Mongolia, its open plains, wild and untamed, and its nomadic people living as one with the land, intrigued me. I grabbed my map, looking for possible backroads around Barnaul. I estimated it was about 5.00 p.m. and I would have three, maybe four, hours of daylight. I could not ride south-east around the city as I'd have to cross the mighty Ob River, the seventh largest in the world, and its multitude of tributaries that zigzagged along its length as it flowed past Barnaul to the Arctic Ocean. There were only two bridges and both crossed at the city's heart. To avoid the main arterial roads, I'd need to stay on the back streets, riding as close to the river as possible before quickly sneaking across the first bridge. My only hope was the police were on a shift change and few, if any, would be on patrol. My guess, after having put the fear of God into me was they'd be sure I was on full throttle heading back to Kazakhstan.

I was about 180 kilometres east of Barnaul heading towards Mongolia and riding through birch forest and past villages of cottage-style timber houses, the delicately carved window frames painted sky blue. I opened the throttle and relished my freedom. Relished being back on the open road; being alone again. With the odds stacked against me, I was also filled with a joyous sense of excitement that I had escaped detection by the Russian police. I opened the throttle and rode on.

Just as light was rapidly fading from the cloudless sky, I passed a double story house made of the same blackened wood common in the Altai. A metal sign hung from a rusted pole: 'Welcome to Altai'. So unexpected were the English words that I screeched to a halt. A sign in English surely indicated the inhabitants spoke English. Maybe it was some kind of hotel, a homestay perhaps. It was nearly dark, and

I needed a place to stay.

'Hello,' I called as a knocked on the door. No answer, so I walked to the back of the house and emerged into a vast garden filled with rows of vegetables, flowers, herbs and an enormous patch of potato plants. The garden backed on to the fast flowing Katun River that flowed from the Altai Mountains to join the mighty Ob. Here the river was wide and shallow as it gushed over the rocky river bed.

'Hello,' I called again. Next to the house was a small log hut the same as the one at Niko and Karina's farm. The residents were in the *banya*. I knocked on the door, and it swung open. A dark-haired man greeted me. He had a towel wrapped around his waist. A pretty young woman with dark auburn hair stood behind him.

'I see your sign,' I said. 'Is this a hotel?' I asked knowing full well it wasn't.

'Ah, welcome to Altai. Yes, you very welcome. Stay with us. One moment,' he said a broad smile breaking across his handsome face. He closed the door, and a moment later they both emerged in loose tracksuit pants and T-shirts.

'I am Varso. My wife is Diana,' he said. 'How you travel here?' he asked, confused.

'Motorcycle,' I said, and I followed them to the front of the house. 'I have travelled from Australia,' I added as they studied the map on the TT's side-cover.

'All the way to Altai. This is very good.' He stood up. 'Come bring your *mototsikl*. We have *banya*, then we eat.'

I'm sure when they erected the sign they never thought it would bring in a tourist on a motorcycle.

I stayed two days with Varso and Diana. Varso could speak, read and write English having studied it as his second language since high school, but Diana knew just a few words. They'd met at university during Soviet times where they both studied agricultural science. They were lucky enough to have jobs in their field and worked for a nearby agricultural research centre. Varso erected the sign, he told me, because the Altai Mountains region had so much to offer, but as yet, was undiscovered by tourists, even Russians. 'You are the first foreign tourist we meet,' he told me. They showered me with hospitality and the most delicious food cooked from their garden. My favourite dish was potato fried with spring onions, tarragon and a mild, sweet garlic called elephant garlic.

Varso spoke excitedly about life in Russia, about its achievements and its future, always translating for Diana, whom he visibly adored. They continually cast loving glances towards each other and witnessing this pure love, I found myself smiling as I basked in the aura of happiness they generated. I thought of my own parents, and this was the same love they shared, but as a child, I'd never noticed it, and later as a young woman, I'd been too busy with my own life. As I sat with them at their kitchen table, the faint light of an electric bulb casting an ethereal glow, I felt no envy, regret, sadness or anger that the love I witnessed would never happen for me. Instead, I felt a sense of peace knowing that true love was real. For a brief moment, I also had an overwhelming sense of knowing that everything would be alright. It was as though something had reached down to embrace me, to reassure me that life was eternal and whatever happened didn't matter.

The next morning, as I was about to leave, Varso gave me a folded sheet of paper.

'It is a poem by Musa Jalil. He is one of Russia's greatest poets. He was a revolutionary. He fought for communist Russia to make us all equal. I translate this poem into English. Musa's words will help you on your journey.'

I opened the folded sheet and read the words out loud:

To My Soul
By Musa Jalil
How is it my soul, you have found the earth displeasing?
Why is it with such passion for the sky you are yearning?
Do you think the heavens hold so many wonders?
All that is false and shallow from your conscience under!
Do you think on seeing a starry light in heaven,
That the moon has secrets full of purest wisdom?

It is from afar the sun appears unruffled,
Only from a distance that it looks a flower.
On this earth or in the heaven's superstructure
Matter's like and one, where you seek in nature.
So back to earth, my soul, return with the assurance,
That both here and there all things are like in essence!
From the sky descend, the earth's a surer resident,
Only on the earth you will find what is of substance,
Seek and you shall find. Use your determination.
Reinforce your soul. Then act on your ambition.

*****

It was nearly 500 kilometres to Tashanta and the border crossing between Russia and Mongolia. I'd started early before Varso and Diana left for work as I wanted to reach the township and cross into Mongolia first thing tomorrow morning. This was the best part of the Chuysky Trakt, the M52 highway, which I'd been riding on since leaving Barnaul. The smooth tarmac cut through the Altai Mountains and was listed as one of the world's top ten most scenic road trips. The Chuysky Trakt was the northern branch of the Silk Road and traders since ancient times had passed through here to reach China. The Mongol armies also used the Chuysky Trakt as one of their routes to Central Asia, but its harrowing passes could only be crossed with horses. It was not widened until gulag prisoners constructed the highway in the 1930s.

The scenery was stunning. Framed with a backdrop of snow-capped peaks, the road cut through grassy meadows dotted with sheep and goats grazing under the watchful eye of a shepherd and his dog. A pale turquoise river bubbled frothy over rocks beside me. I passed through quaint log cabin villages and at mid-day stopped in one to refuel from a rusted bowser. I bought a small loaf of unleavened bread and jar of pickled beetroot from the shop next door. It was all that sat on the bare shelves of the store run by an elderly woman who stared at me as if in a state of complete bewilderment.

'*Pitaniye?*' I asked hoping she'd understand my pronunciation for the Russian word for 'food'. Surely, she sold more food than these two items.

'*Nyet,*' she replied.

Late afternoon, I reached the Chuya steppe. Hemmed by a range of distant snow-capped mountains, these high-altitude grasslands were lush from summer rains. Leaving the tarmac, I turned the TT and headed toward a yurt, called a *ger* this close to Mongolia. It was about a kilometre from the road next to a tree-lined stream. Other than the desert in Turkmenistan where there was no chance of anyone finding me, I never risked camping alone, and this *ger* would offer protection. It would be home to a family, and in their company, I would feel safe.

As I approached, I could see two Ural motorcycles with side-cars. Throughout Central Asia, these motorcycles are the equivalent of the family car. Hearing my approach, several children emerged from the *ger* to watch me. A middle-aged woman joined them, followed by another woman, bandy-legged and bent over with advanced age. A log cabin had been built beside the *ger*, which was covered in sheets of light brown felt and had a look of permanency, unlike the yurts in Kyrgyzstan. Even so, just like those yurts, this too could easily be dismantled and moved by yak, or in modern times by vehicle, to their winter home: a farm on the outskirts of a township. I couldn't see any animals, but horse and sheep droppings littered the ground and I assumed the men were out grazing the livestock on better pastures as the grass here, for as far as I could see, was cropped short as if mowed like a lawn.

A boy aged about ten greeted me with a smile from a smooth round brown face, the skin not yet weathered by the sun.

'Welcome,' he said.

'You speak English?' I asked, and he shook his head.

I leaned to show him the map on the side-cover, pointing to Australia. I hoped it would answer their questioning elongated dark eyes. He moved closer, and there was much discussion, sighs and shaking of heads between him, the two women and the gaggle of children that stood around them.

'I am going to Mongolia,' I said, raising my chin in the general direction of the border. 'Tashanta.'

'Eat,' the boy said, and I followed him into the *ger* through a little wooden door, the two women and children trailing behind.

The boy indicated I sit on an old spring bed against a wall and the younger woman offered a small bowl of tea. As I sipped the salty milk tea, cradling the bowl in my hands, I took in the secret world of nomadic life. The *ger* was bathed in a gentle light cast by a lantern that hung from the ceiling. Other than a few western items, a chest of drawers, a few plastic bowls and metal pots and pans, it was a way of life unchanged since ancient times. A wooden lattice held up the walls, and the ceiling was like the spokes of a wheel, a multitude of thin wood poles angled towards a small opening at the roof's apex where a metal chimney carried away the smoke from the stove, a square metal firebox in the centre of the *ger*. A blackened pot bubbled on top of it. Traditional hand-woven carpets covered the floor and tapestries in bold reds hung on the walls which were lined with thick sheets of felt made from sheep wool. A sheet of felt covered the wooden door so that cold and wind could not penetrate. The elderly woman sat near the entrance and with a stick, stirred *airag*, fermented mare's milk, in a plastic drum. She would stir for a few minutes, leave it to busy herself at a bench preparing some kind of meal, then return to the milk to stir again. I'd tried the slightly fizzy, slightly sour and mildly alcoholic milk on several occasions offered outside yurts in Kyrgyzstan, where it is called *kumis*.

The younger woman lifted the lid on a pot on the stove and ladled a lumpy brown broth into a bowl, handing it to me along with a spoon. She did the same for the elderly woman who sat on a spring bed opposite and then served the five children who sat cross-legged around the fire. I toyed with the broth, but it didn't take me long to figure out what it was—a concoction of grisly mutton and offal: lumps of organs, brains, kidneys, liver and probably a few testicles as well. The small rounded pieces, I suspected, were from the recent de-nutting of the young goats and sheep from the family's herd.

The family watched, waiting for me to start eating and I scooped up a small spoonful and gently chewed the lumps, which were quite tasty; the flavours of kidney mingled with mutton. The family smiled and finished their bowls. The younger woman collected the bowls and placed these on a wooden bench against the wall. The elderly woman moved the broth aside and put a pot of water on the stove. She then returned with a plate of dumplings and once the water was boiling, plopped these into the pot. I figured the bowl of offal was the entrée; the dumplings the main course. Filled with finely chopped mutton and garlic, these were absolutely delicious.

With the meal finished, I retrieved my sleeping bag, map and photo album and gave this to the children. They pored over each photo of my parents, their banana farm in lush tropical far north Queensland, kangaroos, koalas and wombats. There was much discussion about a photo of me on a chestnut horse named Chiquita, on my parent's farm. The mare was stocky and robust like the steppe horses. Without language, the photos answered many of their questions. Who was I? Where did I come from? Questions about my family and life in Australia. While Australians are a nation of mostly coastal urban dwellers living on the fringe of dry woodland and a vast inland desert, there's a whole bunch of people in Africa and Central Asia who believe this land down under is an iridescent green wonderland where we eat an abundance of bananas and are surrounded by strange native animals. At least for this family they could see, just like the Mongols, we also ride horses and motorcycles. I spread my map on the carpeted floor to show where I'd been in Central Asia and where I planned to go.

'Road good?' I asked, pointing to the road from Tashanta to Ulaanbaatar, a thick red line on my map indicating it was, at best tarmac, and at worst corrugated dirt. But whatever it was, my map said it was the main highway to the capital, a distance of 1800 kilometres, and as such should be reasonably passable.

'Da. Gruzovaya mashina,' the boy said.

The words translated to 'large truck' and if such trucks used this road, then it would be passable for my motorcycle. Later the younger woman ushered the children and teenage boy out of the *ger* to the log cabin next door where they'd sleep. The old woman curled up on the bed opposite, and I retrieved my sleeping bag to sleep on the bed where I sat.

After a breakfast of salty milk tea and dumplings, I thanked the family and in the brisk morning air, headed towards Tashanta to cross into Mongolia. I reached the border post two hours later and handed my passport to the Russian soldier on duty. He and his comrade looked with intense interest at my passport, at me and at my motorcycle. They were armed with AK47s and wore battle fatigues over a blue and white striped T-shirt.

'*Nyet* cross. Only for Russian and Mongolian. *Nyet* foreigner,' said the young soldier with short cropped blonde hair and stern, pale blue eyes.

'Visa,' I said pointing to the Mongolian visa in my passport.

'*Nyet*,' he shouted and raised his weapon indicating this rule was not negotiable.

The Mongolian border was a mere 200 metres away, and I knew the Mongol officials would welcome me into their country. I just had to get past the Russians. Opposite the soldiers' guard post was an old truck parked next to a timber shack that operated as a roadside store. A dozen or so Mongolian men and women with bags overstuffed with their possessions sat in the back of the truck under the tarpaulin cover stretched over a metal frame. I parked the TT behind it and asked a man where they were going.

'Ulaanbaatar,' he called down to me.

'The Russians won't let me through,' I called back.

'Mongolia let you. No problem. You follow us. Stay close beside truck. Russians are stupid. They inside drinking vodka. No problem,' he said and the others nodded, some laughing when he'd translated. 'Come. We go.'

As the driver returned, I quickly pulled on my helmet just as he started the truck's engine, crunching its old gears. As it lurched forward, I slowly rode beside it making sure its large wheels hid me from the Russians on the other side. I didn't dare look in my mirror, but as the truck approached the Mongolian border post, a man suddenly stood in front of it waving frantically. I looked behind, and the two soldiers had their AK-47s pointed at me. My plot was foiled, and I had no choice but to turn around.

'Bullets in guns. You *nyet* stop. We shoot you. You dead,' the soldier bellowed when I pulled up beside him a moment later. For my sake, I expect he had overemphasized this possible outcome to ensure I understood the seriousness of what I'd just attempted to do. I fully expected I'd now be arrested and sent hand-cuffed back to Barnaul, but he and his comrade retreated to their hut, and I was left to plot my next move.

I parked the TT next to the small store and headed inside. A middle-aged Kazakh man with a paunch stood behind a wood counter. On the shelves behind him were rows of vodka bottles, cigarettes, soft drink, chocolate bars and not much else. A television sat on a high shelf. A video played hard-core porn. It was so unexpected, I stared at it for several moments, the storekeeper grinned and his hand disappeared below the counter.

'Russians catch you,' he said then leaned forward. 'Easy to cross border on *mototsikl*. Fence finish not far,' and tilted his head to the side to indicate the fence ended a few hundred metres or so to the south. 'Easy, you ride around. Tonight, when Russians go, I show you. No problem for you on *mototsikl*.'

Word had travelled fast about my attempt to jump the border. I looked up at the television and then at the man, his hand still below the counter.

'I don't think so,' I said.

After buying a Coke and Snickers bar, I left the store to eat my treats outside. I looked along the two high fences topped with razor wire that ran parallel to each other and disappeared over a yellow wasteland of dry, undulating steppe. I had no idea what to do, and this dejection weighed heavily. I physically slumped and with this came a feeling of severe tiredness. It may have been the shock of nearly being shot by the Russians; not even the sugar hit from the soft drink and chocolate lifted my spirits. Added to this latest blow, the TT's clutch plates needed adjusting. The ride to the *ger* then back to the main road that morning had finished it off, and the plates were slipping badly. Between the workshop manual and having watched Peter, the motorcycle traveller from New Zealand I'd met in Nigeria, adjust the plates, I knew what to do. But even so, I was delaying the inevitable until absolutely necessary. I'd felt so confident that I'd easily cross into Mongolia where I'd get a visa for China and head down to South East Asia. But here I was stuck in Russia with no legitimate visa; it had expired nearly a month ago. If I rode back through Barnaul and the police caught me, I would not get a second chance. If I slipped by without detection, how would I cross into Kazakhstan?

I opened my map, hoping it would reveal a secret road that would carry me out of Russia. But there was no option other than going back through Barnaul into Kazakhstan. I had no choice but to return to Almaty. It was a 2000-kilometre ride on already worn tyres and there was no chance of buying new ones. The thought of riding back over territory I'd already covered filled me with dread, especially the ride over the flat plains of the northern Kazakh steppe.

Over the past few days, the deep tiredness had gotten worse. The previous day, as I rode through some of the world's most spectacular scenery, I'd had a microsleep and only woke up as the front wheel touched the grassy verge. After that, every time I started yawning, I'd stop and ride off the road, finding somewhere to lie down next to the TT and falling into a deep sleep. On one occasion, I woke just as two men approached. Something had caused me to wake up and bleary-eyed, I got back on the bike and left before they reached me. I could not face such a long ride back to Almaty. A lift on a truck was my best and safest option.

Once in Almaty, I would have several choices: cross into China from Kyrgyzstan at the Torugart Pass and ride to Kashgar through Tibet to Nepal; cross into China from Kazakhstan riding to Urumqi; or fly myself and the TT to Pakistan. Travelling through China depended on getting a Chinese visa with permission to travel with my motorcycle. Permission, I'd been warned, was highly unlikely. The Torugart Pass was my preferred route and had been my plan before meeting the Frenchmen. I remembered again, the British traveller I met at the Orient Hostel in Istanbul who'd travelled illegally for months in Tibet. To avoid detection by the Chinese officials, he'd blended in with the locals; then hid in the back of a truck to cross into Central Asia. He'd given me a white scarf, ripped and worn from its miles of travel. It was an 'offering scarf' called a *khata* and had been given to him by a monk as a blessing for his journey, and he'd given it to me. 'I'll take it back to Tibet,' I'd promised. I'd tied the scarf to the bike's handlebars so the prayers of goodwill bestowed on it could fly free in the wind and bring me even more good luck. I needed it now more than ever, and as I ran my fingers over the scarf untangling the silky threads, a plan began to formulate.

As I lingered at the border, the occasional Russian truck carrying a shipping container lumbered past. Would one give me a lift? This latest plan was the most feasible and I could travel undetected through Barnaul and save some of the tread on my worn rear tyre. After that, I could risk slipping back into Kazakhstan at that apparently unmanned border I'd crossed nearly a week earlier. I may even get a lift in a truck all the way to Almaty. I coiled the scarf around my fingers and prayed to God.

'Tourist,' I heard a voice behind me and turned to see the Russian soldier who'd been so stern with me before. 'Go to Kosh-Agach. Police chief give you permission to cross,' he said. 'Long journey on *mototsikl*,' he added.

'*Spasiba. Spasiba*,' I said and could have hugged him. With this latest information, a rush of new-found energy surged through me. I may just be able to cross into Mongolia after all. Other than the Russian border post, which amounted to a one-room cement block structure and the roadside store with the porn-addicted shopkeeper, there was not much else in Tashanta. I'd passed through Kosh-Agach, fifty kilometres back. It was my only chance of somewhere to stay.

Kosh-Agach was a desolate frontier town of small pitched-roofed fibro houses entangled by power lines hanging from poles leaning at odd angles. The town was built on a barren depression where not a blade of grass could survive, and I wondered why it existed there at all. But in its desolation under an eternally blue sky with snow-capped mountains rising in the distance, it was also eerily beautiful.

After asking a man wandering a dusty street for directions to the *politsiya*, I pulled up outside a white-painted cement building that still displayed the hammer and sickle emblem of the Soviet Union. A police officer, hearing my approach, leaned on the open doorway and a moment later I was seated inside. Resplendent in a grey uniform with gold buttons and red-trimmed epaulettes, he sat behind an enormous wooden desk, his black jackboots resting on it as he flicked through the pages of my passport. I'd been in such a rush to speak with him that I'd forgotten about my expired Russian visa.

'Visa expire,' he said looking up from my passport waiting for my response. This far from Moscow it appeared that news of the dissolution of the Soviet Union had not yet made it. This man was pure KGB, and he ruled this backwater of the Altai.

'I have a Mongolian visa. I'd like to cross the border. I will go to Ulaanbaatar,' I offered. 'I need your permission to cross at Tashanta.'

'Is only for Russians and Mongolians. I cannot give permission. You must get a letter from Altai governor in Gorno Altaysk. If he gives permission, you cross,' he said and handed back my passport with no further mention of my expired Russian visa. I can only assume that detaining me was more trouble than it was worth and would focus undue attention on his kingdom, which he preferred to rule without interference from Moscow.

It was late afternoon, and I need to find a place for the night. There were no hotels in these parts, so my only chance was a spontaneous offer of hospitality. While I'd always tried to travel with something for the table of my hosts, I'd been so preoccupied with getting out of Russia that I hadn't done this for days. I could have easily bought a few extra Snickers bars, and it would be a welcome treat for households always filled with numerous children. The only thing I had to offer was my photo album and tales of my travels when someone could speak English.

I rode back towards the main road and was forced to pull up outside a row of identical fibro houses with pitched iron roofs, the walls painted bright blue. The clutch had finally reached the end of its wear, and under revs, the bike barely moved. I had no choice but to perform 'surgery' right there where I'd stopped. I could only assume that the houses opposite, and the entire town, in fact, was built by the Soviets to house workers for a nearby mine. I'd read the area was rich in gold, which would explain the former-KGB officer's reluctance to draw attention to himself by detaining me as an illegal.

I retrieved my tools and workshop manual and laid the bike on its side. By now a group of children aged from toddler to teen had gathered to watch. One of the older children, a girl aged about twelve with an angelic face, elongated eyes and the long sleek black hair of her Kazakh heritage, could speak a little English and bombarded me with questions, translating my responses to the others. 'Where you come from? What you do here? Where you go? What is your name? Where is your husband? Do you have children? Is there a problem with *mototsikl*? Do you need a mechanic? My uncle is a mechanic!' As I deciphered the workshop manual's instructions, I answered as best I could. Tackling anything mechanical had always frightened me because it just looked too technical. And what if I made a mistake? I didn't want to fuck it up, causing more damage than was already there. But that was until circumstance forced me to do it; in Africa, I had to service and repair the TT. Now I was an old hand, but opening up an engine without the watchful eye of someone who knew what they were doing, was by far the biggest mechanical task I'd yet faced. With the manual and recalling what Peter had done in Nigeria, I dived in and I did it. I was about to replace the engine cover when Aisha, the girl who'd bombarded me with questions, began tugging at my shirt.

'Come. Quick. Not stay here. *Mostiques, mostiques*,' she repeated frantically.

'I can't leave the engine open,' I said and seeing I would not budge, the children dashed into the nearby house as if an apocalypse was about to unfold.

I heard the buzzing first. It was like a squadron of propeller-driven planes straight out of a World War II movie. I looked up, and a black cloud of mosquitos swarmed towards me. As the first enormous blood-suckers landed, each about a centimetre long, boring their needle-sharp proboscises into my soft exposed skin, I quickly pulled on my jacket and helmet, closing the visor and tucking my scarf around my neck. I couldn't put on my gloves as I needed bare hands to fit and tighten the bolts on the engine. The pain was almost unbearable as they feasted without opposition. In a matter of seconds, my hands were a mass of red welts, but once the engine covering was fixed, I dashed towards the house. Aisha quickly opened the door.

'*Mostiques* very bad,' she said, shaking her head as she held my swollen hands.

'Does this happen every day?' I asked.

'Only in summer. At end of the day. *Mostiques* gone soon.'

We waited about an hour then the children all filed out, following me back to my motorcycle where I packed away my tools and asked Aisha if the children could help me lift it. They eagerly agreed.

'Come you stay with us. Very welcome,' Aisha said and I pushed the TT to a flat-roofed one-room white-washed cement block hut at the back of the fibro cottage painted bright blue. The cottage looked unlived in. As we walked past it I asked, 'Don't you live in the house?

'Sometimes in the summer when it is very hot. In winter, too cold. Too big to keep warm.'

Aisha ushered me inside the squat little hut, and I met her mother, a middle-aged petite woman, and her ageing grandmother. Both Kazakh women smiled their welcome, and when Aisha told them she'd invited me to stay, they both nodded. It appeared the tiny room was home for the two women and three children; Aisha, her younger sister and toddler brother. He sat on a single bed, used as a couch, staring at me wide-eyed. I asked about her father, and Aisha told me he and her uncles were out on the steppe grazing their animals for the summer. Tapestries hung on the white-washed walls.

A table, covered in floral vinyl, was in the centre of the room with several chairs. Against one wall was a wood cabinet with pots, pans and plates. Against another was a dung-fired stove. The grandmother opened the door and threw in a dried cow pat. There were two double beds; I expected, one was for the adults and one was for the children. I sat at the table and was offered a small bowl of milky salted tea. Later, we ate a meal of soft white cheese, stale bread with rancid butter and a fragrant potato and herb soup. After the meal, I brought out my photo album and map, and Aisha translated my tales of adventure.

'Tomorrow, I will go to Gorno Altaysk to ask the Altai governor permission to cross into Mongolia. If I can't get permission, I hope to get a lift on a truck to Barnaul,' I said, speaking my plans out loud.

'Uncle Sergei is a truck driver. He drives from Mongolia to Barnaul. He gives me clothes,' Aisha said standing proudly to show off her pretty T-shirt and blue jeans. She then exchanged a few words with her mother and beaming a smile said, 'He stops here tomorrow.'

Just as Aisha promised, the next morning Uncle Sergei arrived bearing gifts. I was about to leave when she came running to tell me the good news. A convoy of six ageing trucks each carrying shipping containers were parked on the dusty street. The drivers climbed out, and a Kazakh man picked up Aisha, swinging her in the air. None of the men spoke English, and Aisha asked if they'd give me a lift to Barnaul. Except Sergei, with his brown skin and smiling dark eyes framed by thick black-grey hair, all the men were Russian.

'What about Gorno Altaysk. The Altai governor?' I asked.

'Is no problem. They stop for you, and if you get the letter, you come back.' It seemed she was not overly confident that permission would be granted.

While Uncle Sergei had tea and snacks with the family, the other men loaded my motorcycle into the empty shipping container on his truck. I was curious about what they transported, and Aisha later told me they'd carried packaged food, medicines and engine parts. These would have been sold to retailers in regional towns on the road to

Ulaanbaatar. With nothing of value to bring back from Mongolia, the containers were empty. In years to come, the route they'd travelled would become the north-western arm of the new Silk Road as China invested billions in its *One Road, One Belt* project in its bid to build a network of superhighways opening up markets for its goods across Central Asia, the Middle East, India, Russia and Europe.

Mid-afternoon, we arrived in Gorno Altaysk, and Uncle Sergei parked outside a large grey Soviet-era building that housed the governor's office.

'Governor in Moscow,' said the stern Russian woman behind the counter.

'When will he return?' I asked.

'Maybe three weeks. Maybe end of summer. He stays at *dacha*,' she replied with disinterest. A *dacha* was a Russian summer house, and yes, he could be there all summer.

Uncle Sergei had taken this detour for me, while the other five trucks carried on to Barnaul. We would catch them up in a few hours when they stopped for dinner by the side of the road. We'd had lunch next to a mountain stream, the men unravelling a meal of meat on bones from a cloth-covered metal bowl. One of the men had peeled several bulbs of Russian garlic to go with it. Dinner, I expected would be the same. As a single woman alone with the six men, I never once felt, in any way, vulnerable in their company. In fact, I felt protected as though they were my older brothers and I, their little sister. When I returned to the truck, Sergei looked at me expectantly.

'*Nyet*,' I said. Governor in Moscow. I go with you to Barnaul.' I would not be going to Mongolia.

With Sergei's very limited English and my Russian dictionary, I learnt that the men worked for a trucking company based in Barnaul and that their trucks also went to Almaty. Yes, it would be no problem to get a lift.

As we drove toward Barnaul on the stunning Chuyska Highway framed against a backdrop of snow-capped mountains, I tried not to worry about how my world was falling apart. Even though Mongolia was closed to me, my prayers for a truck had been answered, but I failed to appreciate this fact. Instead, a sense of impending doom gripped me. I could not shake the fatigue that had settled into my bones; I could not shake the feeling that I was trapped in Central Asia and all borders were closed to me.

21

THE WARRIOR WITHIN

Kazakhstan

A week after the lift with Uncle Sergei I was comfortably delivered, by another truck, back to Almaty, Kazakhstan's capital. This much-welcomed second lift saved me a two-day ride on 1600 kilometres of endlessly boring tarmac that stretched over the vast Kazakh steppe, its grasses yellowed in the height of summer. When the six trucks lumbered into the depot in Barnaul, I'd been ushered into the office of the 'big boss'. He was broad-shouldered with close-cropped blonde hair and piercing ice-blue eyes— a man with an imposing presence that dominated the room. He shot off a few words and almost immediately, a fit stocky young man with the same cropped hair, ex-military I guessed, appeared. I was introduced to Stanislav, who could speak English, and when I asked for a lift to Almaty, it was swiftly arranged.

'In three, maybe four days, truck go to Almaty,' Stanislav told me later. The 'big boss' had also instructed Stanislav to look after me.

Leaving my motorcycle at the depot, Stanislav drove me to his aging high-rise apartment, and after unlocking several cumbersome locks on the thick steel-plate door, I was warmly welcomed by his girlfriend, Irene. Blonde and blue-eyed, she was the classical Russian beauty, tall and perfectly proportioned with slightly elongated eyes and full lips. The couple worked for the trucking company as radio operators coordinating the trucks that ferried expensive western goods and packaged foods from Europe into Russia, Mongolia and Kazakhstan. The 'big boss' was former KGB, I was told—and yes, Stanislav had served under him during Soviet times. After the dissolution of the USSR, 'the big boss' moved into the trucking business, with ice-cream being his most profitable cargo.

'Russians love their Magnums, even in winter,' Irene told me.

For the next three days, I was treated to meals at Barnaul's trendy alfresco restaurants. My hosts looked horrified when I offered to pay my share. Dinner always ended with vodka in their apartment. Another couple often joined us, and each morning I'd emerge bleary-eyed from my room to a table littered with empty vodka bottles. Stanislav and Irene would be bright as buttons, calling the shots on the panel of radios set up in their lounge room.

On the third day, Stanislav announced a truck was being loaded for Almaty. I was sad to leave, and as we said goodbye, I realised I'd fallen in love with Russia.

'I could live here,' I'd told them (although, I had not yet experienced the severe cold of a Russian winter). 'We are the same, Russians and Australians.'

The Russians I'd met had the same positive attitude; the same sense of humour. My time with Stanislav, Irene and their friends in Barnaul reminded me of how life used to be when I lived in northern Australia, in the mining town of Jabiru, a lifetime ago: where it'd been fun hanging out with friends. Those warm days of rest, and balmy evenings of friendship, delicious food, and yes, vodka too, had pushed away the tiredness that had crept into my bones in recent weeks. As I left Barnaul, I felt vibrant and filled with expectation for the road ahead. Hopefully, this would lead me to Kashgar and into Tibet.

The truck driver, Ali, who'd safely deposited me in Almaty, lived on the city's outskirts and had space for my bike in the container on the back of his truck. It was packed with non-perishable food products from Europe destined for Almaty's western-style supermarkets popular with a burgeoning expat population, wealthy Russians and minority of Kazakhs rising to the top. Since the fall of the Soviet Union, one way or another, they were all getting rich off Kazakhstan's abundant natural resources: gas, oil, gold and other minerals too.

Stanislav had told me the 'big boss' had given Ali instructions to look after me—that I was a special guest.

'I don't want to be any trouble,' I said.

'It is no problem. Ali will get a bonus. He is pleased.'

I'd wanted to thank the 'big boss' for all he'd done, but Stanislav told me he'd left for Moscow, for his *dacha*.

Ali couldn't speak a word of English, and my Russian improved considerably over the next two days on that drive from Barnaul to Almaty. However, conversations were painstakingly slow as I still had to translate most words from my Russian dictionary. Rather than trying to explain my expired Russian visa and absence of one for Kazakhstan, I hid in the sleeper cab when we crossed the border. It was the same border I'd crossed into Russia illegally. A few kilometres before the crossing, I advised Ali I was tired and needed to lie down. Fortunately, the Russian official waved him through.

Ali drove late into that first night and stopped at a relative's house in a small township. Late afternoon on the second day, we arrived at Ali's home on the leafy outskirts of Almaty. I was given a room in a bungalow beside their large low-set timber house shaded by apricot and cherry trees loaded with ripe fruit. It was a veritable Garden of Eden. After two days of bread, garlic and meat on bones, I gorged on sweet apricots and large juicy cherries. Ali and his family insisted I stay with them, but I advised I needed to be close to the city to organise visas. The next morning, I rode to a campsite on the lower slopes of a mountain range overlooking the city. It was the same campsite, the Frenchmen and I had stayed at when we passed through Almaty a month ago. They'd discovered it from a listing in their guidebook. It wasn't so much a campsite as two rows of old railway carriages. The owner rented the carriages for drinking parties, and I soon discovered, it was popular with Russian and Kazakh men entertaining their 'girlfriends'. The owners, an elderly Kazakh couple, welcomed me back as if I were a daughter and after tea and honey cake, I set up my tent in the same spot as before.

With the scent of pine from the forested hills, a mountain stream gushing frothy and pale aqua, and the snow-capped peaks of the Tien Shan rising majestic in the distance, I had a birds-eye view of Almaty. I woke early each day just as the sun rose across the distant steppe, and in the crisp, clean mountain air, I sat with a steaming mug of tea to watch the city slowly emerge in all its new-found modern glory.

But not even this view could lift the darkness that had settled on me since I'd arrived back in Almaty. It was the end of my third day in one of the world's most beautiful cities, but I felt trapped and very much alone. Even my idyllic campsite had turned nasty after I'd fought off a drunk Kazakh the previous night. When the group of three men and their girlfriends had arrived, they'd seen me sitting alone writing in my diary outside my tent and insisted I join them. When I'd politely declined saying I was tired, two of the women, one on either side 'frog-marched' me to their railway carriage. It was a few hours later, after sharing an abundance of Kazakh food and vodka, that I thanked my hosts and slipped away only to be followed by one of the men. Just as I'd given him an almighty shove when he tried to push his way into my tent, one of the women came to my rescue, and led him back to the carriage.

When I first arrived in Almaty, the fatigue had returned and filling my passport with visas as I rode around the city each day, had exhausted me. First, I had to get a one-month Kazakh visa, which had been issued on the spot with no questions asked about my expired Russian visa. The Kazakh visa was needed before submitting my application for a Chinese visa. The Kyrgyz embassy showed the same disinterest over my expired Russian visa and also issued a thirty-day visa, which was needed to reach the Torugart Pass and hopefully cross into China and ride through Tibet. This was my first choice. While I did not have permission for my motorcycle, I hoped what I'd been told by the British traveller at the hostel in Istanbul was true. Once halfway across Tibet, if caught I'd be ordered to the next exit point, which would be either Pakistan or Nepal depending on how far I'd ridden undetected. However, word of a woman riding a motorcycle would travel fast, and it was unlikely I'd even reach Kashgar.

But after my travels in Africa and later as a motorcycle courier, I was adept at finding ways around rules or just ignoring them altogether. And this was the point I'd reached on this journey because rules and regulations didn't really matter anymore. What did I really have to lose by giving it a try? The worst that could happen was I'd be refused entry or be deported if I managed to slip into China with my motorcycle. The best was that I'd reach the roof of the world, for some the spiritual centre of our planet—an honourable place to die if this was where I'd meet my end. Just in case I had to cross into Pakistan while in Tibet, if I made it that far, I also applied for a visa for Pakistan.

If I was refused entry to China at the Torugart Pass, I'd head back into Kazakhstan and cross into China on the road to Urumqi, the northern arm of the ancient Silk Road and still used by China as a trade route to reach markets in Central Asia and eastern Europe. Trucks loaded with raw cotton travelled east and returned with barrels of vodka and cheap knock-offs of popular brand-label clothing and shoes. If all failed, my last resort was to fly me and the TT to Islamabad in Pakistan. It would be an expensive option. At the Pakistani embassy in Almaty, over tea and pastries in the luxurious gold-trimmed drawing room, the ambassador himself, along with two of his officials, had warned me of the difficulties I'd face: a single white woman alone in Muslim-dominated Pakistan. When I'd applied for the Chinese visa a week earlier, I made no mention of my motorcycle. I now hoped for a miracle and that somehow, I could sneak it in.

On my fourth day in Almaty, my Chinese visa was ready. I'd leave its monolithic war monuments; its sprawling leafy parks where I'd wandered for hours shrouded in my loneliness. I wore this feeling like a dark cloak as I moved in the shadows unseen by the families whose children played chasing games, their giggles preceding them as the adults followed with picnic baskets. As I wandered unnoticed by the couples who strolled hand-in-hand stopping to share a kiss, I observed a world I was no longer part of. I would never again feel the fullness of a man's lips on mine. I would never be loved. I would never be married. I would never have a baby. I would never feel all this bliss. In a city where just about everyone was either in love, pushed a pram or had a gaggle of children, these thoughts of love, babies and family had dominated my thoughts.

Knowing I would never have the future I'd always expected, the present seemed meaningless. Even the thrill of motorcycle travel—the different experiences, cultures, people and food—no longer held the attraction it once did. For nearly four years, I'd believed, without question that everything would always work out for me. I'd lived devoid of worry. I'd lived energised by a constant sense of knowing an energy moved through me, through us all. It saturated all life. It was a guiding force that helped us fulfill our purpose, our dreams. It was shown to us through chance encounters and coincidences and helped nurture a deep trust in our intuition. With hours alone to ponder these thoughts, I sank deeper into melancholy.

My body, on the other hand, in its desperate search for weapons to fight the war that raged within, was still in partnership with the universal energy and fully embraced its influence. My body spoke to me through my intuition, and I responded unconsciously to these subtle inner prompts. Before heading back to my mountain campsite, I'd stop each afternoon at Almaty's sprawling central market. It was inside the enormous covered food hall I'd discovered the stands selling seaweed imported from North Korea. I'd stopped instantly to sample from the salads and stir-fries in various shades of green and brown flavoured with spices and chilli. Some were crispy, others rubbery, all were salty. My body lapped it up, knowing instinctively these dishes contained the nutrients it so desperately needed. Later I'd read that as well as iodine, iron and a range of vitamins (especially B12), seaweed also contains fucoidan, a type of carbohydrate not found in land-based plants. Fucoidan has powerful anticoagulant and antiviral properties. Too much of a good thing, namely seaweed's high iodine content, would do more harm than good. Fortunately, my seaweed diet only lasted three days.

On one of these afternoons, as I emerged into the brightness of the pavement near where I'd parked the TT, I came across an old woman selling oranges. I handed her a few coins for a bag of four and began peeling one in front of her.

'Nyet,' she said as I picked off the white pith after peeling away the skin. 'Nyet,' she demanded when I ignored her. I looked at her confused, and she began peeling another orange, taking care to leave the pith behind. 'Kushayite,' (eat) she said handing it to me, and when I ate the sweet juicy segments, pith and all, she smiled a wide toothless grin nodding her approval.

I have never forgotten what that old woman taught me that day. At the time, my body craved vitamin C, and I believed this is why I stopped to buy those oranges. Years later, I researched the benefits of pith, that white layer between the skin and fruit of citrus. Pith contains a high concentration of phytonutrients along with just as much vitamin C as the fruit segments. These phytonutrients are packed full of immune-boosting antioxidants, but we peel it off and throw it away.

The morning of that fourth day, when I was due to collect my passport with its visa for China then leave for the Torugart Pass, I felt happier and more energised than I had all week. Maybe it was the seaweed. Maybe the oranges and their immune-boosting pith or perhaps a combination of both. Or maybe it was the expectation that I'd soon be back on the road again. But this reprieve was short-lived.

As if knowing my body was amassing an arsenal, the virus struck back with devastating consequences. It was an attack designed to weaken me to my very core: to use my mind against my body. To tell me I was defeated and no amount of seaweed and orange pith would give me the strength to fight back.

I was in the shower wastefully letting the warm water wash over me as it was likely to be my last hot shower of any kind for several days, if not weeks. I lathered my skin and shampooed my hair, but as I rinsed it off, clumps of hair came away in my hands. I kept pulling at my hair desperate for it to stop falling out. When no more came away, I stood shaking as I watched the last strands wash down the drain. While I saw this as the next stage of my death, my body, in fact, was fighting back. Hair was unnecessary for survival, and so anything that absorbed valuable nutrients was jettisoned. A good few handfuls of my hair washed down the drain that morning.

Even though my light-brown hair with golden sun-kissed highlights was fine, it had a fluffiness that gave it a perceived fullness.

But after that shower, I was left with a few handfuls of mousy thin rats tails and a receding hairline as though I suffered the first stage of age-related baldness.

Self-conscious, I pulled on a hat, packed my motorcycle, paid my camping fees and thanked the old couple for my stay. Then I was gone, riding towards Kyrgyzstan. Riding past the towering snow-capped peaks of the Tien Shan towards the Torugart Pass: riding back into the land of nomads.

22

THE KINGDOM OF THE HEAVENLY MOUNTAINS

Kyrgyzstan

There was a new urgency to my travels. With a good amount of my hair jettisoned, it was apparent I was running out of time. But still, I moved forward as if I had all the time in the world. Rather than take the shortest route to the Torugart Pass, I followed the road east to skirt around the enormous alpine lake, Izzyk-Kul. Its warm, slightly alkaline, waters stretched 182 kilometres long and sixty kilometres wide, and it was bordered on its northern and southern shores by the snow-capped ridges of the Tian Shan, the 'heavenly mountains'.

As if I would be spared the fate of the millions who had succumbed to AIDS before me, I rode away from Almaty with the attitude of my old self: the independent positive-thinking traveller embarking on her next adventure. Even as I faced what I thought were my last days, that innate need to explore was irresistible, and I chose roads that offered twists and turns and vistas of majestic mountains. Or was it denial?

After I'd collected my passport with its Chinese visa, which held such promise, it was almost mid-day when I rode away from Almaty. I had made good time under a cloudless blue sky, the snow-covered Talgar Peak rising nearly 5000 metres beside me as I travelled parallel to the northern arm of the Tian Shan. I rode through a patchwork of cultivated farmland that turned from green to brown when I later crossed a semi-arid expanse and into Kyrgyzstan. After two hours, the road turned south, and I faced a distant wall of mountains that rose like a tsunami of jagged rock, snow and ice and stretched all the way to Nepal. It was the end result of the powerful collision of tectonic plates that started shifting over fifty million years ago and had formed the Himalayas, the Hindu Kush, Pamirs, the Tian Shan and the Tibetan plateau.

As I reached the Tian Shan's scree-covered foothills, the landscape returned to lush pasture and meandering streams. Late afternoon, the narrow stretch of tarmac I'd followed all day turned west, and I passed through market towns bustling with Kyrgyz herdsmen in traditional garb: *kalpaks*, embroidered black-and-white elongated felt hats, and baggy trousers and black waistcoats. Women and girls in floral dresses and bright headscarves mingled with the men, who flashed gold-capped teeth when they returned my smile.

After refuelling and a quick meal of freshly baked flatbread spread with the honey I still carried from the beekeeper's hut in the Altai, I stopped at a sale yard made of rough-cut timber. Climbing onto a railing, I joined a group of boys to watch the spectacle of horse-trading where more than a hundred were penned, their hooves stirring up the fine dust. As I watched the horses, the herdsmen watched me with wrinkled faces, their brown skin pulled taut over high cheekbones and broad noses. They stood around my bike and pointed at me and then my motorcycle, scratching their long grey 'goatie' beards in befuddlement.

I moved on, and late afternoon I reached Izzyk-Kul, which stretched as an enormous dark turquoise inland sea to the distant Pamirs brushed in delicate shades of mauve, pink and orange. As the sun sank beyond the snow-capped peaks, I searched for a place to camp. There were no hotels, not even tourist campsites in these parts, but as if on cue a suitable place was provided. On a low rise overlooking the lake, sat a farmhouse.

I turned and followed a two-wheeled track pulling up outside a low-set brick house with rendered white-washed walls, a pitched red-tin roof and blue-framed windows. On hearing my approach, usually, people would be standing to greet me, but all was quiet. I knocked on the front door and then the back. A cow bellowed, and I followed the sound to a barn where a smallish woman, in her early sixties or maybe older, sat on a stool her back bent as she milked a dung-coloured cow that looked at me with compliant watery black eyes.

'Hello,' I called, and the woman turned, stopped her milking and stood up. She wore a man's shirt and trousers. A floral scarf was tied tightly around her hair, but a few grey strands had escaped. Her lithe gracefulness belied her age.

'Where you come from?' she said smiling her welcome. With hazel eyes and a delicate pale face, I guessed she was Russian from one of the northern states.

'You speak English?' I stammered.

'Oh, yes. I learn it from my father. He was an American and came to the Soviet Union for a better life.'

I quickly did the maths. Her father must have immigrated during the 1930s, during the Great Depression, to escape persecution and unemployment. I'd read thousands of skilled workers with allegiance to America's Communist Party left to take up factory jobs in Russia's emerging car industry. I introduced myself and asked if I could camp, briefly telling my story.

'Please, you are welcome. I have a big house. There is a bed for you,' she said and sat back on the stool to finish milking. Her name was Rachel.

'I grew up in Moscow, but the Soviets moved us here to work in the gold mines. My husband is dead, and my three children are all grown. It is now only me.'

'I'm sorry,' I said.

She shrugged as though it no longer mattered and I got the feeling she had lived alone for many years. After leading the cow out of the barn and releasing it into a paddock, she ushered me to the house and into her kitchen where she de-cantered the milk into several large glass bottles, the thick cream settling on top.

Rachel placed the bottles in an old refrigerator, retrieved one that was chilled and poured two large glasses. I sat down at an oversized wooden table that I expected had seen many family celebrations. She then prepared a simple meal of cheese, boiled eggs, salad and fresh bread, which we ate with a delicious blackcurrant jam and thick dollops of cream. After the meal, I retrieved my things from the TT and showed her my photo album.

'Your family are farmers,' she said, smiling her approval. 'Oh, you ride horses too. Don't show this to the Kyrgyz men. They will see you as a good wife.' We both laughed, but she detected a hollowness in mine.

'I am tired,' I said and stood up. 'I rode from Almaty today.'

Rachael led me to a bedroom down the hall and showed me the outside toilet and where I could wash. The bed with its floral doona was soft, and the moment I laid down, it consumed me into a deep sleep.

It was mid-morning when I woke. The house was quiet, and I went outside in search of Rachel, who was tending her vegetable garden beside the barn. When I apologised for oversleeping and advised I needed to leave to make the Torugart Pass, she admonished me severely.

'I see you are not well. You must rest. I make you vegetable soup with herbs. This will make you strong.'

I ran my hand over what was left of my hair, knowing it had given me away. There was no arguing with her, and admittedly, I could easily go back to bed and sleep the entire day and night too. But instead, I helped Rachel with her chores and watched her make cheese, which she sold at a local market. For lunch, we ate her delicious nutrient-rich soup and late afternoon milked the cow. Rachel attempted to teach me, but the knack of 'push-pull' on the teats didn't come easy, and nor did the milk.

'Don't stay alone for too long,' she said when she'd taken over the milking and resumed the gentle rhythm. 'When your travels are over, find a husband. Have some children. Family is what matters. It is not good to be alone.'

'Yes,' was all I could say.

After a day of rest and her home-cooked food, I thanked Rachel, and when I said goodbye, we hugged like best friends. She had given me enough supplies to last all the way across the Tibetan plateau if I made it that far. My bags were packed with cheese, bread, tomatoes, cucumbers and cherries. I refused the apricots, saying there were many trees laden with ripe fruit growing wild on the side of the road and I'd already eaten my fill on the ride from Almaty.

I followed smooth tarmac that meandered around the lake with its dramatic backdrop of towering mountains, and I made good time reaching the turnoff to the Tash Rabat *caravanserai*, a roadside inn used by Silk Road travellers and merchants for centuries on the route from Kashgar to Osh. Today, it was a forgotten relic as a new road had been forged through the Torugart Pass, a 100 kilometres to the north.

From the main road, the *caravanserai* was an hour's ride along a washed-out dirt track that wound its way through a narrow valley of yellowing grass dotted with the occasional yurt. Small herds of shaggy black yaks raised their horned heads as I rumbled past and in the dimming light, I reached the ancient walled structure of Tash Rabat. Made of stone collected from the surrounding scree-covered hills, it sat lonely and abandoned on a low rise overlooking the valley. An overland truck, the type used by tour companies in Africa, was parked outside. As I pulled up at the cavernous arched entrance, a Kyrgyz man in a traditional *kalpak* and a long black overcoat appeared.

'Come,' he said.

I followed him inside to a huge domed chamber. A group of about twenty tourists sat cross-legged in a circle eating a meal from their camp bowls. This is what travellers passing through the Torugart Pass had done for centuries and in the faint light cast by several oil lamps, I was taken back to that ancient time as though nothing had changed. Leading off from the main chamber were several tunnel-like hallways, but with no light, these further recesses were plunged in darkness.

The tourists stopped eating and looked at me, bewildered by my arrival. A clean-cut young man in cargo pants and polar fleece stepped over several brightly coloured sleeping bags spread over the uneven stone floor, to greet me.

'Come, join us. Have some food,' he said in a jovial American accent.

We introduced ourselves, and I explained my plans to cross into China.

'I have a visa,' I said in answer to his questioning look.

'It is impossible to do this with your motorcycle. Even without the bike, even with your visa, they will not let you through. With us, you might have a chance. We're crossing the Torugart Pass in the morning. Please, stay with us tonight. We have permission to sleep here.'

I retrieved my sleeping bag and Thermarest, a bowl and spoon, and Martin filled it with mutton stew cooked by the caretaker who lived in the little house nearby.

As I ate, Martin told me the tour was the first his company had organised into Kashgar, with the Americans flying to Almaty where they boarded the overland truck.

'It has taken many months to get permission from the Chinese authorities,' he said, and explained the tour would visit a number of historical Silk Road sites on the way to Kashgar; Tash Rabat was the first.

After breakfast of sweet black tea brewed by the caretaker, and muesli bars handed out by Martin, we all packed our things and headed towards the Torugart Pass—and my moment of reckoning. I told Martin I'd be much faster on my motorcycle and would wait for them before I came in sight of customs. He explained my passport would be submitted with theirs and hopefully I'd avoid suspicion by being part of their group.

'Once our passports are stamped, you must ride close beside the truck where they can't see you. Many trucks are crossing at this border so they will be distracted,' he said.

I told Martin he was taking a significant risk by helping me and if I was caught, he might be blamed.

'Not at all. It is nothing to do with me that you were at the border at the same time as us and your passport was bundled with ours,' he said mischievously.

As I approached the border, I passed long lines of trucks loaded with bales of raw cotton and others carrying scrap metal from disassembled ex-Soviet factories. In the chill morning air against a backdrop of the Tian Shan, the drivers stood together smoking cigarettes as they waited patiently for their turn to get through customs. Even though the road was flat, I had reached a higher altitude, and in the thin atmosphere, the cloudless sky graduated from deep blue to dark indigo.

As the road climbed higher, the tarmac was replaced by smooth hard-packed gravel that wound through barren hills. Near the border, I rode beside two impenetrably high barbed-wire fences several metres apart. Towers, now deserted, stood at intervals. The fences, separated by a stretch of bare earth, snaked into the distance to disappear over the rounded hills that rose into mountains.

I stopped several kilometres before the border and in the eerie silence waited for the overland truck, which slowly lumbered towards me about twenty minutes later.

My passport was stamped without question by the Kyrgyz official, and then Martin handed the bundle to the Chinese official who waited with his colleague at another desk in the immigration hall. I stood amongst the Americans hoping I would not be noticed in my dust-encrusted Belstaff jacket, dirty jeans and motocross boots.

'Let's go,' Martin said slipping me my passport as he rushed past. A moment later, I was on my motorcycle, but just as the truck started moving, a Chinese immigration officer ran out frantically waving a sheet of paper. The truck stopped and, through his interpreter, he spoke a few angry words with Martin.

'They realised there was an extra passport not on their manifest. I'm sorry,' Martin said.

'It was always going to be a long shot,' I replied and a moment later waved the truck goodbye as the Chinese official stood glaring at me. I'd done nothing wrong as I had not officially entered China, just nearly slipped past the first stage of entry. Officially, I was still in Kyrgyzstan.

After leaving the border, in a last ditch, half-hearted attempt to reach Kashgar, I stopped at the long line of trucks I'd passed earlier and spoke to a group of drivers about the possibility of hitching a lift. 'Just thought I'd ask,' I said as they smiled, shaking their heads at the preposterousness of such a foolhardy idea. Like the Russians, the Chinese were not to be messed with either.

These were my last days in this magical land of yurts, yaks, wild horses and towering snow-capped mountains; my last opportunity to immerse myself in this nomad kingdom, still unknown to the outside world. I wanted a few final days to hang-out with these nomads with their sun-browned faces, dark elongated eyes and broad smiles. And here in these isolated mountain valleys bordering China was just the place for such an experience.

I looked at my map and could see a small lake in a nearby valley. The lush pasture surrounding Song-Kol would undoubtedly be ideal summer grazing. It was about forty kilometres along a minor road, which I would pass on the ride to the Kazakhstan-China border, northeast of Almaty—my next option for leaving Central Asia.

Three hours later, I reached Naryn, where I planned to stock up on supplies. It was the last township before the turnoff to Song-Kol. This time, I was prepared and would not arrive on a doorstep, or in this case at a yurt, empty-handed. I purchased vodka, a few rounds of flatbread, sweet biscuits, tea, sugar, and several Snickers bars. I also asked the store owner about the road to Song-Kol.

'Horosho. Na mototsikl mojno' he said when I'd unfolded my map and said 'mototsikl da' and pointed to the thin yellow line leading to the lake.

'There are yurts?' I asked.

'Da, yurta,' he replied.

After an hour of riding on a washed-out gravel track skirting velvety-grass covered hills, traversing scree-covered gullies and rocky mountain streams, I reached the last hill, and the road dipped into a wide bowl-shaped valley blanketed with the thick pasture of high summer. The lake shone aqua and was fringed to the west by a low range of rounded mountains.

A small herd of horses scattered as I approached. Close to the lake's grassy edge sat a lone yurt and an A-framed white canvas tent. It was the first yurt I'd seen along the lake's shore, but a few distant specks of white indicated there were others.

As I pulled up, the inhabitants emerged. It was mid-day, and I'd probably disturbed their lunch. An elderly man in *kalpak* and black waistcoat, and a dumpy woman in a floral dress and cream wool cardigan, smiled their welcome from deeply wrinkled brown faces. The three boys who ranged in age from sixteen to five stared at me suspiciously. The adults, I guessed, were the boy's grandparents. And the boys were with them during the summer school holidays to help graze the family's animals, while their parents went to work or ran their farm. In winter, they'd all move back to their home in one of the townships in the lower lying valleys where the boys could attend school, and the horses could graze on pasture not covered in feet of snow. This was their summer holiday, and as a nation of nomads, it was a time of freedom, wide open spaces and living their ancient heritage.

The older boy stepped forward in knee-high black boots made of soft leather, the same type of boots worn by his grandmother. He wore baggy trousers, too short for his lanky frame and a baggy wool jumper. His *kalpak* made him appear several inches taller than he was. The youngest boy sported a shaved head, probably a quick remedy to treat head lice, and his brother, the ten-year-old, threw me a quick smile.

'What you want?' asked the lad in the *kalpak*.

'You speak English?' I asked surprised. He nodded, holding a thumb and index finger together to indicate just a little.

'I'd like to stay. I have my own tent,' I added, and the elderly couple waved their arms to usher me inside their yurt.

'Why you come?' the lad shouted, stopping me dead after I'd turned to retrieve my gifts.

'It is very beautiful here. But maybe there are wolves,' I stammered, hoping this would explain why I did not want to camp alone. I felt I couldn't say I just wanted to 'hang out'; to experience their nomadic life. Saying this would seem like I was here for no other reason than to invade their privacy; to observe them as though they were a curiosity. My made-up fear about wolves, which actually were a possibility, although not in summer when food was plentiful, gave me a genuine reason to be there.

I stuffed the gifts in my daypack, and as I walked towards the yurt, the lad gave me a piercing stare that clearly said he saw through my deception. He turned and strode over to were several foals were tethered to a long line pegged into the ground. A light grey cow stood tethered nearby.

Taking off my boots, I entered the yurt and its ornately carpeted interior. Hand-woven red-patterned rugs adorned the walls, and a large bright red velvet throw covered a pile of mattresses that would be laid out on the floor when it was time to sleep. In the centre was a low table and against one wall a little square stove, its chimney pierced through the ceiling. At the entrance was a wooden barrel of *kumis*, fermented mare's milk, which the old woman stirred with a ladle as she entered.

I sat cross-legged on a sheepskin on the carpeted floor, and the old woman offered a bowl of black tea and indicated I eat a chunk of the unleavened bread from the plate on the table. I spooned thick cream onto a piece from the bowl beside it. She then offered a bowl of *kumis*, and as I unpacked my gifts from my daypack, I introduced myself and handed the bottle of vodka to the old man, who didn't seem all that interested and placed it on the floor beside him. The elongated dark eyes of the two younger boys lit up excitedly when they saw the sweets and chocolates, and the elderly couple smiled warmly. We sat this way for a few minutes until the awkwardness was broken when the lad appeared, stooping to bend his lanky frame as he entered the yurt. A few words were exchanged between him and his grandparents. The old woman stood up and pulled one of the mattresses from the pile, laying it on the floor.

'I have a tent,' I said and looked at the lad to explain.

'You sleep inside. Very cold at night.'

'I have my own mattress and sleeping bag,' I said and got up to retrieve it so I would not deprive one of the boys their bed.

With greetings over, the family went about their chores. The old woman went to milk the cow, and I followed the old man and the three boys to the foals. Further along the shore of the lake, a line of bay and chestnut horses moved toward us. These were the mares returning to their foals, and when they reached the tether line, the grandfather and two older boys harnessed the six horses. Several more grazed nearby. While the old man held the mare, stroking its neck to keep it calm, the lad quickly milked her before moving on to the next, and when all were milked, the foals were allowed to feed.

Over the next two days, I fell into the gentle rhythm of nomad life, which revolved around milking the mares several times a day. Having grown up with horses, I helped halter the mares and settled each to be milked. On the second day, the old man left the boys to do the milking alone and seeing I was of some use, the lad slowly warmed to me. So much so, that he told me his name and that of his brothers. The lad was Taalay, the middle brother Aybek and the youngest was Ulan.

Later that afternoon, my usefulness rose considerably when one of the foals broke free of the tether line. As it dashed past, I dived to grab its lead, its whinny causing its mother to gallop towards us. Taalay quickly tethered the foal as she approached. A kind of friendship developed after this, and the two younger boys were no longer shy in asking for my binoculars to spy on the waterbirds nesting and feeding on the lake's marshy shore.

On the third day, I packed my things and said goodbye to the nomad family. While I felt very much like the intruder when I'd arrived, they had opened their home and their hearts to me. Before leaving, I handed the old man a handful of notes that amounted to about US$10 for my stay.

'No money,' Taalay said. 'You work very hard with us.'

'It was very special to stay with you. Thank you. Many tourists want to do this. Maybe this will make a good business for you one day.'

'Maybe,' he said and gave me a broad knowing smile.

In the near future, there would be yurt camps dotted all along the shores of Song-Kol. Some with ten or more yurts accommodating up to sixty people at a time. Individual Kyrgyz families were also catering for individuals and smaller groups wanting to experience nomad life. Local tourism, such as these yurt camps, brought new prosperity to local families as they shared their cultural traditions with a growing number of people from the west, people that increasingly live and work in cities devoid of wide open spaces, nature and a life lived close to the earth. A nomadic life that we, as humans, once all lived. As I left the family, I hoped that Taalay and his brothers would go on to share their nomadic traditions with others—and find prosperity.

Part 4

CHINA TO AUSTRALIA

23

RESISTANCE IS FUTILE

China

I rode across a semi-arid expanse, the tarmac cutting a straight line to the Kazakhstan-China border. I'd left Kyrgyzstan two days earlier, sleeping at a roadside motel on the outskirts of Almaty. It was mid-day, and I travelled on the northern route of the ancient Silk Road. Shortly, it would veer towards the glacial peaks of the Dzhungaria Alatau Mountains, the far northern arm of the Tien Shan, and through the Dzhungarian Gate. This ten-kilometre-wide barren windswept valley is a natural fault in a wall of mountains that begins in northern China and runs nearly 5000 kilometres to Afghanistan.

The mountain pass was first used by the Chinese during the Han Dynasty around 200BC when a posse of diplomats was sent to investigate the lands to the west. On their return, a trade route was formed, linking China to Central Asia all the way to the kingdom of Parthia, a region in modern-day Iran. But when the nomadic tribes of the steppe began to pillage the trade caravans, the merchants favoured the more difficult route to Kashgar. The deserts and the high windswept mountain plateaus lacked the banditry of the steppe, and the valley pass was then mostly used by migrants. Genghis Khan's army also rode through the Dzhungarian Gate, a mass of men and horses numbering more than 100,000 by the estimates of some historians. His armies travelled through it in the early thirteenth century to invade Central Asia where they slaughtered millions of citizens and razed cities to the ground when the leaders of those cities refused to surrender.

Today, the Dzhungarian Gate is the route of the Soviet and Chinese-built railway that transports mostly freight, but also passengers travelling from Almaty to Urumqi. Unlike the migrants of antiquity, I would not leave the magical land of Central Asia through this pass as the road I followed had been blasted by Soviet engineers.

As I neared the border, I passed convoys of trucks that slowly crept towards China and stopped at a row of three carrying shipping containers parked a short distance from the back of the queue. The drivers, not Chinese, but Kazakhs or Uyghurs I guessed, sat on their haunches smoking cigarettes and drinking tea they'd brewed on a small gas stove.

As I approached, one of the men offered tea served in a small bowl. Another offered a cigarette. I pointed to my motorcycle and a truck before flipping through my Russian dictionary in search of the words for: 'Is the truck empty?' and 'Can I get a lift?' The words for 'One hundred dollars' are universally understood.

'Nyet,' they said. 'Mototsikl nyet, Kitay (China) nyet.'

I then pointed to the map drawn on the side-cover and opened my passport with its bright red ink-emblazoned Chinese visa.

'Mototsikl in mashina?' I asked my voice quivering in desperation.

'Nyet,' they said again.

When I finished my cigarette and tea, they waved me off as I rode towards the border.

I was resigned to the imminent refusal for entry and mentally prepared for the long ride back to Almaty where my last option would be to fly to Pakistan.

After I passed through Kazakh immigration, I pushed open the door to the Chinese customs hall and presented my passport to the waiting official. I was out of deception and willingly offered up my motorcycle, advising that I was on a long journey. The official walked outside to inspect my bike and announced: 'You with Mobil?'

For a few seconds, I looked at him dumb-founded, unable to comprehend the significance of what he'd just asked.

'Mobil,' I stammered as my brain rapidly grasped this overlooked opportunity. An opportunity available all this time, but one I had not even once considered. My Mobil letter of introduction was buried under my other travel documents inside the Pelican case. I quickly retrieved it. The letter had not seen the light of day since Baku when I stayed at the international oil workers compound at Mobil's expense.

'Mobil,' I said, handing him the laminated letter Mobil UK had given me for the ride from London to Hanoi. It was an update of what I'd received from Mobil Australia for my ride through Africa.

'Come,' he said and once inside the customs hall, disappeared behind a door into an office with lightly frosted windows where he spoke to another man who then reached for a phone.

After about ten minutes, he returned and handed back my Mobil letter.

'Welcome China,' he smiled 'You go Urumqi.' As I looked at him unable to speak, he explained my motorcycle and I would be transported by the Chinese government to Urumqi where it would be impounded at the customs depot until I had permission to travel with it across China. 'You are guest. Driver look after you.' He then called over a Chinese man sitting on his haunches chatting to several other Chinese men at the front of an old truck that looked like a furniture removal van.

The official spoke at length with the driver pointing to me and at the bike, and the man nodded several times. I imagined, the official was saying my motorcycle was not to be released to me under any circumstances.

My motorcycle was the driver's only freight, and several ropes secured it to latch points. I climbed into the cab, and we headed out across the dry plains towards Urumqi, travelling parallel to the distant snow-capped peaks of the Tien Shan.

The driver spoke no English, and I soon gave up trying to make conversation using the Mandarin phrasebook I'd bought in Almaty. My pronunciation of this tonal language was incomprehensible to him, and he'd looked at me confused, probably thinking I was speaking English.

Throughout the day, the drive was broken by several stops to drink tea or eat noodles prepared and cooked in huge woks on open fires at roadside cafés made of mudbrick and corrugated iron. The free space in the back of the truck did not go to waste, and we soon made a quick detour to a railway siding. Several men appeared, and large hessian bags filled with pumpkin seeds were quickly loaded from a carriage. The driver offered me a handful of seeds from a bag that had split open.

'Pumpkin seeds.'

'*Nánguā Zĭ*,' he replied.

'*Nánguā Zĭ*,' I said, and we both smiled, having at last, broken through the pronunciation barrier. I sat nearby and without realising it, nibbled on the seeds, adeptly removing the outer shell as frantically as the men loaded the truck. My nibbling was so automatic I soon finished the handful and went back for more. Even though I'd consumed lashings of pumpkin seed oil while working in St Johann, Austria, I didn't give a thought to the health benefits of the seeds as I busily nibbled that day. But these health benefits were something over a billion Chinese knew almost innately.

Along with sunflower seeds, pumpkin seeds are eaten everywhere in China and the husks litter streets, footpaths and railway platforms. The raw pumpkin seeds I nibbled were high in phosphorus, magnesium, zinc and omega oils—all substances my body desperately needed. Since my body had jettisoned a good amount of my hair, the pendulum in my will to survive had swung towards a resigned acceptance of my demise. It was an acceptance that came without worry and with this acceptance came a sense of peace.

As I sat on a mound of dirt nibbling off the husk, one seed at a time, I was acutely aware of my surroundings. There was no beauty in this far-flung part of China, a semi-desert region where the sky was no longer a deep blue, but a pale dirty grey from the dust that hung in the air, hiding the Tien Shan twenty or so kilometres to my right. Even so, I felt a heightened sense of awareness to be 'in' this very moment. Since leaving London nearly a year ago, my emotional journey had been just as diverse as the landscapes I'd ridden through. Denial, shame, worry, fear, hope and now acceptance.

With the truck fully loaded, the driver waved me over and we bounced over the dirt road back to the stretch of black tarmac. Just on nightfall, we reached a township and pulled up at a four-storey nondescript cement-block building where the driver and I were shown to a six-bed dormitory by a uniformed official. Inside, the walls were stark white, the iron spring beds neatly made with white sheets, a flat pillow and a grey blanket. Two men and a woman occupied three of the beds, and as the driver chatted with them, I claimed the bed near a barred window.

As I thought about dinner, they all rose and indicated I follow them. After noodles in the cafeteria downstairs, I pointed outside and rose to leave, but the driver shook his head and walked me back to the room. It was then, I realised, the driver was not letting me out of his sight until I was safely handed over to customs in Urumqi.

We left the hotel at daylight, and by mid-afternoon, the landscape changed from semi-arid desert to cultivated farmland. The driver stopped in a township to fill the remaining space in the truck with large oval-shaped watermelons, stacking the melons on top of the bags of pumpkin seeds that surrounded my motorcycle. As the men worked, I sat nearby under a shady tree eating half a melon, it's bright pink-red flesh sweet and juicy.

We reached Urumqi during rush hour. This sprawling city on China's remote far western border was home to nearly a million people (this would swell to more than four million in 2019). With 80 per cent of the city's population Chinese, the Uyghurs, the traditional people of this region, are a minority. Urumqi is the capital of Xinjiang province, which became part of communist China in 1949 and was later renamed as the Xinjiang-Uyghur Autonomous Region, but there was nothing autonomous about it with Beijing calling the shots. Once the railway reached Urumqi in the 1960s, the Chinese stamped its claim on the city. A mass migration of Han soon followed, and the Uyghurs found themselves in the same situation as their Tibetan neighbours: overwhelmingly outnumbered. Throughout history, the region has been home to many nomadic tribes, the largest being the Uyghurs, who briefly gained independence as Uyghuristan in the 1940s.

But Urumqi also has a Chinese past. It was established as a major trading post on the Silk Road by the Tang Dynasty, which ruled in the seventh and eighth centuries, known as the 'Golden Age' of prosperity, creativity and discovery in China's history. However, as we drove through Urumqi's streets choked with cars, trucks and buses belching black smoke, I only saw a city enveloped in a haze of dust and traffic pollution so thick it hid the nearby ragged peaks of the far north-eastern arm of the Tian Shan.

After the pumpkin seeds and watermelons were unloaded, perhaps as a bit of side trade shared by the officials, my motorcycle was locked in what can only be described as a prison cell. The customs compound comprised of an office building and two long rows of about ten cells, each with steel bars. Most of the cells contained bulging checkered-plastic bags filled with Chinese goods awaiting customs clearance. I retrieved my daypack and stuffed it with clothes and things I'd need over the next few days as once the cell was locked, it would not be opened until I was given permission to ride across China.

Adjacent to the compound was an ageing three-storey hotel that was busy with mostly Russian, Kazakh and Uyghur traders. Once inside its dark corridors, I requested a room and was told there were no single rooms and I'd have to share for 25 yuan (about US$3) per night. The communal bathroom and squat toilet were at the end of the corridor. It was a ground-floor room with large windows, which I immediately opened to get some relief from the stifling heat. Several stacks of bulging checkered-plastic bags were stacked against the walls and on my bed; I removed and stacked these with the others. My roommate, a middle-aged, dumpy Russian woman with short, wiry black hair, arrived a short time later. She greeted me with a rant as she launched herself at the window, clamping it shut. 'Nyet window. Nyet open. Many thieves.'

'It is very hot. I need air,' I replied, but I was soon silenced.

'Thieves come. Shoot you. Bang bang. You dead.'

We introduced ourselves and I was so pleased she spoke English that I rambled on about my travels. I'd not spoken English for more than a week, the Americans at Tash Rabat and the Torugart Pass being my last conversation.

'You are very brave,' she said when I finally stopped. Lidiya was from Moscow and proudly told me she was a 'business woman' buying

Chinese-made clothing and shoes to sell at her market stall. The two bags she'd carried into the room where stuffed with Nike shoes of various sizes and colours. 'Very good quality,' she said, holding up a black and white Nike basketball shoe.

The next morning I asked a motorcycle taxi to take me to the Mobil office, but when I showed him my letter and pointed to the Mobil logo, he looked at me confused. Assuming there was no Mobil office in Urumqi, I gave him the slip of paper from customs for the main immigration office in the city. It was a ten-minute ride, and once there I filled out the appropriate forms and was told to return the next day. When I returned, I was told my application was still being processed and to come back tomorrow. The following day I returned and the day after that too. Each morning, the official politely told me the same thing.

It was too hot to stay inside the hotel. Besides, the room I shared with Lidiya was now filled wall to ceiling with bags bulging with her purchases and there was just a narrow corridor from the door to our beds. In the heat, I had no energy to wander around Urumqi, but on my first day, I had visited Urumqi's main tourist attraction, a 700-year-old, nine-storey pagoda perched on a hill of red rock that gives 360-degree views of the city shrouded in dust and smog.

With nothing else to do and nowhere to go, I'd patiently wait at immigration hoping my presence would prompt a quicker decision. I'd break up the hours with a lunch of dumplings from a street vendor outside and refilling my jam jar from the hot water urn at the end of the hall. With tap water unsafe to drink, and bottled water expensive, like most Chinese, I drank tea from a jam jar with a metal screw-top lid. I was particularly fond of chrysanthemum flowers as I loved the way the dried flowers opened to float in a spectacular display of delicate, fluffy creaminess. I'd get several seeps from one brew, and in the heat, the tea was surprisingly refreshing. I later read it had antiviral, antifungal and antibacterial properties, which provided an added boost for my immune system.

My evenings were spent sitting on the footpath, on the gutter edge, with a mixed group of Russians, Kazakhs and Uyghurs. These were men and women all doing business one way or another; either in the process of buying goods or waiting for customs clearance. With my motorcycle imprisoned, we shared a common bond in that we had no choice but to sit it out. I was surprised how many spoke a little English, but it made sense as English was the common language for 'doing business'. The Russians and Kazakhs complained how difficult it was to deal with the Chinese. 'They treat us like dirt,' spat a Russian man.

Mostly, I found myself chatting to a group of three young Uyghur men and the Russian. They'd befriended me the first day when I'd sat outside the hotel eating my dinner of noodles purchased from a nearby street vendor. The Uyghurs, with their thick black hair, high cheekbones and long straight noses, were nomads, and I could easily forget I was in China, but instead, was still in Central Asia, which I actually was, from a historical perspective. They shared nothing in common with the Chinese: neither looks, customs, food nor religion—they were Muslim.

'You must tell the world what the Chinese do to us. They take our country. This is our land,' the Uyghur men told me proudly defiant during our long conversations each evening.

'China never take Russia. We crush them like insect,' said the Russian, thumbing a meaty fist into his other hand.

'Yes,' I told them. 'I will tell the world.' But outnumbered and up against a superpower, this was an unwinnable battle, I thought.

'You are lucky Australia does not share a border with China,' the most outspoken of the Uyghur men said one evening. 'The Chinese will take Central Asia. They want their oil and gas, and their land. See how much they eat. They never stop. All the time, they eat, eat, eat,' he said and pointed at the people milling around the numerous food vendors along the street.

'China has big plans to build pipelines, roads and railways on the old Silk Roads all the way to India and the Middle East. And these nations will welcome the Chinese. They will think this will bring them money,' added his friend. 'Europe will be next. Then America. They make one-hundred-year plan to take over the world. It will not be a battle with bullets, but a silent invasion. This is what they did to the Uyghur nation.'

'So does this mean resistance is futile?' I asked and explained its meaning from Star Trek where the Borg, an alien race, absorbs other races into its own.' 'Resistance is futile. You will be assimilated,' I said, quoting the famous line.

'Yes, this is what the Chinese do to us,' said the third man and the others nodded, except the Russian.

Maybe these Uyghur men were right and what happened to their people could happen to other nations too. Maybe like the Uyghurs, the native-born citizens of the new independent nations of Central Asia would slowly be outnumbered. Nepotism would then seal their fate, excluding them from positions of power and influence.

What would Australia be like in a hundred, a thousand, years from now? Would we too be outnumbered: second-class citizens in our own country; renters rather than home-owners; service workers rather than professionals? Would China, through the hard work and determination of its people, emerge as the new superpower and America fall like the Roman Empire? After months of riding mostly through wild and wide open spaces and villages with only a smattering of people, to being surrounded by a mass of Chinese so dense one could barely move on the streets, the Uyghur's prophecies undeniably held substance.

A week after I'd lodged my application, I still had not received an answer from immigration. Permission had neither been refused nor granted. Each day, I was just told to come back tomorrow. At about this time, I also moved to another hotel after a Russian man was shot and killed on the second-floor of the hotel where I shared a room with Lidiya. She told me he'd been murdered for the US dollars, rumoured to be $25,000, he carried to buy Chinese goods. It wasn't the first gunfire I'd heard at the hotel and while it felt like I was deserting the TT, I no longer felt safe. Lidiya, I'm sure, secretly welcomed my decision as she desperately needed the extra space for the last of her purchases. We wished each other well and I hailed a motorcycle taxi to ferry me to a cheap hotel close to the city centre.

On the tenth day, I finally received a response from immigration.

'You pay US$1500 for permit. When you leave, you get refund,' the official said.

'Sure,' I thought. After ten days in Urumqi, its air thick with dust and smog; its mass of people, many of whom looked too exhausted to smile; its language that I had no hope of understanding or being understood in; and its road signs with indecipherable Chinese characters, I had to question: 'did I really want to travel through China?' Besides, the Uyghurs I'd befriended had already warned me that different rules applied to different autonomous regions and provinces. Each was like a separate country, and any permit was likely to be invalid once I left Xinjiang. Once I'd handed over my US$1500 it was highly likely I would never see it again. I would ride 1200 kilometres on an unforgiving stretch of tarmac in the height of summer between two of the world's hottest and driest deserts— the Taklamakan on one side and the Gobi on the other—only to be refused entry to Gansu, the neighbouring province.

'I'll take the train,' I replied to the official.

'Yes, very good,' he smiled back. 'Customs will escort you to the station. The train leaves this afternoon.'

As he handed me a slip of paper to give to the official at the compound, I suddenly got the feeling that this was a cleverly devised plan to get rid of me.

My motorcycle was released and for the first time in nearly two weeks, I was free to ride. But it was constrained freedom with customs officers in two cars, one leading the way and another following behind for the ten kilometres to the Urumqi train station. This was an imposing three-storey building that rose up from the barren earth on what was then the outskirts of the city. In future years, it was all but replaced by another station built closer to the city for a new high-speed rail line, the world's longest, that connected Urumqi to Beijing. An officer walked with me into the cavernous interior to arrange a sleeper ticket and freight for my motorcycle all the way to Nanning near the Vietnamese border, a seven-day journey plus an overnight stop in Chengdu.

When the official explained the prices for the different class of sleepers, I chose a hard sleeper in third class. He looked at me horrified, but the ticket was 960 yuan (about US$120) including the TT, which was half the price of the second-class sleeper. The train departed in two hours, and after I'd paid my ticket, the customs officers escorted me to the freight yard where my motorcycle was loaded into a carriage and tied down. Would I ever see it again? I had no choice but to put my trust in China's railway system, one of the world's largest and most complex, but also one of the most efficient.

I asked one of the customs officials to walk me to my platform as the Chinese characters were meaningless to me. My train was waiting, and he helped me find my carriage and sleeper compartment. It was a small area open to the passageway and had two narrow bunks of six beds with thin vinyl mattresses covered with a starched white sheet. At each end of the carriage was a washroom and squat toilet. Also, at one end, was a samovar, a large urn with boiling water. I settled into the bottom bunk and nibbled on the pumpkin seeds I'd bought outside the customs compound.

Before collecting my bike, I'd stocked up on supplies as an afterthought. My entire food supply for the week-long journey was a bag of dried chrysanthemum flowers, pumpkin seeds, sweets and two round loaves of bread. But the train would stop at several stations throughout each day, and I'd be able to buy food from the hawkers on the platform.

It wasn't long before the carriage filled with passengers and I found myself sharing with a Chinese family of five travelling to Chengdu. It was a stroke of good fortune that the sixth bunk was free, unless the customs official had ordered that one of the family members be allocated another seat. The family was made up of a petite elderly woman, and another woman and three men, all of whom appeared to be in their mid-thirties and forties.

'Our grandmother is very old. Please, can you give her your bed?' one of the men asked.

'Of course,' I said and moved my things to the top bunk, which gave me privacy as the man who took the bunk opposite was rarely in it on that journey.

Late afternoon, the train pulled out of Urumqi to head across the flat expanse of dry plains. Soon after, the family laid out a feast of fried chicken, noodles, boiled eggs and watermelon and insisted I join them. I had nothing to share and apologised to the man, who could speak a little English.

'Please, you are welcome,' he said.

Over the next four days, I fell into a routine of sleeping, eating with the Chinese family, nibbling on pumpkin seeds, filling my jam jar with boiling water and buying food from the hawkers when the train rolled into a station. I'd join the other passengers, leaning out the window calling over a hawker to inspect what was on offer. I would have starved if it were not for the generosity of the Chinese passengers who always insisted I eat with them as I wandered about the carriages. The only food sold by the hawkers were bags of sweets, salted snacks and boiled eggs. I'd bought four from a hawker, but these were no ordinary boiled eggs! I nearly threw up when I peeled one to reveal its dark green gooey centre and gave all the eggs to the grandmother, who smiled her thanks. The three men shared a joke as they briefly looked up from their game of cards, which they played continuously like most of the other passengers.

After three days, the landscape slowly changed from brown to green, and the train passed through forested valleys. The towns and cities became more frequent, and soon there was barely a break where one ended and another began. As the train neared the populated east and its megacities, the sky was always a dirty grey from the pollution belching from a billion cars, factories and coal-fired power stations.

We rolled into Chengdu just after midnight on the fourth day, and I found myself standing outside the train station in search of a hotel, but none would give me a room as I did not have the required booking. Eventually, one allowed me to sleep on a threadbare couch in the lobby, and I woke at dawn covered in bites from bed bugs.

Scratching, I headed back to the train station where I jostled and shoved with a throng of Chinese to reach the ticket window for seat allocation. It was one of the most frustrating and confusing experiences of my life. No one spoke English. I just kept repeating 'Nanning' to the woman behind a barred window. At one point, the man behind me physically picked me up and tried to hurl me away from the window. I gripped its bars and refused to budge. A call must have gone out for someone who could speak English as a teenage girl suddenly appeared. I was issued with a ticket, and the girl advised my train would depart at 1.00 p.m. from platform three and to be there early. 'If you can't find it, show someone your ticket,' she said and then disappeared.

It was about 9.00 a.m. and I headed to an open-air café where I ordered two steamed buns stuffed with pork. As I ate my breakfast, a smartly dressed Chinese man joined me. He appeared to be in his late thirties and advised he was waiting for a train to Shanghai. I told him about my travels and that I was on my way back to Australia. He nodded approvingly, but I got the feeling he wasn't really interested in my story and that he'd only joined me to spruik the virtues of China, the new superpower. I'd already been told this several times on my train journey from Urumqi. Mostly, by young Chinese who took great pleasure in telling me the west was finished.

'China will be the next superpower, not America,' he said interrupting me. 'You've had your time. It is our time now. The Chinese people know this, and we work together for the future of China, and the future of the world. We help the poor nations. In ancient times, we were the most powerful civilization. China was the most advanced on earth, and we will be again. We make what the world wants, and China grows rich.'

'But what about the pollution?' I asked. 'What will happen when the Chinese people can't breathe the air or drink the water?'

But he ignored my question as though it was irrelevant. He then checked his watch, stood up and disappeared into the mass of humanity that was continually pouring into and out of the cavernous entrance to the Chengdu train station.

Two days later, as the train neared Nanning, the scenery grew greener and more tropical, and we rumbled through valleys and past a patchwork of rice paddies and ponds where men herded flocks of white ducks as though one would herd a flock of sheep. We rolled into Nanning, a city of 1.5 million (this would swell to nearly seven million in 2019) at pre-dawn and I emerged from the station's enormous hall into a modern city of high-rises that was in stark contrast to what lay at my feet.

As I made my way to the city centre in search of the Vietnamese consulate, I was forced to step over an endless row of people sleeping on the pavement on their grass mats cocooned in their blankets. These were China's massive army of rural migrant workers: the new arrivals who had not yet landed a job and a bed in a factory dormitory. The scene I witnessed was likely repeated in all of China's megacities.

After nearly a week of sitting, I enjoyed this early morning walk and was surprised to find Nanning was a city of parks and in the grey dawn, groups of people practiced Tai Chi. In the centre, I found an upmarket hotel and asked for directions to the Vietnamese consulate. It was still several kilometres away, and I hailed a motorcycle taxi giving the driver directions written on a note from the receptionist who spoke perfect English.

My Vietnam visa would take ten days to process at a cost of US$25. What would I do for ten days? My dilemma was quickly solved once I'd found the tourist information office in downtown Nanning. I should go to Yangshou to visit the limestone karsts and one of the most beautiful places in China, I was told.

The journey was an exhausting overnight ride on an overcrowded bus. It deposited me on the outskirts of Yangshou, an ancient village nestled in a valley of iridescent green rice paddies and surrounded by an endless forest of limestone karsts. These conical formations rose up to eighty metres high and were densely covered in lush sub-tropical vegetation. Coiled in wisps of early morning fog, the sun bathed the scene in a gentle orange hue. The village was made up of narrow cobblestone streets and quaint three-storey houses with ancient clay-tiled roofs. At last, I'd arrived in the China of old: the authentic China I'd imagined. It was just like in the paintings that adorned the walls of Chinese restaurants back home.

But then I reached the centre, and as I stood at the top of a side-street, I gazed opened-mouthed at what lay before me. The scene was a kaleidoscope of colour: souvenir stalls of thongs, sunglasses, T-shirts and sarongs; magazine and books stands; tour placards advertising bicycle and tube hire, bus and train tickets. Lining the street were alfresco cafés with menus in English: banana pancakes, milkshakes, hot-dogs, hamburgers, pizza and beer. Western backpackers sat at little wooden tables on the narrow pavement eating breakfast in the warm morning sunshine. 'How did they find this place?' I wondered.

But like me, the backpackers of the mid-1980s, when China opened its doors to independent travel, had unwittingly stumbled upon Yangshou. Since then its scenic beauty and 2500-year-old history had become a backpacker haven in a China that exhausted even the most hardcore and experienced travellers. Yangshou was where they came to chill out; to eat western food; to escape the chaos; to escape the language barrier; to speak with their own kind. As I stood reading a menu, I heard not only English but German, French, Hebrew and what sounded like Danish. I ordered a chocolate milkshake and banana pancakes and ate alone. The backpackers sat huddled in their familiar groups and had no time for a lone traveller. Besides, against their rainbow-coloured T-shirts, cargo shorts and fake designer sunglasses, I looked like a hobo in my faded jeans and dark grey T-shirt. I hadn't showered since the train nearly two days ago and my hair, what was left of it, was lank and greasy. I felt drab, and in my drabness, I felt ugly. It was like the light was slowly dimming inside me, and soon it would go out. Humans can innately detect disease in another. It is a survival mechanism to stay clear of what can harm them. As I ate, I caught the occasional glimpse from the backpackers who sat nearby, but they quickly averted their gaze as if they feared I might ask to join them.

After I'd eaten, I found a cheap backpacker hostel. I was the only person in the dormitory room of four beds and after a lengthy shower, I fell into an exhausted sleep for the entire day. I woke to movement late afternoon when a slim blond girl dumped her backpack on the floor next to the bed opposite.

'Hi, I'm Anna' she said in a thick German accent, flicking a strand of long blond hair from a delicate pink face that glistened with sweat. 'Are you hungry? Let's go eat.'

If it wasn't for Anna during my wait in Yangshou, I doubt I would have left my bed. During the past week, I'd become so incredibly tired and wanted to do nothing more than sleep, which is what I mostly did on the train journey from Urumqi. But rather than being well rested, this heavy cloud of fatigue had followed me. It appeared Anna did not sense that I was unwell or if she did, chose to ignore it. Her abundant energy was contagious, and somehow I mustered the last reserves of strength to join her on several sightseeing adventures.

Like me, Anna thrived on independent travel and refused to go on an 'organised tour' to explore the Yangshou valley. Like me, Anna was also travelling on a tight budget. We opted for stir-fried noodles, pork and vegetables from the food stalls in the local market instead of the backpacker cafes. Instead of hiring a taxi, we hired bicycles to ride to Xianggong Hill to watch the sunset over this mystical valley of karsts.

Our last adventure together was tubing down the limpid River Li. We'd hired inflated tyre tubes from a friendly Chinese family who ran a grocery shop next to our hostel. The husband gave us directions to reach the river explaining that it would take about five hours to float on the current to the village of Puyixiang, where we could catch a bus back to Yangshou. As we'd be in the water all day, we decided to take nothing but a few yuan coins for the bus fare. We'd eaten a large breakfast of noodles with vegetable and fatty pork at the market, and would not need to eat till dinner. We both wore swimsuits and sarongs, which we'd draped over our shoulders as shade from the hot sun. From the shop, Anna also bought an umbrella, and I wore my hat.

All went well for the first two hours, but then the current hardly moved, and we slipped into the water to swim, pushing the tubes, then quickly retreated when several turds slowly floated by. These, I expect, were from the cruise boats, overcrowded with Chinese tourists that chugged up and down the river. By late afternoon, there was no sign of Puyixiang village and wet through, we began to shiver.

'We need to get out of the water,' I said. Anna agreed.

Up ahead was a flat cement platform flush against the riverbank; we paddled over, and as soon as we'd dragged our tubes on to it, several children surrounded us.

'Hello. Speak English?' Anna asked. We both stood shivering, our wet sarongs wrapped around us.

'Yes,' said a boy aged about twelve and we explained our predicament and that we needed a place to sleep and food.

'Pay money,' he demanded, his eyes devoid of all compassion.

'We have no money,' Anna said

I held out my hand with my few coins: 'For bus fare from Puyixiang to Yangshou.'

'Pay money,' he repeated.

The children stood chatting amongst themselves, pointing at us and then laughing. After several minutes, one of the younger boys picked up a stone and threw it at us. The older children did the same.

'You go,' the older boy hissed at us.

'We can't go. It will soon be dark,' we said, dodging the stones. Suddenly the children left as if they'd been psychically summoned. A few minutes later they returned each carrying a bowl of rice and vegetables. They all took great pleasure in eating in front of us. Apparently, they were not convinced we did not have any money and thought the sight of food would weaken our resolve.

'We will give you the umbrella,' Anna said, and the older boy stopped eating to consider the trade.

'Pay money,' he said and resumed shoveling the rice with chopsticks into his mouth. We watched mesmerised as our tummies rumbled.

Once they'd finished eating, the younger children hurled a few more stones, and then they all left. Just as we'd resigned ourselves for a long cold night, the boy returned with his mother, a petite Chinese woman with her black hair tied in a thick ponytail.

'Come,' the boy said and grabbed the umbrella from Anna.

The family lived in a small cement house that appeared to have just two rooms. The woman gave us some clothes and pointed to the second room. After squeezing into the pants, which came halfway up our calves and the shirts with the sleeves ending just below our elbows, we sat like two giants on little bamboo stools to warm ourselves at the open fire where the mother squatted on her haunches as she cooked a meal of fried rice with vegetables and egg in a fire-blackened wok.

'*Xiexie*,' we repeated, to thank her, when she handed us each a bowl.

After we'd eaten, the boy led us up the narrow steps to the flat roof where two grass mats were laid out. He gave us each a thin cotton sheet and then was gone.

'We would've froze to death out there,' I said as we both laid down and curled up close to keep warm.

'Yes, if the children hadn't told their mother,' Anna said, her voice still shivering.

After a breakfast of rice and fried eggs we thanked the family and resumed our slow float down the river arriving at Puyixiang at midday.

Anna left Yangshou the next day, and I missed her immediately. She'd brought light into my dark world, and when she left, I retreated to my bed grateful I had the room to myself for my last two days before I caught the overnight bus to Nanning.

On the tenth day, I arrived in Nanning at dawn, collected my Vietnam visa and was on a train to the township of Youyizhen a few hours later, arriving just after 4.00 p.m. After the passengers had gone, I stood on a deserted platform fearful my beloved motorcycle never made it on what had been a journey of epic proportions for both of us.

'Foreigner, come,' called a Chinese man dressed in a railway uniform. Two men, railway labourers, I presumed, stood beside him.

'Your motorbike,' he said when he opened the railway carriage.

And there he was. Other than a fine coating of dust and a hole in the front brake line where a rope had rubbed, he had made it.

'What do I do now?' I asked once the TT was rolled out of the carriage and handed to me.

'You go to border. Ten kilometre,' he said pointing to a road that would take me south.

I needed no further prompting. The TT fired after a few vigorous kicks, and there I was riding free in China. Free to go anywhere I wanted, anytime I pleased. Maybe in a different life, I would have taken a chance and headed north-west towards Tibet and fulfilled a long-held dream to ride through the high Himalayan plateau to Nepal and India, but China had worn me down, and I welcomed my escape. I had no energy to play cat-and-mouse with the Chinese, and it was likely I would not get very far before Chinese government officials found me.

I reached the border just before it closed. The official stamped my passport and not a question was asked about my motorcycle. Then I was in no-man's-land, riding towards the Huu Nghi border gate. This narrow strip cut through dense rainforest for about a kilometre and was neither officially China nor Vietnam, although China appeared to control it.

I'd made it to Vietnam. Alone, I'd travelled across half the planet. I smiled at my achievement, because I never thought I'd make it this far. I had survived. Maybe I would survive HIV too.

24

ROAD'S END

Vietnam

When I reached Vietnam's Huu Nghi border gate, it was closed, and I had no choice but to spend the night with a Chinese roadworks crew. I'd passed their campsite of dirty white canvas tents set up near a ditch of red earth as I rode through no-man's-land on my way to the gate. It seemed China had big plans for this obscure border crossing and the two-lane strip of tarmac would soon become a four-lane transit point for trucks hauling Chinese goods into South East Asia. With a number of hand signals, I indicated the border to Vietnam was closed and asked the men if I could camp with them. They nodded and flashed yellowed teeth from broad, friendly smiles. It was only later I realised how much of my hand signals had been lost in translation.

After I'd pitched my tent, I returned to their camp with my cooking pot and things to make tea and instant noodles. Several men, all smallish, in ragged mud-encrusted work clothes and worn runners sat around a wood fire smoking cigarettes. A small stool was quickly vacated, and a clear alcoholic spirit was poured into my cup. I gingerly took a sip of the firewater, and the men nodded approvingly. I'd read about Chinese vodka, *baijiu*, which averaged an alcohol content of around fifty per cent. The Russian vodka I'd unwittingly become quite fond of in Central Asia was like lolly water in comparison. I shook my head when a man offered a refill. Another took my cooking pot and spooned in rice, stir-fried vegetables and meat, the origin of which I couldn't quite make out. It was neither chicken, pork or beef. Maybe duck or something else entirely. Other than a handful of pumpkin seeds, I'd not eaten since the steamed pork buns for breakfast in Nanning, so I gobbled it up without another thought.

After eating, I thanked the men and retired to my tent only to be annoyed, for there was no other way to describe it, a short time later. One of the men adeptly unzipped my tent, climbed in and threw a US$20 note at me. 'Sex,' he announced.

'Fuck off, you little bastard!' I screamed and pushed him out, throwing the twenty after him. I quickly zipped my tent and prayed he would not return with the others.

I left at daylight and waited two hours for Vietnamese immigration to open, but while my entry was straightforward, customs required I have special permission for my motorcycle. And this document had to come from the district office in Lang Son, a fifteen-kilometre ride by motorcycle taxi. I was forced to make the death-defying trip twice on a road of rough tarmac that wound through forested hills peppered with villages. The import papers had to be signed and stamped correctly in triplicate, but I was missing a signature on my first attempt. The officials at both ends were apologetic, and no money was demanded.

Once I was free, it was all downhill to Hanoi, nearly 200 kilometres to the south. With no front brakes and the rear drum brake almost non-existent on this model of the Yamaha TT600, it was an exhausting ride made all the worse under a blazing tropical sun in high humidity. When the road levelled, lured by a Coca-Cola sign, I stopped at a roadside café. After peeling off my sweat-soaked jacket, I headed inside.

A man sat near the counter plucking the brown speckled feathers from a large native bird. It was a curlew—and it was alive. It looked at me with its large yellow reptilian eyes, I immediately felt its pain. I moved so fast, the man holding the bird had no time to tighten his grip, and in one swift action, I wrung its neck.

'What sort of people are you,' I screamed as I tossed the now dead bird into his lap. My sudden appearance and what I'd done was so unexpected, so entirely out of their normality that the man with the bird, as well as the shop owner who stood behind the counter and another man who sat at a nearby table, looked at me completely dumbfounded.

'Have you no compassion? The bird was still alive. Can't you see it was in pain?' I ranted. And then I was gone.

As I rode towards Hanoi, I could not forget the bird and all that I'd felt when our eyes had met. Living in Australia, I'd grown up with curlews and would lay in bed at night listening to their sad wailing songs. The curlew is a nocturnal bird with long spindly yellow legs and cryptic plumage, perfect for hiding amongst bushes and leaf litter during the day. Different species are found all over the world. While in Australia, Aboriginal people avoided the curlew for its reputation as a harbinger of death, here in Vietnam and perhaps right through China, South East Asia and India, it was seen as a meal.

In the Aboriginal Dreamtime, the curlew was once a woman whose baby died when she'd left the infant in the hot sun while she went into the bushes with her husband's brother. Her husband killed her and then committed suicide. The woman became the curlew doomed to forever wander the earth wailing at night for her dead baby. Through the language of pain, the bird and I had communicated on a level that united us as one. I'd felt this intuitively, and the feeling had gripped me so firmly, I knew it to be true. In its last moments of life, the curlew had reached out to me, not only to end its suffering, but to share a universal truth: that we are all connected.

I'd come so far since leaving Australia, nearly four years earlier. Not just in the distance travelled, but in my own growth too. As a child living in outback Australia, during a mouse plague, I'd thrown hundreds of mice to their death, splattering each one against a white brick wall in a kaleidoscope of blood and guts. Just before leaving Australia, I'd gone fishing with friends and threaded a hook through the back of a live fish so it would swim away as bait on the end of my line. Back then, I'd perceived the lives of such creatures as insignificant and not given a thought to their suffering, not even to their right to exist.

As I rode through villages busy with people in conical straw hats, past bicycles overloaded with produce being peddled precariously to market, I said a prayer for the curlew and wished it well on its journey back to the source.

9 I had no map to lead me to Hanoi and often stopped to ask directions, but as darkness approached, I found myself on a back road that cut through fields of rice paddies with not a village in sight. The only sign of civilisation was the occasional thatched-roofed bamboo hut surrounded by a sea of green. I turned the TT and rode towards one, following a maze of raised walking tracks fringing each water-soaked rice field. A hut sat on a small square of raised earth.

Hearing my approach the family stood waiting for me: an elderly woman; a husband and wife; a girl in her late teens; and a gaggle of younger children. They seemed a delicate, gentle people—in complete contrast to the Vietnamese man who, without compassion, plucked the feathers from the live curlew just hours before.

Once I'd stopped the engine and pulled off my gloves and helmet, the teenage girl in ankle-length pants and a pretty floral blouse stepped forward and smiled warmly. Her straight black hair trailed to her waist, and a fringe partially covered her large doe eyes. I explained I was on my way to Hanoi, but had taken a wrong turn and was now lost. I told her I had a tent and asked if I could camp as it would soon be dark and I could not ride my motorcycle at night. 'I'll be gone first thing in the morning,' I said, hoping she understood.

'You are welcome,' she said in faltering English and grabbed my hand, which appeared overly large and rough in hers. She lead me inside their hut. I was seated on a raised bamboo structure covered with several thin mattresses and large enough to sleep the entire brood. A mosquito net that would cover them all, hung coiled from a beam above it.

The family filed in behind us, the old woman first, followed by the husband and wife and then their children in no particular order. When I took off my jacket, I hoped I did not smell. The adults sat on little bamboo stools, and the children sat on the reed mats covering the dirt floor. The teenage girl gave me a small bowl of green tea and then a larger bowl filled with rice, a few pieces of chicken, and vegetables, mostly greens, flavoured with lemongrass. It was absolutely delicious, and as I ate, the family watched, mesmerised by my every move. I'd arrived after their dinner, and all wore clean, casual clothes as if ready for bed.

To break the silence, I retrieved my map and album and explained to the girl, whose name was Thang, where I'd travelled. An oil lamp was lit, and there was intense discussion over the photos. When they'd finished, I told Thang I wanted to set up my tent, but she insisted I sleep with them on the raised platform under the netting. 'Mosquito, very bad,' she said. Later we all laid out our bedding and settled in. Surprisingly, I slept soundly.

At dawn, we all stirred and after tea and leftover rice with a fried egg, I thanked the family, offering them a fist full of Vietnamese dong about US$5, but the mother looked horrified and Thang told me I was a guest. 'You have a long journey,' she said.

'So many people have said these same words,' I told her, but for the first time, I felt these would be the last.

Following Thang's directions (drawn on a sheet of paper torn from my diary) I rode into Hanoi mid-afternoon, entering the city at the start of rush hour. With no map, no guidebook and no idea where to go, I pulled over. It was a momentary reprieve from the traffic chaos of he-who-is-bigger rules. Luckily, with next to no brakes, I ranked third in this hierarchy after trucks and cars, both in the minority. Scooters came forth and outnumbered all traffic by about a million to one. I had only to give way to larger vehicles, while the scooters let me through, miraculously parting like a school of fish avoiding a predator.

Across the road was a billboard advertising Mobil. I looked up and smiled my thanks—it seemed in my last desperate hours of need, Mobil was there reaching down from its gilded tower to help me. I had visions of the Mobil guesthouse in Lagos, Nigeria, in Africa, where I'd lived in luxury for three weeks while I waited for spare parts to arrive from Yamaha Australia. But I didn't want three weeks. I just wanted a few days to get my thoughts and health in order before I tackled South East Asia. Despite a lack of both enthusiasm and energy, I held on to the last threads of my plan to ride all the way home through Laos, Thailand, Malaysia then island hop on ferries through Indonesia to Timor. With only about US$500 left, I was also in desperate need of an American Express office, where I could withdraw cash to top up my funds.

I waved down a guy on a scooter and asked directions to the Mobil office. 'Follow!' he yelled over the din and after weaving through the mass of scooters and past numerous buildings under construction, the new Hanoi rising from its French colonial heritage, we pulled up outside Mobil's Hanoi office. 'No money,' the young man said when I offered to pay.

Inside, I handed my Mobil letter of introduction to the Vietnamese receptionist, a delicate creature of immaculate refinement. She disappeared into a side office returning a moment later. 'The manager will be with you in a moment.'

While I waited, I spied a copy of *News of the World* on a coffee table, but as I reached for the newspaper, my heart stopped. Shaking, I sat down on the plush two-seater. The headline read: Diana Dead. The People's Princess Killed in Car Crash. Princess Diana had died nearly two weeks ago on 31 August 1997. It was 12 September, and I'd heard no news of her death while I travelled in China.

'Is this true?' I stammered. Tears welled up in my eyes.

'Yes,' the receptionist replied. 'It was a car accident in Paris.'

As I turned the page to read the full story, the door to the office opened and a middle-aged man with white skin flushed pink and the beginnings of a paunch appeared. He held my Mobil letter.

'What do you want?' he asked curtly. His Australian accent was so unexpected, it momentarily stunned me.

'Nothing,' I said wiping away the tears that had begun to stream down my cheeks.

Leaving my letter on the counter, he turned and closed the door.

'Will you be alright?' the receptionist asked as if apologising for her boss's rudeness. But he had not been rude at all. What right did I have to turn up, and with a wave of my magic letter, expect to be welcomed into the Mobil fold? I had no right at all. I'd come to Mobil in desperation, in the hope they would save me.

'Can I sit for a moment to read this?' I asked the young woman.

'Yes, of course,' she said and handed me a packet of tissues.

After reading the details of Princess Diana's death, at first, I could not understand why I'd been overcome with such deep sadness. I cried as if a close relative, friend or beloved pet had died. At the time, I had no idea that my own outpouring of grief was shared by billions of people globally. On the news of Diana's death, a tsunami of grief had washed over the world as a united humanity mourned her loss. We'd lost a shining light; a crusader fighting for the weak and vulnerable—fighting for people who were shunned and rejected. Fighting to stop HIV stigma and fighting to help those who were dying of AIDS. Fighting against the world's most powerful to end the use and manufacture of landmines that kill and maim so many innocent lives. Even in her pain of a failed marriage, mistreated from the very beginning by the royal family, shackled by her own demons, perpetually hounded by the media's insatiable desire for her image, she did not give up... or go mad. Instead, she harnessed her power, focusing the world's attention on those in desperate need. And the most desperate were the millions infected with HIV. Millions who slowly wasted away to die from AIDS in a world that had only just discovered effective treatments to control the virus to undetectable levels. Princess Diana was The People's Princess', and in her pureness of spirit, she had connected us all like no other person in history.

Mobil's receptionist gave me a city map and advised I go to Hanoi's old quarter. 'There are many hotels there,' she said when I asked where I'd find a place to stay.

I joined the stream of scooters and rode with the flow, turning down a side street when the city sprawl changed to long narrow streets lined with the architecture of Hanoi's French occupiers, who conquered the city in 1873. They'd used it as the capital of French Indochina until 1945 when Vietnam regained its independence. In just seventy years, the French left a significant mark, and as I entered the old city, I entered a scene reminiscent of something out of nineteenth-century France. Narrow three-storey buildings in pale pastel yellows, pinks and greens lined the streets. Some boasted delicate wrought ironwork and tall French windows opening to balconies. A spiderweb of power lines hung from the colonial facades and crossed the streets busy with both scooters and pedestrians as there was no room to walk on the pavement. Every available space was taken up by street vendors, canvas awnings, neon signs and alfresco dining where Vietnamese and tourists alike drank beers.

It was just after 5.00 p.m. and the tropical heat was still oppressive. As I had no hope of riding through this bedlam, I pulled up at a café and ordered an iced avocado smoothie after pointing at the adjacent table occupied by three young Vietnamese men and asking what it was. On this warm tropical afternoon, it was surprisingly delicious and refreshing. My motorcycle was parked close enough for the men to see the map on its side-cover and they nodded their approval. I asked about a budget hotel, one where I could take the bike inside, and I was given a name and directions. It was just around the corner in the next street.

Three low steps lead to the hotel's gleaming white-tiled foyer, and the owner was only too happy to help me push the TT down the corridor and under the stairs that lead to the rooms upstairs. For US$10 per night, I had my own room with queen-sized bed and ensuite. It was the most luxury I'd enjoyed since leaving Europe. It was also the first time in as many months that I'd stood naked in front of a full-length mirror.

After showering, I'd dropped the fluffy white towel at my feet and stared horrified at what stared back at me. Thin mouse-brown strands of wet hair clung to a bony skull; its eyes were sunken into sockets. My body was almost skeletal, and I estimated I weighed under fifty kilograms. At 165cm, I was usually sixty. How had I managed to ride a motorcycle, fully loaded, weighing around 200 kilograms? How had I come so far?

As I stood staring at this stranger, I knew I did not have the strength to continue the ride through South East Asia. This was obvious. My body was losing its fight. With my immune system almost completely destroyed. I was defenceless against the multitude of pathogens that circled waiting to attack. I now had AIDS.

Over the past week, I'd had frequent bouts of diarrhoea. A raised reddish-brown oblong spot about three centimetres long had appeared on my left shoulder. Later, I found out it was Kaposi Sarcoma, a cancer that grows in the cells lining the blood vessels under the skin and is caused by the herpes virus. Most of us carry it in one form or another, but it is generally kept in check by a healthy immune system. I'd taken the last of the Bactrim antibiotic as a prophylactic against PCP pneumonia in Urumqi. This type of pneumonia was another common pathogen unable to penetrate a healthy immune system. But now I was defenceless. It was just two years, almost to the day, that I'd been diagnosed on 14 September 1995. I did not get five years as the doctor in London had told me. Instead, mine had been a rapid decline. Maybe there was something in the Australian Aboriginal 'bone pointing' ritual when the accused willed themselves to die after the *kurdaitcha* man, the tribe's ritual executioner, pointed the bone at them. Had my decline been accelerated by my constant internal chatter: 'I'm going to die'?

But I could still see some semblance of hope in my eyes. It was a faint glow that had been fanned by the winds of circumstance as events seemingly always fell into place for me on my Silk Road journey. Even as the pendulum of my emotions swung between denial and depression; fear and acceptance, I still held on to hope that somehow I would be saved.

As the sad emaciated creature in the mirror stared back, it was obvious what I needed to do. I needed urgent medical help. I needed to go home NOW. On the next available flight. I was done with denial; I was done with giving up. Instead, I was gripped by an overwhelming sense of survival. This was a new urgency and with it came a new sense of purpose.

It was almost mid-day when I woke. Sun streamed through the large French window. The sheets were soaked with my sweat as overnight my body had thrown itself into a fever to fight yet another pathogen. I'd suffered a few night sweats since Kazakhstan, but this was by far the worst.

After I'd showered and dressed, I formulated a new plan. I needed to find safe storage for my motorcycle. Then a one-way ticket on the next flight to Australia. I headed downstairs and asked the hotel manager about storage companies. He flicked through a phone book and wrote down the address for the Hanoi office of Transpo International, a freight and storage company.

Once he'd helped me push the TT outside, I hailed a motorcycle taxi and asked its rider to lead the way.

At the cavernous warehouse of Transpo International, I was advised storage for my motorcycle was US$300 a year. I paid one hundred dollars up front, and it was pushed to rest against a wall. With my newfound sense of purpose came renewed enthusiasm for the ride through South East Asia. I would return in a few months, I believed, to complete my journey.

Except for the Gearsack bag, filled with a few clothes, camera, sleeping bag and other personal items, left at the hotel, the rest of my things, including tools, spares, and boots, were locked inside the two leather panniers, with my helmet tied to the luggage rack. I patted the TT's fuel tank and silently promised I would return, casting one last look at my dear old friend as I left the warehouse.

At the old city, I asked the motorcycle taxi to drop me off at a travel agency where I used my Amex card to buy a one-way ticket to Cairns, in far north Queensland. Cairns has an international airport and is an hour's drive from my parent's banana farm. The flight departed the next morning, and a day later, I would be home.

As I walked back to my hotel, I was suddenly overcome with an enormous sense of loss. My travels were over; my motorcycle was gone. The life I had lived for the past four years had ended. I feared going home to face my parents. I feared their shame and rejection, but there was no turning back now.

I stopped at a street stall selling straw hats and bought a 1920s-style cloche hat with a narrow brim and navy ribbon. It hid my hair loss, and with foundation and a splash of lipstick, I may even look pretty. The stall also sold dresses, and I picked out a blue denim shirt dress with short sleeves that hung straight to my knees and perfectly hid my bony frame.

'I'll wear it now,' I said to the woman as I stood in front of the mirror. My disguise was complete.

25

DYING DAYS

Australia

'Is it lamb for lunch?' I asked my mum. I'd phoned her from a bus stop a short drive from their banana farm. My mouth watered with the thought. It was mid-morning, and my parents always had a roast on Sunday. As farmers, Sunday was their only day off.

'Yes,' she said. 'Why?'

'That's great. I'm at the bus stop. Can you pick me up?'

There was a moment of silence as her brain reeled to comprehend what I'd just said. She thought I was still in Central Asia. My last letter was sent from Kazakhstan nearly a month ago when I explained I wasn't sure where I'd travel next: Tibet, China or Pakistan. But there I was in far north Queensland. A mere fifteen kilometres away.

I arrived unexpectedly on my parents' doorstep after the flight from Hanoi via Singapore landing in Cairns late the night before. The cute little straw hat and the blue denim dress achieved its purpose. My parents were oblivious to the fact I was just a few steps away from being one of the walking dead. Yes, there was a short intake of breath when I took off my hat, but I convincingly blamed my hair loss on the stresses of travel. And when they both hugged my bony frame, I advised I'd picked up a bad stomach bug in China.

'A course of antibiotics will sort it out,' I said later as I toyed with the delicious lamb roast with all the trimmings that would soon end up in the toilet.

My parents were in their fifties, people of the land who farmed the fertile red volcanic soils of the Wet Tropics. Driven by my fear of their rejection, as well as the shame I perceived I'd bring on my family, I faked wellness. They had brought me up, and therefore I was a 'good girl': a smart girl. This was my fight, and I needed strength, not an endless stream of questions that all asked, how could you be so stupid? There was another reason too. I simply did not want to worry them. I did not want to burden them, to hurt them; to take away all their dreams for their only daughter even if it was one who'd had a crazy idea to travel the world on a motorcycle. One who'd believed in that dream and followed it without question.

The lingering bout of gastroenteritis was confirmed by the family doctor with a diagnosis of the intestinal bacteria shigella, which I'd most likely picked up from river water contaminated with human faeces in China. The antibiotics soon cleared it, and within a few days, food no longer slipped straight through me. Having recouped its ability to retain nutrients, my body regained some ground in its battle.

Despite knowing I'd travelled through Africa, a hotbed of HIV, our family doctor failed to make the connection. Not even the Kaposi Sarcoma, which sat as an oval-shaped reddish-brown spot on my left shoulder, raised suspicion. It was a common condition in AIDS patients and had grown larger since I'd noticed it just days earlier in Hanoi. The doctor saw it as skin cancer, a basal cell carcinoma from years of sun exposure starting as a child, and surgically removed it.

My mother was not deceived quite so easily, and while we washed up one evening, she asked outright if I had AIDS. I just scoffed and said no. My father worked from dusk to dawn ending each day with several beers, dinner and then bed, usually by 8.00 p.m. He never asked any questions except when I planned to get a job. In the meantime, I too was woken at daylight, as it was expected, I too would work in the banana paddocks and packing shed, just as hard as he and my mother. The shigella, treated with a course of antibiotics, was my escape from their rejection and their shame.

As the weeks passed, the violent battle raged silently inside me: silently killing me. At first, it was a stalemate, but the virus was always going to get the upper hand. After three months, I could no longer pretend wellness. My body was a wasteland of dead soldiers, its T-cells, the foundation of my immune system, were all but destroyed. I would force myself to eat the dinners lovingly cooked by my mother, which would only later end up in the toilet as vomit and diarrhoea caused by a number of factors. This was due to a lack of stomach acid, a common condition in people with AIDS. And also HIV enteropathy, a breakdown of the neurons within the nervous system that governs the intestinal tract. It was likely I had cytomegalovirus (CMV), which is carried by half the population, but lies dormant in the healthy. I was also riddled with candida so much so that this yeast-like fungus covered the inside of my mouth and throat with a thick fury whitish coating. The fungus left the mucous membrane red and raw and made eating and swallowing painful. At first, I managed to hide all of this from my parents, but I soon reached that point where I could no longer fake wellness, and I knew I needed to leave.

It was Sunday, and over roast chicken, I told them I was moving to Cairns on the pretence of a job offer through a friend of a friend. I explained it was time for me to 'do my own thing'. Secretly though, I'd phoned the Queensland AIDS Council (QUAC).

'I've got HIV. I'm very sick. I can't tell my parents,' I'd said feebly into the phone cupped close to my ear.

'Get yourself up here as quick as you can. We'll take care of everything,' the young man told me. QUAC, a support organisation for people living with HIV and AIDS, understood without explanation.

The following morning, I packed my car and with my few possessions, I said goodbye to my parents, faking the best look I could of a young woman about to begin the next chapter of her adventurous life.

A few weeks after I'd arrived home, I'd bought the car for $3000, a second-hand Holden Camira station wagon I called Martha. I bought it because I knew I would need an escape. I plotted another escape too—an exit that would leave no shame on my parents or me. My seemingly untimely death would be deemed a sad, but unfortunate accident. It would be from the bite of a taipan. It is the world's third-most venomous snake and is common on the banana plantations and sugar cane fields of the tropical north where it hunts its favourite food: rats. I'd searched for one when my parents had gone away on a business trip for a few days and left me in charge. I'd scoured gullies, looked under rocks and logs, but did not find one as fortunately for me, the taipan is an elusive reptile.

When this escape failed, I plotted others too, but I could not follow through as a small part of me would not allow it. Even when all hope seemed lost; a small part of me still believed in the guiding hand of that higher force. It had often been a faint voice urging me not to give up, but nonetheless, it had always been there. When my parents were away, it became louder. There was a sudden urgency to it as though the universal energy, God or Allah, saw just how close I was to ending it all. 'Go to hospital! Go to hospital!' the voice boomed.

When I arrived at the QUAC office on Monday morning, they took charge. Leaving Martha with them, I was driven by a volunteer to the Sexual Health Clinic at the Cairns Base Hospital. I was immediately ushered in to see Dr David Bradford, one of the world's leading HIV specialists. He'd moved to Cairns from Melbourne three years earlier.

'You won't be able to hold on much longer,' he said looking at me over the top of his reading glasses with pale grey eyes. 'It's remarkable you've lasted this long.'

There was no need to explain. He'd seen it many times before. Young gay men, mostly, who also faked wellness hiding both HIV and their homosexuality from families until the very end. Families who were often incapable of understanding due to an impossible, unbridgeable generational divide. 'I want you to go straight upstairs,' he said reaching for the phone. I felt the strength drain from my body as though it knew I was, at last, in safe hands and it could relinquish its fight to a higher power in the form of the medical staff upstairs.

I slumped back in the chair and doubted I'd have the energy to walk to the elevator that would take me to where I could, at last, rest—where there would be no more pretending.

'Who is your emergency contact?' Dr Bradford asked, his pen poised over the section on my patient form that I'd purposefully left blank.

'No one,' I replied. 'I can't tell my parents.'

'You should. You're very sick,' he said with a seriousness that changed his pale eyes to steely grey.

'I'm not going to die,' I replied with a conviction that came from some deep hidden place inside me. 'I've got to be out of here by Christmas. My parents will be expecting me.'

That was ten days away, and if I didn't return home on Christmas Eve, my carefully planned deception would topple. I would be exposed.

'We'll do all we can,' he said, but I could see he shared none of my optimism.

Within the hour, I was upstairs hooked up to an intravenous drip comprising a concoction of medications (a powerful antibiotic and a combination of HIV antiretrovirals), in a private room set aside for AIDS patients who mostly came there to die.

The Cairns Base Hospital sprawled along the northern end of the city's palm-fringed foreshore. Outside tourists sweated in the humidity of a tropical summer. Our worlds could not be further apart as I lay shivering on the third floor. It was my second day and already several nurses, one after the other, had tried to convince me to contact my family. I insisted I was not going to die. I would get over this. But I could see they held little hope for my precious young life, which would soon be lost.

'Another blanket,' I whispered to the nurse who leaned close to check the drip.

'You need to let us phone your parents,' she said with the authority of someone frequently dealing with those in denial. She firmly tucked the blanket, the fourth that morning, around my skeletal body. The HIV had destroyed most of my immune system leaving me defenceless against an infinite number of invading pathogens intent on consuming me. A test later revealed I had forty T-cells: forty soldiers fighting a massive unstoppable force. A healthy person has around a thousand. I would likely die from the PCP (pneumocystis pneumonia) smothering my lungs. At an advanced stage, it signalled I was close to the end. There was no pain, just weakness—and cold

DYING DAYS — AUSTRALIA

that penetrated deep inside. It was the cold of death that no amount of blankets could fend off.

'Would you like to see the chaplain?' the nurse asked, pausing at the door. It seemed a question born out of hospital protocol more than concern for my journey into the afterlife.

I shook my head, rolling it slowly from side to side. I knew I would survive. I had always survived. It was the same feeling of certainty I had five years earlier when I blurted out to friends, for no apparent reason, that I would ride a motorcycle across Africa, and later along the Silk Road through Central Asia. I knew I would be okay because when I took that first step towards Africa, everything fell into place. Just as I believed then, I believed now things would work out for me here too. I knew the cocktail of drugs, saquinavir, a protease inhibitor, along with a combination of existing HIV drugs, being drip fed into my dying body would control the replication of HIV. Protease inhibitors, a new generation of medications, were only discovered by scientists a year earlier, in 1996, the year everything changed in the world of HIV. This new HIV drug was the key to suppressing the virus, but was only effective when used in combination with two of the older antiretrovirals such as AZT and 3TC. It was just in the nick of time for me. But too late for the millions who had already died since the early 1980s when HIV first spread its tentacles on an unsuspecting world. The nurse left the room with a backward glance of deep sadness for me—and also for my parents, especially my mother, who it was assumed would not have that last goodbye.

Rather than improve, my condition only worsened, but my body, with its forty troops, gallantly continued to fight. It fought a ruthless invader that gloated with malignant pleasure about to celebrate victory. As I lay shivering under a pile of blankets, I felt a sense of timelessness as though I floated in weightless bliss. Propped motionless on the stiff hospital pillows, an oxygen tube breathing air into my pneumonia-smothered lungs, I teetered on a precipice between life and death and gazed with hollow eyes at the wall opposite. All morning it had slowly morphed into a state of fluidity, and I was mesmerised by its constant movement. There was something there.

For a moment I saw it. I squinted, trying to see the dark shapes that seemed to mill about as if waiting to embrace me back into the pool of energy where all life began—where we all came from, and where we would all return. I smiled weakly with a sense of deep gratitude for my travels; for all the people I'd met and the kindness I'd been shown; for the realisation that there is an energy, a force, that flows through us, around us and is there with us, helping us chase our dreams. It is an energy that connects us as one. I was no longer afraid: death was not the end. The dark figures reassured me that all I believed in, was in fact, true. Over the next three or four days, I drifted in and out of consciousness. The fluidity hovered for brief moments and then began to recede. The figures began to fade, and the wall regained its true form. The shivering too subsided. The battle had turned.

Epilogue

Ten days after admitting myself to Cairns Base Hospital, I rose from my deathbed, discharged myself and collected my car Martha. I was home for Christmas Eve, my parents none the wiser they'd nearly lost me. Rather than being a celebration with champagne, prawns and roast turkey it could so easily have been filled with sadness and funeral plans. Instead, a combination of powerful HIV medications were rapidly suppressing the virus. I would take these treatments every day for the rest of my life.

A week after Christmas, I returned to Cairns and moved in with Jackie Frost, a QUAC volunteer, who recently retired as their client services officer. Jackie offered me a room and cared for me in those early weeks of my recovery when I still kept HIV secret from my parents. She became a close and dear friend.

I still weighed around forty-five kilograms and my hair was still months away from regaining its previous fullness, but each day my battle-weary body grew stronger and more vibrant. Dr David Bradford's parting words when I left hospital were: 'Eat lots of hamburgers'. And to this high fat, protein and carbohydrate-laden diet, I added tropical fruits, banana smoothies, rump steak and fresh fish. Yes, food occupied my every thought in those first weeks out of hospital, for those were the weeks dedicated entirely to my body and its recovery.

The combination of four HIV medications, prescribed by Dr Bradford on my discharge, soon suppressed the virus to undetectable levels. In those early days, taking these treatments was often complicated as some had to be taken with food, some two hours before food, some at four-hour intervals and some with grapefruit juice. There were also the occasional horrendous side-effects: sudden diarrhoea, especially in the mornings, early stage peripheral nerve damage, fatigue, bouts of dizziness and headaches. Through a combination of trial and error, Dr Bradford's recommendations and my own online research (for I had discovered the internet!), we eventually found a combination that worked in perfect harmony without side-effects.

Since then, scientists have discovered more effective treatments and my most recent combination is Maraviroc, Atazanavir, Raltegravir and Ritonavir. There are numerous combinations available today and some are combined into one pill taken once per day. While a cure and a vaccine to prevent HIV infection is on the horizon, for those living with HIV, these antiretroviral treatments are as good as a cure.

Early in this battle, I had decided to face my enemy alone. I could not tell my parents at the time of diagnosis—when my world, my hopes and dreams for the future, fell apart and collapsed into a black void of despair. I could not tell them even as I lay dying in my hospital bed as the nurses kept insisting I should.

Mostly, I did not want to worry them, but I also feared their rejection and their admonishment for the perceived shame I'd brought on our family. Together, I believed this would crush me. This was the power of stigma. This was HIV's greatest weapon because it guaranteed silence from its victims. Stigma has kept millions upon millions of those infected isolated from love and support, from getting tested after an unguarded moment and getting the medications that could save them from a slow death as they waste away to nothing.

In 2017, scientists finally endorsed the undetectable = untransmittable message (U=U). This breakthrough in ending stigma came after more than twenty years of scientific evidence that clearly demonstrates people living with HIV on treatments and who have an undetectable viral load cannot transmit HIV. If testing was universally available and utilised, and all those diagnosed positive had access to HIV medications, we could end HIV, just as we ended polio. Unfortunately we are still years away from universal access to treatments, and ending stigma is a battle that will not be easily won. In the UNAIDS report from 2017, there were more than thirty-seven million people globally living with HIV. Women accounted for more than half of this number, and every week, around 7000 young women became infected with HIV. Only twenty-two million of all people infected have access to treatments. And it looks unlikely, the global target of thirty million people living with HIV on treatment by 2020 will be reached.

I kept my secret from my parents for another two years after I left hospital. When I told them, they were devastated but their fears for me were born out of a lack of knowledge. Of course, they still loved me unconditionally and were there to support me. I kept my secret from my extended family and most of my friends for nearly twenty years. Like millions of people living with HIV today, I too lived under a dark cloud in fear that my secret would be found out. But when I became a mother, my fear of stigma was not just for me, it was also for my sons. Such is the insidiousness of HIV stigma—it affects simply by association. My boys were all born without HIV, because the combination of medications I take meant there was no risk to them being infected in my womb or during their birth.

In 2015, I decided enough was enough and broke free of stigma. I stood strong, ready for the onslaught when my first book *Ubuntu: One Woman's Motorcycle Odyssey Across Africa* was published in April 2016, and revealed that surprising 'twist' in the Afterword. But the onslaught did not come. My boys were still invited into the homes of their friends, and without question, their friends came to our house too. And my book, *Ubuntu*, was embraced, and I received praise for my courage. My aim then was to write this second book, *Timeless On The Silk Road*, in the hope that it would not only take the reader on an odyssey along the fabled Silk Roads of antiquity but also pique their own search for meaning, leave them considering their own mortality. I also hope my story will help make right an injustice against millions of people. I hope it has answered questions, raised awareness and in so doing, helped end HIV stigma once and for all.

HIV entered me—I'm sure—in Africa, when it took advantage of an unguarded moment. It happened just a month before I left that continent where the virus ran unchecked, and few took notice of prevention campaigns in a world where tomorrow is too far away.

When I was diagnosed in September 1995, there were no effective medications to control HIV and rumours that scientists had made a breakthrough had not yet filtered down to patients. Back then, those of us living with HIV still believed death was inevitable. Just like it still is, in 2019, for fifteen million people who are yet to receive these life-saving antiretroviral treatments.

As I headed home in November 1996, still healthy, I was told nothing of the discovery of protease inhibitors, the new generation of HIV medications that saved millions from certain death. But even though I was in good health, doctors would have seen no need to tell me. I didn't know about the internet either as it was still emerging back then. Besides, I was isolated from it in a world of unforgiving deserts, high mountains and ancient cultures—and my passage through China.

But even if I had access to the internet, would I have searched for news of medical breakthroughs? I travelled home, weighed down by a combination of denial and acceptance of my inevitable death. However, there was always a glimmer of hope on that journey. I could not deny what I'd come to believe in so completely first in Africa and later as I travelled the Silk Roads—an unwavering faith that some higher force was out there. As I travelled alone, I had no one to fuel any doubts. There was no one to criticise my decisions—my beliefs—and so I was free to trust what I felt was real. Unexplainable, but nonetheless, real. What I felt intuitively as a result of my travels was a slow awakening. Each experience, chance encounter and coincidence built on the previous until it reached a point where I could not ignore what was being slowly revealed to me. When I started this journey, first across Africa, then Europe to Asia, I was twenty-eight, a naive young woman who worked as a radiation safety technician at a uranium mine on the fringe of Kakadu National Park in Australia's Northern Territory. I never gave a thought to the deeper meaning of anything. There was no realisation of that elusive thing we call universal energy. The only energy that I was aware of was the radiation levels detected by my monitoring instruments, which similarly could not be seen or felt, but nonetheless was real.

Two months after I discharged myself from the Cairns Base Hospital, I enrolled in a Bachelor of Journalism at the Cairns Campus of James Cook University. I'd discovered writing, and journalism seemed the obvious choice. Within months, I was the editor of *Bedlam*, the student magazine. Soon after, *The Cairns Post*, the far north's regional daily operated by News Ltd, offered me a student cadetship after I enthusiastically turned up in their newsroom every Sunday afternoon to write fillers for Monday's paper. Such was my success, that university authorities invited me to be part of its inaugural mentor program.

I also joined the student environment club because I knew I was in a position to make a difference. The Australian government had just given the go-ahead for the Jabiluka uranium mine in Kakadu National Park. It was near the Ranger uranium mine where I'd worked for nine years. I no longer agreed with uranium mining and certainly did not agree with mining so close to the Magela Wetlands, the womb of Kakadu and the traditional lands of the Mirarr Aboriginal people. Jabiluka holds particular significance as a sacred site. I could not ignore my inner call to action and organised the Jabiluka Kombi Convoy. After raising funds from a dance party to pay for fuel and food to get us there, I lead a motley crew of protestors to join the blockade.

I'd been given a second chance and gripped life with an energy and passion more powerful than I'd ever felt before. In my mind, there were no bounds to what I could achieve. I merely had to put my ideas into action and everything would fall into place. And those shadowy figures, milling about ready to receive me as I neared death in my hospital bed, had confirmed my belief.

When people learnt of my travels by motorcycle, there were always questions about how I felt to no longer be living such an adventure. 'The adventure hasn't ended,' I'd say, looking at them confused as I struggled to understand why they didn't see the thrill of it all—this journey called life. And this journey has carried me through many adventures over the decades since Africa and the Silk

Road: student, protester, journalist, wife, mother, single-parent, HIV educator, motivational speaker, motorcycle road safety advocate, writer and author. The adventure continues.

As for my beloved motorcycle, the TT. In 2002, I shipped my loyal friend from Hanoi to Melbourne, Australia where it waits patiently in my shed for our next odyssey.

Acknowledgements

In 1992, when the idea to ride a motorcycle across Africa and beyond came to me 'out-of-the-blue', I never thought I'd write one book, let alone two. I believe it was my destiny to do those journeys and later share my experiences with the world. I am always humbled to receive messages from readers advising that I have inspired them to embark on their own adventures. And that the sharing of my journeys and those, on occasions, ethereal experiences, brought about a sense of believing too.

From the very beginning of my travels, I owe a great deal of thanks to my parents, Kitty Ellis and the late John Ellis. As a mother myself, I now understand the immense worry I caused you both during those four years from 1993 to 1997 when I travelled the world venturing into some of the more dangerous places on our planet, mostly alone.

Thank you also to my sons, Ethan, Morgan and Ashton for your continued patience with having a mother who is a writer—one who spends far too many hours at the keyboard! From now on, we will have many weekends mountain biking together.

I owe deep gratitude to all those who helped me on my travels along the Silk Roads from London to Hanoi. Some I am still in contact: Fabrice Perez and brothers Patrick Mikos and Frédéric Mikos. Some, I never exchanged addresses, but wish I had. If this book finds its way to you—thank you. And sadly some have passed away. After my travels, I wrote to Alan Kendall, the English truck driver I met in Turkey. It was in early January 2019, while editing the manuscript that I searched for him online. But I was one month too late. I learned Alan passed away on 1 December 2018. RIP Alan Kendall.

My deep gratitude also to ExxonMobil UK for providing me with a Letter of Introduction that helped me many times on my journey, particularly in Baku, Azerbaijan, and secured entry for my motorcycle into China.

During the course of writing this book, many people and

organisations have come into my life to help me at just the right moment. A manuscript cannot become a book without the services of a skilled editor and proofreader. I am indebted to Nadine Davidoff for her structural edit. I first came across Nadine while searching for an editor for my first book, *Ubuntu*. When I was seeking the services of a proofreader, Nadine recommended Katia Ariel, who weaved her magic with great skill giving my manuscript that final polish. Katia, in turn, recommended typesetter Libby Austen, who completed my book's journey to perfection, to print. Thank you Nadine, Katia and Libby. And also to Tony Wheeler, Susan Paxton PhD, Ted Simon and Chris Scott for picking up those errors that had managed to slip through this process.

My thanks also to those who gave advice and feedback on historical medical facts: Susan Paxton PhD, David Menadue AO, Dr David Bradford and Dr Richard Moore. John Hall from Thorne Harbour Health also deserves special mention for his ongoing moral support and advice, which dates back to 2017.

I am also deeply grateful for both the financial and ongoing networking support from Positive Women Victoria, Thorne Harbour Health and Living Positive Victoria. These three organisations have been with me every step of the way during the publishing journey and all that follows in raising awareness and bringing about an end to HIV stigma.

And thank you to Cath Smith and Daniel Brace who reached out to help me in those early days, and for your continued support in getting my story out there. Finally, thank you to the many other people, I have not mentioned here.

Above: Andy and me in London where we both worked as motorcycle couriers.

Left: Don inside *Hedgehog*. We met through the Mole Valley Moto Guzzi Club after I bought a Moto Guzzi V50.

Below: Me and my very overloaded Yamaha TT600 on the day I left London to ride the Silk Roads.

Above: Steering *Hedgehog* through Cowley Lock. She was the 64-foot narrow boat I called home in London.

Below: These Georgians and their friends offered an abundance of food, vodka and a room when I was caught in a hail storm near Kutaisi, Georgia.

Above: Mike, the Greek-German motorcyclist I travelled with through Greece.

Below: I pay homage to the fallen Anzacs at Gallipoli, Turkey. This statue honours a Turkish soldier who braved gunfire to carry a wounded Allied soldier to the Australian lines.

Above: I try on an *ushanka* (Russian fur hat) on the shores of the Caspian Sea near Baku, Azerbaijan.

Below: Alan Kendall, the British long-distance truck driver, I met in Turkey and then again in Azerbaijan.

Above: With Ramiza at her apartment in Baku. My red face is a side-effect of Bactrim, the antibiotic I took to prevent PCP (pneumocystis pneumonia).

Above: A spider from the Karakum Desert, Turkmenistan. Unknowingly, I slept on the ground with these spiders!

Left: The French motorcyclists, Fabrice, Patrick and Frédéric in Bukhara, Uzbekistan. We travelled together from Uzbekistan to Kazakhstan.

Below: The ruined walls of the ancient Silk Road city of Merv, Turkmenistan. Once known as the 'Queen of the World' until it was destroyed and its citizens slaughtered by Genghis Khan's army in 1221.

Above: Horses graze in the Alay Valley at the base of the Pamir mountains, Kyrgyzstan.

Right: This family invited me inside their yurt when I stopped to rest on the road to Tash Rabat, Kyrgyzstan.

Below: The Frenchmen and I enjoy a bowl of *kumis,* fermented mare's milk, offered by Kyrgyz nomads.

Above: The hut in the Altai Mountains where the Frenchmen and I stayed with the Russian cattlemen.

Below: Patrick, Frédéric and Fabrice in the Altai Mountains on the road to Karagay, Russia.

Below: Me with Elena, Alexia, their son and a neighbour on the front step of their house near Ridder, Kazakhstan.

Right: Varso and Diana at their home near Gorno Altaysk, Russia.

Above: Sergei (first on the left), the other Russian truck drivers and I share a meal on the road from Kosh-Agach to Barnaul, Russia.

Right: Irene, another Russian couple, Stanislav and I enjoy a farewell meal and several vodka toasts on my last night in Barnaul.

Below: The Kyrgyz family I stayed with for a few days on the shores of Song Köl, Kyrgyzstan.

Left: Anna from Germany with local children. We met in Yangshou, China and spent a week together exploring this magical land of limestone karsts.

Below: Market day at a village on the road to Hanoi, Vietnam.

My mother, Kitty, and my late father, John, at their banana farm near Cairns, Australia. Photo taken April 1996.

At a beach near Cairns walking Jackie's dogs. Photo taken January 1998, a month after I nearly died from AIDS.

Made in the USA
Lexington, KY
08 September 2019